Esquire's HANDBOOK FOR HOSTS

Esquire's
HANDBOOK
FOR HOSTS

BLACK DOG
& LEVENTHAL
PUBLISHERS

This edition published by arrangement with The Hearst Corporation Inc.

Published by
Black Dog & Leventhal Publishers
151 West 19th Street
New York, NY 10011

Distributed by
Workman Publishing Company
708 Broadway
New York, NY 10003

Manufactured in the United States of America

ISBN: 0-57912-043-1

h   g   f   e   d   c   b   a

Library of Congress Cataloging-in-Publication Data
    Esquire's handbook for hosts
            Esquire guide to the perfect party: a time-honored hand book
    on how to eat, drink and be merry / by the editors of Esquire magazine.
            p.   cm.
            Orginally published: Esquire's handbook for hosts. New
    York: Grosset & Dunlap, 1949.
            Includes index.
            ISBN   1-57912-043-1
            1. Entertaining.   2. Dinners and dining. 3. Liquors
    4. Wine and wine making. I Esquire II. Title. III. Title: Guide to the
    perfect party.
    TX731.E85   1999
    642'.4--dc21   98-51702

Contents

vi

Eat

THE WORLD'S BEST CHEFS
WEAR PANTS

"He's sort of continental—kisses your hand, orders in French, and gives you the check . . ."

The world's greatest cooks are men. Since the beginning of time, he-men have always prepared the savory dishes that caress the palates of epicures of every nation.

Some have taken up the culinary art as a new twist on the old "come see my etchings" routine. Some have come to the kitchen out of necessity: even bachelors must eat. But all have remained to reap the pleasures from (and the praises for) good food thoughtfully prepared.

For the "emergency" cook whose kitchen prowess begins and ends with frying an egg, but who would like to be prepared for some pleasant emergency—say a snow-stranded damsel with an appetite . . . For the man who knows how to prepare only one dish well, and is beginning to notice that friends and wooed-one pale at the mention of spaghetti . . . For the man who is overcome by righteous rage at the thought of cafeteria meals, folderol dishes, women's magazine salads and the theatrical bill posters' paste which passes for sauce . . . For every man, everywhere, who appreciates fine food . . . For gourmet and gourmand alike, Esquire has assembled this guide. "Read, mark, learn and inwardly digest" and you'll emerge as a chef supreme, a wine connoisseur who can spar with the smuggest sommelier.

You won't find doily tearoom fare here: no radish roses, no menus designed for their calorie content. Esky has concentrated on food of, for and by MEN. Nor will you find vitamin charts or how long to roast lamb or how to make an apple betty; we recommend that you have a standard, womanly cookbook for reference in such routine matters, for this book is concerned not with the kind of food you can get anywhere but instead with unusual dishes. Esq. suspects that you'll prove nothing (and improve nothing) if you compete with three-meals-a-day cooks on their own territory. So here are the little-known recipes of internationally famous chefs, the unexpected touches which transform an ordinary food into an extraordinary dinner, the *super* dishes that will establish your reputation as a cook even if you *never* learn to bake a cake or disguise a left-over.

"Be different, host-cook, and let he who will forever serve fried chicken."

[11]

"Quick, Gaxton, fix up a warm drink—I found this poor girl
out in the snow"

How to Use This Book

READ IT THROUGH FIRST, for ideas . . . pick out the dishes which most appeal to you . . . then try the recipes on yourself, in an off-night's solitude, so you'll be confident and assured when the time comes to perform for an audience. And if you rank as a rank beginner, you may need this basic dope even before you start to read and practice.

Boiling is cooking in water at a temperature of 212 degrees Fahrenheit; simmering is cooking in water at a temperature of 180 to 210 degrees Fahrenheit, or below the boiling point of water; stewing is simmering either in very small amount of liquid or no liquid at all; steaming is cooking in the steam generated by a small amount of boiling water in the vessel. Broiling is cooking over or under direct heat; pan broiling is cooking in a pan greased only enough to prevent the food in it from sticking. Baking and roasting are practically the same—cooking in the oven at various temperatures required by the food you are cooking. Frying is cooking in a bath of hot fat, while sautéing is done in a small quantity of fat; fricaseeing is a combination of sautéing with stewing or steaming.

[13]

DON'T "IMPROVE" ON THE RECIPES, AT FIRST — On the first time around, we suggest that you follow the recipes exactly. If 1 tablespoon of flour is called for, measure exactly 1 level table-spoonful. If "flour to thicken" is the order, note the precise amount required so you'll have a starting point for future experiments. Then, when your first test shows you what the recipe was working toward, you're in a better position to . . .

ADD A TOUCH OF IMAGINATION, LATER — It's like painting. Matisse wouldn't have got anywhere if he hadn't sat those long hours in the Louvre copying Delacroix. The real artist adds his own interpretation to the matter at hand; and if the metier is the kitchen range, his dash of this or that is as individual as the painter's brush stroke. So learn the rules lightly, and then throw them away, one at a time. Only then can you take the real creator's pride in your dish and put it out as a little thing of your own.

Of course, leave us face it, in the first rush of inspiration you're apt to court failure, grand or small. Until you've cornered that major ingredient of good cookery—experience—*things don't always come out the way you plan them:*

. . . BUT in case of failure you can always (a) have another pitcher of Martinis, (b) call the nearest caterer, or (c) exit, laughing. But whatever you do, spare yourself and your guests that other Great Fault of women cooks: apologizin' and a-fussin'.

But, whether paying strict attention to a recipe or cooking freehand . . .

USE YOUR COMMON SENSE — Actually, this bride-boner couldn't happen to a man—but it can't hurt to remind you that no good cook follows a book slavishly. A bride takes up cooking because she must, whether she's an eat-to-live gal or just medium-bored with the whole idea. But a man takes to the stove because he is interested in cooking, therefore he has long been interested in eating and therefore he starts six lengths in front of the average female. A vague direction like "season to taste" makes more sense to him than "add ¼ teaspoon salt." We suspect that your chance of error lies in the other, casual direction—but don't say we didn't warn you: a recipe is a guide, not a law.

When you've practiced enough on yourself and your enemies, you'll be ready to take on your friends. You'll find the cook-and-host job easier if you . . .

PLAN EVERYTHING WELL IN ADVANCE:

Don't trust to luck or to supplies-on-hand. Go over your menu and wine list carefully, check to make sure you have everything you need in the way of equipment and supplies, then you can confidently attend to your guests with no time out for worrying.

Best bet is to do your planning on paper, too. To a host who wants his cooking to appear effortless, *memory is a poor substitute for schedules and shopping lists:*

Do all of your table-setting and as much as possible of your cooking before your guests arrive, so you won't have to rush around during the cocktail period. A written time schedule is a big help, if only because such a carefully-thought-out plan is a constant reassurance that you haven't forgotten anything. As you'll learn for yourself the first time you discover your prize salad or your special dessert still in the refrigerator on the morning after—only because you forgot to serve it—it doesn't pay to become infatuated with the taste of your own martinis unless you have a concealed LIST to do your thinking for you.

REMEMBER THE SAW ABOUT TOO MANY COOKS—It's true: too many cooks not only get in your hair but may spoil your fare. Particularly in the early stages of your cooking experience, onlookers will rattle you; and if they insist upon rattling pots and pans as well, you'll wish you'd stood in the restaurant set.

So if you can get away with it, keep your gallery out of the galley. A display of temperament might work; a fresh supply of cocktails set out as far as possible from the cookstove is more certain to leave you a clear field in the food department.

If your best efforts fail and your busybody guests prevail, you can either (a) crowd them into a kitchen corner, (b) force this book into their hands, to keep them occupied or (c) make a point of bumping into them at every turn, until they suspect that they're in the way. But, whatever you do, *don't let them help.* Let a woman fix so much as a cracker and she'll soon take over. Whose hobby *is* this, anyway?

Equipment

A man's kitchenette should contain the following necessary utensils: a kettle, a set of aluminum saucepans, preferably with long handles; a frying pan, a roasting pan, a double boiler, at least one earthenware casserole, a wire sieve, a wire salad basket, an egg beater, mixing bowls, three kitchen knives, a small wooden chopping board, a vegetable brush, a wooden spoon and fork, a spatula, a long fork, a grater, a funnel, a pepper mill, a pair of scissors, an aluminum measure, a basting spoon, a coffeepot, a teapot and a wooden salad bowl. If your oven has no heat control, by all means get an oven thermometer. And even if it does have a broiler rack, you may want a sizzle platter, which both broils and serves such foods as steaks and chops. Individual casseroles are nice to have, for soup-serving as well as miscellaneous cooking. A pressure cooker is helpful for vegetables; you'll want a potato masher or a food mill for potatoes, etc. Gadgets galore—from onion-chopper to wire whisks—will ease your course; and of course you'll want a *good* can opener. You'll

[16]

save on temper, too, if you latch onto one of the new openers made to handle vacuum-jars. If you go in for electrical appliances, a good toaster, a waffle iron and a coffee-maker that does its work at the table make a good kick-off.

Then, depending on the tack your cooking takes, you may add special equipment: skewers for shish kabab, say, or an alcohol-flame chafing dish for almost anything dressy. You may need a deep-fry kettle and basket; rolling pin, pastry board, baking pans; special molds for baba au rum or the like; small, shallow frying pans for crêpes Suzette; an omelet pan.

Ample equipment, and the best, is a pleasure to work with, but like the good photographer who can make salon pictures even with a box camera, the good cook can turn out gourmet viands on a hotel hot plate. If you're limited in the pots and pans department,

DO THE BEST YOU CAN WITH WHAT YOU HAVE . . . And if your space is limited, MAKE YOUR EQUIPMENT DO DOUBLE DUTY.

Your casserole can double as a stewpan. A small saucepan floated in a larger one makes a double boiler, a pint bottle can pinch hit as a measuring cup, a frying pan can be used as an oven dish and so on. Be wise . . . improvise!

When it comes to TABLE EQUIPMENT, you'll probably want service for 6 or 8. We suggest you go in for . . .

MODERN DESIGN—modern china and linens were made for men: simple and striking, they are utterly devoid of pink rosebuds and fancy volutes. Your tablecloth or runners will probably be in solid color linen—wine, gray, bright blue or rust being the most popular. These may have contrasting borders, or your monogram in big bold letters. For brunch or very informal entertaining, you might invest in some bright colored cellophane mats, or the new cork mats, neither of which ever have to go near a laundry!

Your china will be plain white or gray, with block initials or a modern striped border, and your silverware will be decidedly streamlined.

PEASANT DESIGN—This allows a lot of latitude. You may use gay Czechoslovakian linen cloths in raucous plaids or checks, or rough cottons that look like dish towels. Your china may be Mexican pottery, California pottery in vivid sun-drenched colors or French Provencal or Italian pottery, really charming and unbelievably hardy. With this you might use colored glassware—effective and inexpensive.

Allow yourself such whimsies as wooden-handled cutlery or salad forks with bright painted handles. Have a large, impressive wooden salad bowl, and lots of copper utensils. Don't be afraid to use color lavishly at your table: it has a great brightening effect.

As for EQUIPPING YOUR SHELVES, here are some of the staples and condiments you'll want to keep on hand at all times: butter, flour, sugar, salt, pepper, onions, oil, vinegar, baking powder, gelatin, parmesan cheese, coffee and tea, cocoa, mustard, ketchup, Worcestershire sauce, anchovy sauce, Hungarian paprika, curry powder, capers, bay leaf, garlic, cloves, vanilla, caraway seeds, raisins, rice, macaroni, black peppercorn, nutmeg, prunes, brown sugar and arrowroot. The major wines and liqueurs used for cooking are: Chablis, Claret, Marsalla, Sherry and Maraschino.

In addition, try always to have . . .

SOMETHING TO FALL BACK ON...

Just in case you ever come down with unexpected guests (or with the sort of hangover that knocks out your to-market plans), keep a supply of canned goods at home: soups, vegetables, fish, meat, a pudding or two, fruits, condensed milk. Pick out a favorite quick dish—rarebit, omelet, corn-beef-hash-with-poached-egg or what you will—then make sure that you always have the necessary ingredients on tap. If you keep a close watch on your "emergency shelf," and make a point of replacing each item you use, your hospitality needn't be a sometimes thing.

How to Serve

WHEN YOU PUT YOUR
BEST FOOT
FORWARD

Your kitchen-conquest will go for naught if you fluff the follow-through.

Attractive, knowing service makes good food taste superb; even indifferent fare takes on an epicurean air if it's set forth in the proper setting. So don't miss any of the tricks which weave an atmosphere of good living around your dining table. F'rinstance . . .

PUT A LIGHT IN HER EYES—But not the kind that comes through the courtesy of Mr. Edison. Candlelight is perfect for mood-setting and food abetting. Have enough candles to eliminate the Braille system of eating, but not so many as to brighten the corner where you're not. See that the candle tops are above eye level, and her eyes will center on you—and your magnificent food. She'll say "This is all so beautiful"—and *mean* it!

[19]

GIVE HER MUSIC, MAESTRO, PLEASE—Make it soft music, background music, the unobtrusive kind of music that stimulates rather than irritates conversation (*and* digestive juices). Thus you'll have to put your jazz collection aside during the dinner hour, and even your favorite symphonies if they're by Shostakovich. Play instead a quiet tone poem by Debussy, a stack of gypsy-violin recordings. Note the notes' relaxing effect on yourself as well as on your guests!

ACT AS THOUGH YOU HAD 10 SERVANTS—Your guests know you cooked their dinner, and they're already impressed with your talent or your courage, as the case may be. So you needn't keep reminding them of your chef role by hopping up and down, running back and forth between table and kitchen, during dinner. There could be no other point in such nerve-wracking antics, for it's a simple matter to arrange things so that "Dinner is Served" means for the cook-host as well as for the guests. Plan a menu of minimum courses so that everything can be either on the table or on the sideboard or serving table before you announce dinner; make full use of your chafing dish if it's necessary to keep one course warm while another has the floor . . . Use a dressed-up "family style" of service, with food for second helpings left on the table rather than returned to the kitchen after the first time around . . . Use trays for clearing the table, bringing in the dessert and coffee . . . and you'll find that you can play the lord of the manor at the head of the table, undisturbed by kitchen-calls, even if you *are* the cook.

AND DON'T NEGLECT THE LITTLE THINGS—The newly polished silver, the sparkling glassware, the crackling (non-smoking) fire in the grate, the cigarettes at each place, the heated dinner plates—all the little things combine to make a big thing of your food and wine. The atmosphere can be varied according to the menu—spaghetti might call for checkered tablecloth and operatic arias, while coq au vin might inspire the full formal treatment—but "atmosphere" it must be if you would give your dinner the showcase it deserves. "Showcase" is right: the proof of your pudding is in the way you present it. When you put your best food forward, remember . . .

IT ALL BOILS DOWN TO SHOWMANSHIP!

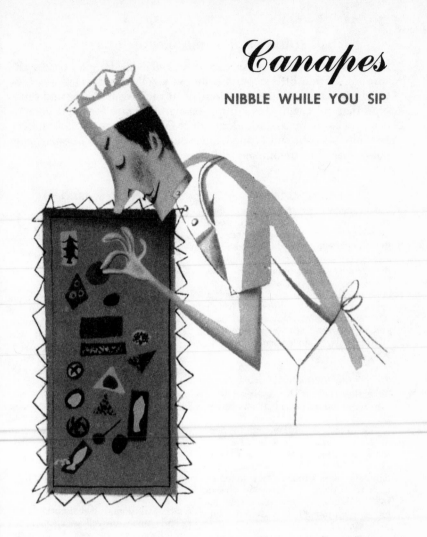

Canapes
NIBBLE WHILE YOU SIP

Everything from potato chip to caviar is nibbled in the name of canapé, so the host who would complement his cocktails (and draw compliments from his guests) need be inhibited by only one rule: the tidbit served to whet appetites should not dampen the dinner to come. That is, your canapés should neither foreshadow flavors to be featured at dinner, nor take the appreciative edge off your guests' appetites. Eliminate tomato canapes if tomato sauce is on the dinner menu, scorn a filling cheese if a heavy dinner is en route, and then you're on your own. For if there's any course which courts imagination, it's this prelude to dining.

After you've tried the cocktail—accompaniments below, branch out: soften your favorite cheese with beer, or mash an avocado with onion and tabasco . . . sample the 1001 cocktail crackers on the market . . . jazz up a bottled mayonnaise with all the condiments in the pantry, then offer dip-privileges with crisp raw vegetables . . . arm yourself with a can-opener and explore the epicure-shop shelves: miniature artichokes, all the patés, shrimps, anchovies,

[21]

little sausages, beefs, mushrooms, deviled ham, tongue, pastes and spreads. With a little experimentation, you'll soon develop a canapé repertoire equal to any occasion: from the cream-cheese-and-olive-type that goes with sherry flips, chaperoned meetings and your "I-can't-think-of-you-as-an-undergraduate" line . . . to the pickled-herring-on-sea-biscuit-type which supports your virile-bachelor, not-prepared-for-feminine callers pose.

CANAPE MARGUERY

Take four pieces of toast, cook (preferably in a silver platter) with sweet butter until crisp. Chop together: one hard-boiled egg, six filets of anchovies, half a green pepper, one peeled tomato, and as much tuna fish as about the weight of an egg, and spread this mixture flat on top of toast. Add a spoonful of Russian dressing (which is composed of mayonnaise and chili sauce). Garnish with several drops of Worcestershire sauce, serve immediately.

HAM AND CHEESE ROLL

Take thin slices of ham, spread with mixture of roquefort and cream cheese. Roll, fasten with toothpicks, place in icebox to chill till firm enough to slice. Slice fresh tomatoes, cut bread circles the same size as the slices. Toast bread discs, butter, spread thinly with mayonnaise and place a tomato slice on top of each toast disc. Cut ham and cheese roll in thin slices and place one on top of each tomato slice. Sure-fire hit.

OLIVES ROLLED IN BACON

Take large sized olives stuffed with pimiento and roll in slice of lean bacon. Secure with toothpick and bake in quick oven.

OYSTERS AND MUSHROOMS

Take a fresh oyster and place in a large mushroom that has been peeled. Dip in olive oil or butter, sprinkle with salt, pepper, paprika and a dash of celery salt, then place under a hot grill. Serve on half shell or a piece of thin toast.

PATE (EL BORRACHO)

1 lb. of butter	1 laurel leaf
1 onion, chopped	salt and pepper
¼ lb. of lard	dash of red pepper
1 jigger of sherry	1 jigger of brandy
½ lb. of calf's liver, diced	
(soak 24 hrs. in cold water)	

Brown meat in fat; remove, and sauté onions with ½ lb. of butter, ¼ lb. of lard and a jigger of sherry. Combine meat, laurel leaf and seasonings. Mix thoroughly all together and let it simmer slowly for ten minutes. Then strain through cheese cloth or fine wire strainer. Now mix remaining ½ lb. of butter and jigger of brandy.
Place this in a mold and cover top with a few tablespoonfuls of clear dissolved gelatin. Put into refrigerator and chill until firm. Serve on hot toasted squares, or crackers. Serves eight.

PETITE RAREBITS

Grate half pound Swiss cheese, half pound American yellow cheese, mix with the yolks of two eggs and one cup of rich cream. Spread on crackers or toast cut in rounds. Broil under quick flame and, before serving, sprinkle with paprika.

PICKLE DILLIES

Use a small-mouthed glass to cut circular pieces of bread. Lay one or two slices of dill pickle on each bread-circle, then sprinkle liberally with grated cheese. Bake in oven until cheese melts. Serve hot.

PIGS IN CLOVER

Wrap a slice of lean bacon around a large oyster. Sprinkle with salt and pepper, paprika and garlic salt. Secure with plain toothpick, place under a hot grill and serve when bacon is done.

SOUP SANDWICHES OR CANAPES

Combine and mix thoroughly: 1½ cups grated cheese; ¾ cup finely ground ham; 1 can condensed tomato soup, 1½ tsp. prepared mustard, 1½ tsp. grated horse-radish. Spread generous amount of mixture on slices of bread or toast. Grill open sandwiches under broiler until lightly browned. Garnish with parsley.

SPREAD SUGGESTIONS

Put equal parts of Bermuda onion and good Swiss cheese through a meat grinder; spread on buttered bread, cut into small pieces.

Fry bacon crisp, let it dry out, then chop it into fine pieces. Mix with peanut butter and spread on crackers.

Mix chopped ham, hard-boiled egg and mayonnaise for another good spread.

Mix red or black caviar with cottage cheese and a dash of garlic.

Mix chopped lobster and crabmeat with mayonnaise and anchovy paste. Spread on unsalted crackers.

STUFFED CLAMS

Boil clams with onions, red and green peppers and cream. When thick, roll with bread crumbs and fry in small balls. Place on clam shells and serve.

STURGEON SLICES

Dust very thin slices of smoked sturgeon (or smoked salmon) with white pepper, then decorate with a few chopped chives.

TOASTED CRAB MEAT

Take fresh or canned crab meat and mix with chili sauce, celery salt and a little pimiento. Spread on crackers or toast strips, or put mixture in pastry shells (they come from bakers or in boxes from the grocer) and bake under the grill for a few minutes.

TOMATO CANAPES

Cut 3 large tomatoes in half. Cut 6 rounds of bread and toast. Spread upper side with thin layer of anchovy paste mixed with creamed butter, then with thin layer of mayonnaise. Place tomato halves (or slices) on each. Dust with salt and pepper and cover tomatoes with thick layer of whipped cream to which 2 tablespoons of well-drained horse-radish and a little grated onion have been added. Dust with paprika and grated carrots.

TONGUE TIDBITS

Spread English mustard, red pepper and olive oil on sliced tongue. Then pack the slices together and put the whole business in the icebox until the mixture soaks into the meat. When ready to serve, pull the slices of tongue apart and fry in butter. Serve hot, with thin slices of bread.

"Go back to him, Bernice—he needs you!"

Caviar

FROM STURGEON WHO SELDOM NEED URGING

Since the spawn of the Volga sturgeon is best when no other flavor disguises its own peculiarly sweet and pungent, slightly salty and pleasantly fishy perfume, the real gourmet takes his caviar "neat"— spread on extremely thin buttered black bread ('tartine', to the French). Others squeeze lemon juice over the fish-eggs, spread the caviar on thick slices of hard-boiled egg or even on wedges of cheese, or sprinkle the crumbled yolks of hard-boiled eggs across the top of a caviar "sandwich."

If caviar in any form reminds you of your childhood's cod liver oil, it may be that you haven't tasted the good, "real thing," considered the greatest delicacy in the world of edibles. Only the sturgeon yields real caviar: the so-called "red caviar" is merely salmon eggs, and a processed caviar which comes from catfish, whitefish, shad or mullet has been artificially dyed. But even among the real caviars there is a confusing variety—so here's a translation of the words you see on caviar cans:

Beluga—large grains
Ossiotra—grains from a sturgeon weighing not more than 700 pounds
Sevruga—from a fish about 200 pounds
Sterlet—from the smallest sturgeon—the tiniest eggs
   o—black caviar
  oo—medium black
 ooo—fine gray

FRESH CAVIAR

Whole eggs. Fish ovaries are cleaned of all fatty matter, the membranes are skillfully removed, then the eggs are strained through seven sieves before being put into seasoning brine, then into kegs, then into cans.

PRESSED CAVIAR

Made from either premature ova, or from eggs damaged on the sieves. Because pressed cavier is less attractive, the eggs being broken, it is much cheaper than fresh. But it is less salty, more tasty and considered to have a more interesting consistency.

[25]

"They're a sensitive people, Clara. Smack your lips after
the yak-butter course"

Soups
DUCK-SOUP WAYS
TO BUILD A REP

When the automatic can opener crowded out the fine art of soup-making in most homes, cagey male cooks realized that the field was wide open to them. Not only did they yearn for un-standardized soups of character themselves—soul-warming soups of appetizing bouquet and myriad ingredients—but in the disappearance of the beauteous bowl they saw the ideal starting point for their own kitchen-pleasing. These days, all you have to do is make soup at home and you're labeled a cook. Make a *good* soup, a distinctive soup, a soup your friends can rely upon, and you're a *chef*.

Here are countless soups from which to choose your specialty: thick onion soup to forestall hangovers and restore good fellowship after a hard night's pub-crawling . . . rich bouillabaise . . . aristocratic vichyssoise . . . companionable chowders. Here are soups to serve as meals in themselves, soups to pave the palate for entrees to come, soups to tuck away in the refrigerator for sudden hunger. Here, too, are suggestions for lifting canned soups from the expected to the taste-treat. So take your time and take your choice. And when you find *The* Soup with which to anchor your culinary reputation, when you add the personal touch which makes it yours, "you, too, can be a soup-er man!"

CANNED SOUPS

To give your lazy-man's soup that indefinable "umpf," try mixing can with can. For example: a can of bean-with-bacon soup mixed with a can of condensed pea soup (plus a can of milk); or bisque of tomato with clam soup; chicken soup with cream of mushroom; mock turtle soup with pea; chicken with celery soup; cream of oyster and tomato, diluted with milk and seasoned with paprika and sherry; chicken gumbo with vegetable, dashed with Worcestershire; onion soup with chicken gumbo; pepper pot with chicken noodle.

Look for the unusual varieties of soup—cheese soup, for example, or haddock chowder—as well as for the best brands of the classic favorites. In solo or in combination, all canned soups are the better for imaginative seasoning, too. Try sherry, bitters, mustard, Worcestershire, chopped chives, lemon slices wherever they seem appropriate—and sometimes where they don't. Or try . . .

BRAZILIAN CONSOMME

Ever try nuts on your soup? Take 4 cups of canned consommé, ½ cup whipped cream, ½ tsp. paprika, ½ cup finely cut brazil nuts. Heat soup, put cream on top of each cup and sprinkle with paprika and finely chopped brazil nuts. Or open a can of creamed pea soup, add a dash of onion, ¼ tsp. nutmeg and sprinkle with brazil nuts.

CRABMEAT A LA NEWBURG SOUP

You can go very gay on this with a minimum of effort. 1 can cream of mushroom soup, 1 can asparagus soup, 1 cup milk, ½ cup cream, 1 can crabmeat and 3 tablespoons sherry.

Not Canned but MANNED Soups

ALE SOUP

Try this one on your next stag gathering. 1 quart of ale, juice of ½ lemon, dash of lemon peel, 1 stick cinnamon, 1 tbsp. potato flour, salt and sugar to taste. Put ale in saucepan with lemon juice and cinnamon and season to taste. Stir continuously, and when hot add the potato flour diluted with a little of the hot soup. Stir and serve.

BEER SOUP

One bottle of beer . . . when hot add a pint of hot milk in which yolks of 2 eggs have been stirred plus salt and sugar to taste. Serve with fried bread. Or slice or grate some black bread (pumpernickel) into dark beer, with sugar, lemon peel, a sherry glassful of *Kümmel* liqueur, and a small piece of ginger. Let it come to a boil, then strain. When ready to serve, add a lump of butter and salt according to taste.

BOUILLABAISSE

While there are many women cooks who can prepare a fairly presentable bouillabaisse the dish reaches the heights only in the hands of a man. And for every lover of the dish there is another recipe, in fact there are as many bouillabaisse schools as there are for juleps. This recipe permits variation and exceptions.

Begin with a white fish, haddock preferred, allowing one pound for each guest. Remove the head, tail, fins and backbone and place them in a quart of water and boil until the eyes fall out of the head. Strain the juice and you have a soup stock. Replace the stock in the kettle and add:

One clove of crushed garlic
Two sliced onions
One cup of olive oil
One cup of white wine (Chablis, Rhine or Moselle)
One green pepper chopped
One teaspoon saffron
Salt and pepper to taste.

If you have any or all of the following they may be added:

One dozen oysters with liquid
One dozen clams with liquid
One cup of lobster, crab meat or shrimps (fresh only)

Start your liquid cooking and add the vegetables and the fish and later the shellfish. Let it simmer twenty minutes, stirring slowly so that the fish does not break up, and serve on top of coarse toast.

BILLY THE OYSTERMAN'S BOUILLABAISSE

1 lb. sea bass, ½ lb. kingfish, 1½ lbs. boiled lobster, ½ lb. smelts, ½ lb. porgy (no relation to Bess), ½ lb. shrimps, boiled, hot olive oil, 1 cocktail glass each of brandy and sherry, 2 large onions, 5 stalks leeks, 3 stalks celery, 2 medium-sized carrots, 2 tablespoons butter, 1½ cups canned tomatoes, 1 tsp. salt, cayenne pepper, 1 tsp. saffron, 3 buds garlic, 1 tsp. chopped parsley, 3 bayleaves, 3 cups water. Clean the fish, remove bones, cut off heads. Cut flesh in pieces about 1½ inches long. Season with salt and fry for 10 minutes in hot olive oil. Remove the lobster meat from shell, cut same way, remove shrimps from shells, remove black line from their backs. Fry lobster and shrimps in another pan, also in hot olive oil for 5 minutes. Let cool and add brandy and sherry . . . cook 5 minutes. Dice onions, leeks, celery and carrots. Fry in butter until tender. Mix fish, lobster and shrimp, add onion mixture, put in tomatoes. Add seasonings. Cook for 20 minutes and serve on buttered toast. A meal, gentlemen, a meal.

CANJA SOUP
(A Brazilian Specialty)

Salt and pepper a fat hen, and let it stand for half an hour. Meanwhile slowly fry a sliced onion in fat; add a minced garlic and go on frying until the onion is a golden brown. Add the jointed chicken, and let it fry under close cover until lightly browned on one side, then turn it and fry the same way on other side. Wash half a cup of rice thoroughly, and after draining it add to the chicken together with a quarter of a pound diced ham. Cover the pan and continue the slow frying process but shake occasionally to prevent sticking. Add two quarts of boiling water and one bayleaf, some parsley, and a sprig of marjoram. Simmer until the chicken is tender, then take it out and remove all bones, cut the meat into pieces and return it to the soup.

CARAWAY SEED SOUP

(The most healthful soup on record, according to Joseph Knoepffler of the Passy Restaurant in New York.)

Brown a tablespoonful of flour in a little lard or butter, stirring it constantly so it won't burn. Add a teaspoonful of caraway seeds (for four helpings). When the seeds begin to crackle—in about a minute—pour four waterglassfuls of cold water over them. Cook for ten-fifteen minutes, salt and pepper, strain, and serve with croutons.

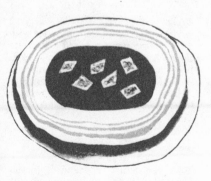

CLAM CHOWDER

20 clams	1 teaspoon salt
1 slice fat salt pork	2 tablespoons
1 onion, sliced	butter
4 potatoes, diced	1 tablespoon
1 cup fish stock	Worcestershire
2 cups scalded	sauce
milk	4 pilot biscuits

Wash clams and scald in their own liquor. Then remove clams and strain juice through cheesecloth. Cut pork into cubes and fry out. Cook onions in pork fat five minutes, then strain fat into soup kettle. Parboil potatoes in one cup water and add water and potatoes to fat. Cover and simmer ten minutes. Add fish stock and clams. Add hot milk, salt, butter and Worcestershire Sauce. Split pilot biscuits, soak in a little cold milk and add to chowder. And also, for Sunday morning—add two teaspoons of Worcestershire to a raw egg.

CONSOMME A LA ROYAL

Bring to boiling point two quarts of good stock; remove it to one side of the fire and add a tablespoonful of beef extract, one quart of scalded milk, salt and cayenne to taste. Mix well, and add two teaspoonfuls of onion juice; place where it will keep warm, but not boil. For garnishing beat the yolks of two eggs until light, add a half gill of stock, mix; add a dash of white pepper, and a grating of nutmeg, pour into a greased pie tin; stand this in a shallow pan of hot water; place in a moderate oven to harden, do not brown. When firm, cut into diamond-shaped pieces; put them into the consommé and serve.

COLD CREAM OF CHICKEN
INDIENNE

4 chopped onions, 2 stalks celery, 2 bayleaves all smothered in butter with 4 tbsp. curry powder mixed with white flour. Add 4 cups canned chicken broth and 4 glasses milk. Put mixture in your icebox and let mellow for 2 or 3 days (this is the secret of its success) before serving. From Armando's, New York.

CREME DE LEGUME
(For Four)

Take two tomatoes (canned, if you like), three leeks, one large onion, two large potatoes, two carrots, a quarter of a measuring cup of split peas, a few leaves of cabbage, a little celery, one small turnip, a few string beans, a half teaspoonful of thyme, a very small bay-leaf, and any bones you might have handy — turkey, chicken, beef, lamb, ham, etc. If you have no bones, a tablespoonful of fat or butter will do, or even left-over gravy, except for lamb or mutton gravy. After washing everything thoroughly, put the ingredients in a casserole; the vegetables have to be diced. Add two quarts of water, warm or cold. Allow it to simmer for two hours. When it has cooked, strain through a very fine sieve. Correct the seasoning and serve. You may add a little milk at the time of final seasoning.

CREOLE GUMBO
(Roosevelt Hotel, New Orleans)
(For Four)

Stay home some week-end and get to work on: 1 oz. butter, 3 oz. lean, raw, diced ham, 1 small white onion and 1 green onion, a leek, a green pepper and a stalk of celery, a clove of garlic and a dash of parsley, a shallot, a clove and a dash of paprika; then a ¼ can cut okra, ¾ lb. raw shrimps, peeled, 2 hard-shell crabs, 1 small can tomatoes, 2 quarts of stock, salt, pepper and bouquet garni.

The secret of the whole thing is in the ¼ tbsp. gumbo *file*—a powder made by the Indians of the Louisiana bayous from the roots of the sassafras tree. The *New Yorker* tells us that you have to send to Louisiana to get the file . . . The New Orleans Import Company is the concern which keeps it on file, so to speak; you'll have to send to Louisiana for it.

Here's the way you put the stuff together: fry white and green onions, leeks, green peppers and celery in butter, add shrimps and crabs and fry until all liquid has been rendered and nearly dried; add dry shallots, garlic, parsley and fry a little longer, then add paprika and tomatoes. Empty in pot containing the stock and bouquet garni, the latter consisting of celery, bay leaves and thyme all tied together. Season to taste and let cook for 1½ to 2 hours. Last few minutes add the gumbo file, being very careful not to let the soup boil while adding the file or afterwards. Serve with dry sherry.

CUCUMBER SOUP

Make a cream sauce, add 3 large cucumbers peeled and sliced thinly. Cook slowly until soft and transparent, then rub through a sieve. Reheat, season with salt and pepper, add ½ cup cream and 2 tsps. of bitters just before serving.

FISH FUMET

Two pounds of trimmings and bones of sole or whiting, ½ pound of sliced blanched onions, 1 ounce parsley roots or stalks, ½ pint of white wine. Preparation: Butter the bottom of a thick tall saucepan, put in the blanched onions and the parsley stalks and upon these aromatics lay the fish remains. Add the juice of a lemon, cover the stewpan, put it on the fire and allow the fish to exude its essence, jerking the pan at intervals. Moisten in the first place with the white wine, then with the lid off, cook until the liquid is reduced to about half; now add 1 quart of cold water, bring to a boil, skim and then leave to cook for 20 minutes only, on a moderate fire. The time allowed is ample for the purpose of extracting the aromatic and gelatinous properties. You might try a *Bâtard-Montrachet*, 1929, with this or a *Clos Ste. Odile*, 1929.

LOBSTER STEW

Another New England concern goes to town on deep-sea lobster . . . effectively tinned by an exclusive process . . . only selected portions of the claw and tail meat used. Put as much milk as you need in double boiler with lump of butter and seasoning. Add contents of a can of deep-sea lobster (cut in small pieces). To secure rich, red coloring, lobster may be fried in butter for a few moments before adding to the milk.

ONION SOUP

Stay-uppers in Paris have known for years of the curative properties of *onion soup* and have trundled themselves down to the markets for a bowl alongside the truckmen. This is not the Paris onion soup but comes from Burgundy, and is made according to the old Tisseyre formula.

For six persons take about five pounds of onions. Cut them thin. Put in an iron pot or French cooking dish. Add six bouillon cubes (or better yet, a cup of soup stock or a can of beef broth), then take a loaf of French or Italian bread, break into small pieces and put in the pot. Cover this with enough water to submerge the ingredients. Put a lid on the pot, let it come almost to a boil, and then push to the back of the stove to simmer all day. (Peasant households sometimes allow this to simmer for several days.) Just before you are ready to serve, add one pint of thick cream. The bread by this time is dissolved, and the soup the consistency of purée.

OYSTER STEW

Plunge freshly opened, plump oysters (at least 6 per person) into a pan of rich cream. Add gobs of sweet butter and heat over low flame until the oysters' edges crinkle into smiles. Never let the cream boil. Serve with great crunchy seafaring biscuits. Variation: toss in a handful of live oyster crabs to give it sea spice.

PEANUT BUTTER SOUP

Wash and scrape a large bunch of celery, put through food chopper together with medium-sized onion. Melt 5 tbsp. butter in saucepan, add celery and onion. Cook until it turns slightly brown, add 4 tbsp. flour and a tsp. of salt and dash of pepper. Put in tbsp. of sugar, stir until mixed and add 2 cups of boiling water as well as 3 beef bouillon cubes. When cubes have dissolved add 3 cups of scalded milk. Now mix 5 tbsp. peanut butter with half cup of cold water until a smooth paste is accomplished, then add to hot mixture. Cook a few minutes and serve with chopped egg yolks and finely chopped ripe olives and chives.

[31]

"When do you want your eggs — Sport, Editorial or Financial page?"

. . . lunch meat, crackers, cherries—and a fifth of milk!"

PETITE MARMITE
FAMILY STYLE

Wash six pounds of shin of beef in cold water, as well as some beef bones, place them in an earthenware pot, cover with cold water, and season. Boil and skim thoroughly. Now add to it carrots, turnips, a well-peeled onion, some cabbage, leeks, and eighteen whole peppers. Taste and season again. Let it cook on very slow fire for two hours and a half. Strain carefully, add to it a whole chicken, after which cook adding them to the soup at the end. Boil your marrow bones separately, it an hour and a half longer and serve.

POTAGE "BILLY BY"
(For Four)

Take a quart and a half fresh mussels, wash them; also two onions, chopped, a little parsley, and some freshly ground pepper. Add a bottle of good dry white wine and put on a high flame for fifteen minutes.

In a deep bowl beat eight egg yolks with a good pint of thick cream and a generous piece of sweet butter. Add to this the strained liquid in which the mussels cooked. Now remove the mussels from their shells and mash the meat firmly, adding this to the rest. Cook on a low fire, constantly stirring with a wooden spoon. When the concoction begins to stick to the spoon—just before boiling—strain once more through a cloth, throw in another piece of butter, season to taste, and serve very hot.

POTAGE SANTE
(For Four)

Melt one and a half tablespoonfuls of butter or fat in a casserole, and add a chopped onion. Cook for five minutes. Add a palmful of sorrel, and cook for another five minutes. Throw in two large potatoes diced small, salt, pour in five cups of hot water, and cook for forty-five minutes. When cooked, strain. Take the yolks of two eggs, mix well with a small amount of milk or cream, add to this a little of the soup, mix well again, and add it to the soup. Correct seasoning and serve with fried croutons.

POTATO SOUP WITH MUSTARD

Next time you open a can of potato soup, or make it yourself—add mustard. If you make your own, pare 3 potatoes, cook with 1 onion and 1 stalk celery in 3 cups boiling water. When tender mash through purée sieve and add 2 cups thin white sauce and 2 tsps. mustard, just before serving. Gives it considerable élan.

PUREE OF TOMATOES
(From The Players, Hollywood)

Dice a strip of bacon, half a carrot, half an onion, and a bayleaf, and fry this in a little butter. Cut into pieces eight tomatoes and add to the concoction together with a little sugar, two ounces of rice, two cups of consommé, and simmer. Rub through a sieve, add some consommé, and a lump of butter just before serving and just after you garnish the soup with peeled, diced tomatoes fried for a minute in butter.

SEMOLINA SOUP
(Quick)

Brown a tablespoonful of semolina or hominy grits, per person in a little lard or butter, stirring the concoction all the while with a spatula. Pour a measuring cup of water per person over it, and season to taste. Cook for five or six minutes, and serve. You may cook a few vegetables in a different vessel, adding them to the semolina soup.

VICHYSSOISE
(For Six)

Set 6 leeks, sliced, 1 small sliced onion, 2 medium-sized potatoes, sliced, 2 spoonfuls of butter, pepper and salt to taste, in a covered saucepan; place over a slow fire in order to cook slowly until the whole is reduced to the consistency of a paste. (Be sure not to brown.) When ready, put through a sieve, add one quart of chicken or beef consommé; mix well and allow to cook off. Then add 1 cup of sour cream; again mix and place in the refrigerator. When serving, sprinkle lightly with chopped chives. (Especially recommended for the warm months.)

VICHYSSOISE

(from New York's Hotel Plaza)

Chop finely the white parts of four leeks, place in a pot with a lump of sweet butter, and brown very lightly. Add a finely chopped small onion, four finely sliced potatoes, and a quart of chicken broth (if you have any), or consommé (the canned variety will do), or water if you must. Add salt to taste. Simmer for a good half-hour, and when the potatoes and leeks are done, take the pot off the fire, crush the vegetables, and pass through a fine sieve. Return to the fire and add two cups of boiled milk, two cups of cream and a tiny lump of butter. Correct the seasoning, bring to a quick boil, cool, and again rub through a fine strainer. Add a cup of cream (heavy if possible), chill, and add finely chopped chives at the moment of serving. (Serves six generously.)

WATERCRESS SOUP

(Chinese)

Wash and cut into two-inch lengths one bunch of watercress. Chop one-half pound pork. Cook the pork until tender, in enough water to make a soup, then add the watercress and cook for ten minutes. Add two tablespoons Chinese sauce, salt and pepper, and green onion sprouts.

CREAMED WATERCRESS SOUP

1 small bunch watercress, 3 cups water, ½ small onion, 1 tsp. salt, ¼ tsp. pepper, 4 tsp. butter, 3 tbsp. flour, 3 chicken bouillon cubes, 1 cup cream, croutons. Wash and chop watercress. Add to water and onion which has been sliced, add salt and pepper. Boil slowly for ten minutes. Remove from fire and rub through coarse sieve. Melt butter and add flour, add bouillon cubes to soup, then add to butter and flour. Add cream and serve.

Fish

Dangle bait like this before your guests, and they'll bite—with delight. After suffering steam-table tastelessness or misplaced housewifely economy, any palate will perk up at the taste of fresh fish, properly prepared—by a man. (Women don't seem to understand fish—and, we suppose, vice versa.) Call upon your fishing-trip memories to guide you in selecting only the freshest fish at the market: gills should be bright red; fish should sink, not float, in water. Then hook onto the suggestions, plain and fancy, below. You won't have to fish for culinary compliments once you've served these sea beauties:

BAKED FISH

A satisfactory way to prepare any fish is to sprinkle some flour in the buttered pan, so that the fish won't stick. Then place the fish in the pan, together with shallots and parsley chopped fine, and butter on top; bake for twenty minutes; and a few minutes before it is done, pour a glass of dry white wine and the juice of a half lemon on it. It is against culinary principles to use garlic in cooking fish, except smearing a crouton or two with a clove, not unlike the method used in salads.

[35]

CARP A LA POLONAISE

(Courtesy of the Polish Restaurant in New York)

One lemon
One stalk of celery
One onion
Two lumps of sugar
Six seeds of black pepper
One pinch of ginger
Half quart beer
Half quart water
Two oz. gingerbread
One and one-half oz. butter
One spoonful of prune jam
One oz. raisins
One oz. currants
One oz. almonds
One oz. nuts
One glassful of red wine

Clean the carp well and cut into pieces of one and one-half inches each. Slice the celery, the rind of lemon, chop one onion, put in skillet with half quart water and boil. When the celery is soft, squeeze in some lemon juice and place the carp in the mixture. Boil for forty minutes, then take out the carp carefully and put it on a plate; keep it warm.

Strain the remaining mixture and put back in the skillet; add the chopped-up gingerbread, beer, butter, prune jam, sugar, raisins, sliced almonds, peeled nuts, and other ingredients and boil. Pour this mixture over the carp, and some of the remaining sauce may be served separately.

COURT-BOUILLON

Although it is most important in the alchemy of fish cookery, few people know the secrets of a good *court-bouillon*. It is the united cooking of fish, water, wine, vegetables, and seasoning. But the vegetables must be put on about an hour before the fish, otherwise they won't get done and their perfume will not infuse the fish; in other words, the fish must cook in the vegetable water that already is so good that it could be eaten as is. Then before you put the fish in, envelop it securely in a thin piece of linen or any other kind of thin, clean rag. If you don't do this, the fish might fall into little pieces. Don't ever cook fish too long; it isn't meat. If you want to retain all the flavor and perfume of the fish, do not cook it over a large flame; just simmer. The liquid of the *court-bouillon* is used for soups and sauces, or if strained, it can be put away in bottles if all of it is not needed immediately. The fish is eaten hot with a sauce and vegetables, and what remains is eaten another time, cold, with a sauce that complements cold fish.

Here are several ways to make *court-bouillon:*

1. Simmer together two quarts of water, a pint of milk, a generous quantity of salt, and the juice of a half lemon. Place the fish in this after about twenty minutes and simmer till tender.

2. Two quarts of water, salt, vinegar, two carrots sliced in small round shapes, two small onions, a *bouquet garni,* peppercorns according to taste; cook for a half hour before you add the fish.

3. Two quarts of red or white wine, one quart of water, and all the other ingredients mentioned in recipe No. 2. (This *court-bouillon* is very good for making fish sauces.)

4. Two quarts of water, salt, garlic, one carrot, one branch of celery, one onion, one clove, a *bouquet garni.* Cook very slowly for a half hour. Strain, and add a quart of milk. Now put in your fish and simmer, don't bring to boil. (This kind is excellent for soups.)

And here's what to do with the leftover liquid:

COURT-BOUILLON SOUP

Place your *court-bouillon*—minus the fish, of course, for you've eaten that—in a pot together with an equal amount of water. Add potatoes, diced, carrots sliced, leeks, watercress, and a bit of sweet cicely. Cook till vegetables are tender, add a glass of white wine and season with salt and pepper. Finally, add a small piece of butter and pour it over small pieces of toast in the tureen.

CRAB MEAT RAVIGOTE

Mix the fresh crab meat with cold Ravigote sauce, made the following way: Add finely chopped chives, tarragon, chervil and parsley to a half cup of mayonnaise. Stir in a little spinach juice for coloring, add a little garlic and capers.

FILET OF FLOUNDER HOLLANDAISE

Put half of a chopped carrot and a quarter of a small onion in salted water and boil slowly. Wash and dry the fish, salt it, and roll and fasten it with the aid of toothpicks; then cook it in the boiling water for ten minutes over a medium flame. While the fish is cooking, make your sauce the following way; Melt—do not brown—one and a half tablespoonfuls of butter, stir in it a half tablespoonful of flour, one egg yolk mixed with one-eighth cup of milk, a few drops of lemon, pepper and salt to taste, and four tablespoonfuls of water in which the fish was cooked. Pour the sauce over the fish.

FILET OF SOLE-ANYMAN

Get some filet of sole (real lemon sole is well worth the added cost over flounder). Put it in a pan with some butter, one tablespoon of vinegar, one thinly sliced onion, salt and pepper and a cup of white wine. Cook for ten minutes covered. In the meantime have a half pound of mushrooms sauted in butter, with perhaps a taste of good oil. After the fish has cooked, pour the mushrooms over it, and more wine, then bake in an oven for another ten or fifteen minutes. You'll probably have to eat this with a spoon.

FILET OF SOLE MARGUERY

Poach the filets in a liquid made from one square of butter, four ounces of white wine and two ounces of water. (If you have a good culinary sense, you don't have to measure.) Coat the filets with a white sauce, and garnish with mussels, mushrooms, shrimps, which have been previously cooked. *To make white sauce:* The liquid left from poaching the sole is called fish fumet. Add to this liquid two yolks of eggs and some butter. Cook slightly, and strain, season to taste. Then add a little whipped cream, and glaze.

FILET OF STRIPED BASS
Bonne Femme

Take a flat sauce pan and butter it well. Place in it some chopped shallots and parsley and then lay the fish in the saucepan. Season with salt and pepper and add some sliced mushrooms. Sprinkle some cooking wine sauce and fish broth over the filet of

bass. Bake ten minutes. Place the fish on the serving dish and pour over it the sauce of the cooking pan after it has been thickened with the yolks of three eggs and a little butter. Serve very hot.

FISH IN DARK BEER

3 pounds of fish (carp, pike or bass. In winter, large fat pickerel)
1 tablespoon vinegar
2 chopped onions (large size)
4 tablespoons of butter
2 tablespoons of flour
2 tablespoons of brown sugar
5 peppers (whole)
2 ground cloves
1 teaspoon Worcestershire sauce
2 cups dark beer

Clean and scale fish, cut in three-inch slices. Brown onion in butter, add flour and cook for three minutes. Add beer and all other ingredients except the vinegar. Boil this sauce to the thickness of thin cream and put fish slices into it, and continue boiling till the fish is well done. Finally add vinegar and continue boiling for another two minutes. Pour sauce through strainer and serve separately.

FISH MAYONNAISE
(Excellent leftover fish dish)

Use any cooked fish. De-bone and cut in pieces. Make a mayonnaise, and cover thinly the bottom of a dish with it. Place a layer of fish on this, and cover the fish layer with mayonnaise, and so *ad infinitum.* Place the dish for two hours in the refrigerator. Chop some sweet pickles, olives, capers and a little tarragon and mix well. Add this to a cupful of mayonnaise which you saved, mix well and pour over your fish. Serve cold.

"I guess that's what they mean by 'The Good Old Days'!"

FISH RAGOUT
(Matelote)

You can make this dish with one species of fish or several. Best combination is haddock, cod and eel. Cut the fish in about three-inch squarish pieces; remove the skin. Put a few slices of bacon (diced) in a pot, together with chopped parsley, small onions, salt and pepper, a glass of white wine, a glass of water, and your fish, and bring to a boil. After this, put in a moderate oven for 20-25 minutes. Take out the fish, place on a dish and keep warm. Add a glass of good red wine to the liquid, bring to a boil, add a piece of butter mixed with a little flour to thicken. Correct the seasoning, pour sauce over the fish and serve.

CANNED LOBSTER
A LA NEWBURG

Heat two teaspoonfuls of butter in a pan. Add to this three tablespoonfuls of flour, and mix it with the butter with a wooden spoon. Take care that it does not burn. Add a pint of hot milk and, stirring constantly, mix it thoroughly with the flour; otherwise it will get lumpy. Cook and stir for fifteen minutes over a low flame.
Open a can of lobster, and dice it. Heat one teaspoonful of butter in another pan; add the lobster, salt and pepper it, and add a bit of paprika. When you see it is getting hot, pour in a wineglassful of sherry. Now pour the sauce you have prepared over the diced lobster, but not too much of it —just enough to cover it. (If you have some sauce left over, you may use it the next few days, for this cream sauce keeps, and goes with most entrées.) Cook over low flame for ten minutes. If the sauce seems too thick, add a bit of milk. Add some cream a few minutes before serving.

LOBSTER ESCALOPES

Cook the lobster in a court-bouillon. When it cools in the liquid, remove the tail, cut in escalope sizes and plunge the slices into hot butter in a pan. Take the rest of the lobster meat, break it up into little pieces, pass through a sieve, add to this hot tomato sauce, a small glass of brandy or whisky, heat and mix and pour this sauce over the lobster escalopes.

LOBSTER XAVIER

Boil your lobster and, after it has cooled, split lengthwise in two. Remove the shell remains intact; dry the shell. Dice the meat and put the small pieces in hot butter. Add a little cream to it and a cup of Mornay sauce, prepared the following way:
Beat the yolks of two eggs together with a cup of Bechamel sauce (melt 3 tablespoonfuls of butter, add to this 3 tablespoonfuls of flour, cook till golden brown, add gradually 2 cups of milk, stir constantly and add a slice or two of onion. Cook for one hour over low flame and strain through fine sieve), add a tablespoonful of butter, and a little grated cheese.
Mix the diced lobster meat with the Mornay sauce, fill the shell with the preparation and cover the top with another cup of Mornay sauce. Sprinkle with grated cheese and brown in a hot oven.

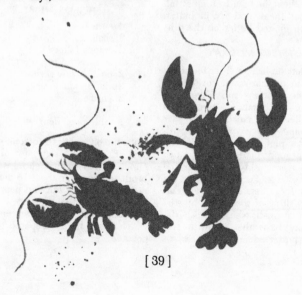

OYSTERSNACK

Sauté finely chopped celery in a little butter and when it is tender add one wineglass of sherry (for each dozen oysters) and stir until very hot. Into this drop your oysters (½ doz. for each guest), and let them cook until their little edges start curling. Then arrange six oysters on a piece of toast and pour the liquid over them and serve, preferably with a glass of sherry.

BROILED OYSTERS

Drain the oysters and lay them on a napkin to dry. Pepper and salt them, and broil them on oyster broiler or small gridiron. The oysters must not smoke, and they must be cooked quickly. Put a bit of butter on them just before serving.

DEVILED OYSTERS

1 pint oysters, 1 tbsp. butter, 3 shallots (a garlic ally), 2 tbsp. flour, ½ cup milk, ¼ cup cream, salt, nutmeg, cayenne, mustard, worcestershire, chopped mushrooms, parsley, egg yolk and buttered cracker crumbs. Wash and chop oysters, cook shallots in butter 3 minutes, add flour and stir until well blended, then add milk and cream. Bring to boiling point and add oysters and remaining ingredients except yolk and crumbs. Let simmer 12 minutes. Add egg yolk, put mixture in deep halves of oyster shells, cover with butter crumbs, bake 15 minutes.

DUTCH OYSTERS

Roll the oysters in yolk of egg, and then dip them in bread crumbs, salt and pepper them, and fry in butter. Serve with melted butter on the side.

OYSTERS MORNAY

Bake oysters on half shell for four minutes. Remove from oven, cover them with sauce Mornay and bake until brown. To make sauce Mornay, boil one pint Bechamel sauce (see Lobster Xavier recipe, use half quantities) with one quarter pint of oyster liquor. Reduce by a good quarter and add two ounces Gruyère and two ounces grated Parmesan cheese. Put the sauce on the fire again for a few minutes and insure the melting of the cheese by stirring with a small whisk. Finish the sauce away from the fire with two ounces of butter added by degrees.

RUFFLED OYSTERS

Take a pan or casserole. Toast a piece of bread, cutting the crust off, put the toast in the bottom of the pan, and moisten it with the liquid of the oysters. Put eight oysters on the toast, pepper and salt them, adding a bit of butter. Place the pan in hot oven, cook until the oysters "ruffle." Serve with slices of lemon. And don't bother to serve on plates; Ruffled Oysters taste best out of individual pans or casseroles.

OYSTERS RAREBIT

Bring one cup of oysters to the boiling point and save the liquor. Melt two tablespoons of butter, add ¼ pound of fresh cheese, cut in small pieces; ¼ teaspoon of salt and a sprinkle of Cayenne. When the cheese has melted, add the oyster liquor and two eggs slightly beaten. When smooth, add the oysters and serve at once on toast.

OYSTERS A LA ROCKEFELLER

Bake oysters on half shell for four minutes. Remove from oven and cover the oysters with very fine chopped spinach and onion, bread crumbs, cheese and a few dashes of Herbesaint. Bake until brown and serve.

SHRIMPS IN BEER

4 cups beer
3 shallots
2 onions (sliced)
3 ounces butter
2 pounds raw shrimps
Sprig of parsley
Bayleaf
Celery
1 tablespoon flour

Cook the beer with the onions, shallots, bayleaf, parsley, celery, for about 15 minutes; add peeled shrimps to the broth and cook for about 15 more minutes; season with salt and pepper. Remove the parsley bouquet and bind the sauce with the butter and flour which has been prepared into a pomade.

Steak

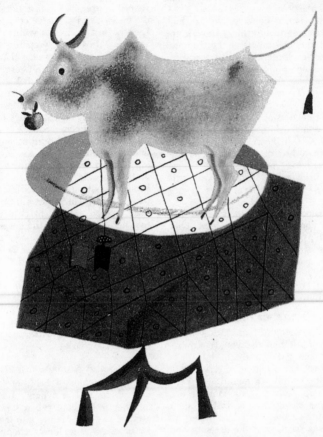

Ah, steak—plain, unadulterated beef—is paradise enow. You no doubt have your favorite method of preparing the queen-beef: perhaps you sizzle it briefly beneath a hot broiler flame to produce a cut-with-a-fork, uniform tenderness; or maybe you throw it into a smoking skillet to form a crusty surface encasing the steak's juices. But if ever you should tire of the wondrous pleasure to be found in such unadorned beefsteak, get into the specialty-sweepstakes with these variations:

BACHELORS' BEER STEAK

1 thick Porterhouse steak
Olive oil
salt
pepper
2 cups beer
4 tablespoons butter
2 tablespoons flour
1 pound fresh button mushrooms

Marinate steak in oil, season on both sides and broil to desired doneness. A few minutes before the steak is done, fry mushrooms in butter, season with salt and pepper, add flour, then steak juice from broiler pan and beer. Stir well while cooking. Let come to a boil, then pour over steak and serve.

[41]

MAC NAMARA BEEFSTEAK

(Ideal for picnics, but can be emulated at home. For a starter, try spring onions, radishes and celery. For dessert, the indicated tidbit is a baby lamb chop broiled over the charcoal. It may sound silly—but try it!)

Procure from a good butcher a steak at least three inches thick. Have it cut from the choicest part of the cow and take nothing inferior. When ready for the food part of the picnic, take the steak and cover both sides with pepper and salt. Then completely encase the steak in a coating of wet coarse salt to the thickness of a quarter inch. Next place some white paper napkins on top of this, to keep the salt in place. Prepare a fire of wood, or charcoal preferred in a pit edged with stones. Place the steak in a heavy wire grill and cook for about ten minutes on each side.

Now knock off the outer layer of salt, which comes off in one piece. Then slice the porterhouse and sirloin down in thin strips. Throw these in a pan of butter which you have set on the fire. Serve the slices of meat on a half slice of bread which has been dipped in the butter.

STEAK CAPUCHINA

Make a dressing of four chicken livers, a dash of salt, half an onion, four mushrooms chopped fine, three almonds, a little butter, a squirt of sherry. While this simmers for ten minutes, brown a filet of tenderloin steak on a broiler, just long enough to seal in the juices. Then take a piece of white paper, lay the steak on it, pour the dressing over the steak, then fold the paper into an overall covering. That goes into a greased pan in the oven. When the paper is light brown, the steak is still rare. When it's a dark tan, the steak

is medium, and when the edges of the envelope begin to char, the steak's well done. That takes about five minutes.

SURPRISE STEAK

Choose your favorite cut, which should be free of bone. A thick rump, if you can find a tender one, is ideal. Lightly dust each side with salt, then apply a thin film of prepared English mustard; English, because that is the fieriest variety. Next—and here you are going to be scandalized, as I was when the editor told me, and before I had tried it out—cover both sides of the steak as thickly as it will stick on, with *powdered sugar.* Sounds terrible, doesn't it? But wait! Burning sugar produces an intense heat. Ask any visiting fireman who has fought a conflagration in a sugar refinery.

Broil your steak about three minutes on each side. The sugar will first melt, then harden into a blackened shell that hermetically seals the pores of the steak, preventing the loss of a drop of juice, or a whiff of flavor. Crack and peel off the sugar shell, and carve, the "blood following the knife." Contrary to your fears, the steak will *not* taste sugary. The intense heat will have absorbed all the sugar into its protective shell, and at the same time have charred the surface of the steak beautifully.

STEAK A LA MARY MULLER

Get a thick filet of beef, broil it on one side for four or five minutes; while the filet is broiling, rub a bowl with a clove of garlic, empty into it a small jar of caviar, very finely chopped onions, and the juice of a lemon on top, and mix thoroughly. Then turn your steak, spread the mixture on the undone side, and continue to broil for another five minutes. Serve hot.

PLANKING

Take a large plank, as large as will fit comfortably in your oven. It should be of non-resinous and well-dried wood—birch and maple are the best— and the top side scooped out to the depth of half an inch. If this is too much trouble you may be able to purchase an already prepared plank at the hardware store. Place the plank in the oven and let it get hot enough for butter to melt immediately. Arrange

your fish, skin side down and fully spread (or your meat with the best side up) in the center. About it lay the vegetables that are to accompany the main piece, then replace them all in the oven. Do not worry about the smoke; it's all a part of the flavor and if the wood chars that is to be expected. Planking is a fine art and it is advisable to try it on the family before inviting the neighbors in.

Stew

HOW TO DO RIGHT
BY A MAN'S DISH

Second only to steak in its standing as a Man's Dish, stew has been much maligned by the coy-type hostess who says, "I'd love to have you for dinner, but we're only having stew." That stew—rib-sticking, heart-warming—should be spoken of in such deprecating fashion! Properly made, stew surpasses most entrées. Accompanied by a bottle of wine and a green salad, followed by a cup of strong coffee and perhaps a hunk of cheese—who could ask for more?

Some stews may indeed be "only" stews—thin, watery, with microscopic amounts of meat. But not these samples below, and not the stews you "invent" when you're familiar with the two basic types:

The *White Stew Family*, includes all stews made of lamb, veal, fowl or hare, sautéed with onions, bacon or butter, and salt and pepper; sometimes potatoes are cooked in these stews, and occasionally thickening is added. The liquid is usually a light stock (or water), or a white wine.

[43]

The *Brown Stew Family*, consisting of stews made of beef, usually cooked *with* carrots, turnips, onions, peas and other vegetables, and herbs and salt and pepper. Red wine is more often used than white; the stock is usually bouillon—although, of course, water may be used for both types.

Here are samples of each. Take it from there!

BOEUF BOURGUIGNON

Get two pounds of beef, lean, for four people. Cube the meat. Make a pickle out of a quart bottle of red Bordeaux wine, small onions, carrots, celery, garlic, thyme, one bayleaf, three cloves, parsley. Marinate meat in this pickle overnight. Then take out the meat (sorry, you can't use the pickle for anything else afterward), sprinkle the meat cubes with a dash of brandy or whisky, salt and pepper them, and sauté them in a pan with finely diced bacon and some flour over a brisk fire for ten minutes. Then pour in a new bottle of red wine, adding mushrooms and small onions. Cook for about two hours over very low flame. Don't open the lid, and don't forget that a stew boiled is a stew spoiled!

This uncommonly good stew belongs to the glorified class. It does not cost much, however, if you use a domestic Bordeaux.

IRISH STEW

Wash and drain the mutton, removing the skin, gristle, and excess fat. Cut meat in square pieces. Put them into the pan with half of the already prepared (quartered) potatoes, and onions. Add seasoning and water or stock, remembering that the liquid must cover no more than half the food. Stew slowly. Add the rest of the potatoes one hour before serving; these will cook gently, and will not lose shape like those put in earlier. Serve hot, with the whole potatoes around the edge, meat in the middle, and the gravy poured over.

OXTAIL STEW WITH AMERICAN BURGUNDY

Cut the oxtails into small sections. Brown them in butter. Add carrots, celery, onions, mushrooms, potatoes, a bayleaf, salt and pepper. Cover with wine and cook until the meat is done. Thicken with butter that has been browned in a pan with lemon juice and parsley. (*Beurre Meunière*)

HUNGARIAN PORKOLT

Get one and a half pounds of shoulder of veal, dice it, chop up two large onions, brown them in a pan with a tablespoonful of lard on a very brisk fire—do not burn—and add a half lump of sugar. Put the meat in the pan, and turn down the flame. After fifteen minutes add one tablespoonful of paprika, one tomato, one green pepper cut up, salt to taste. Let it simmer for one hour. Do not open the lid! Do not add any water or liquid! Serve with boiled rice or boiled potatoes.

This same pörkölt (which, in rough translation, simply means singed) may be made with suckling pig, pork, mutton, fowl, duck, turkey and goose.

(**Note:** In the goulash category there are three specific branches: goulash, which is in reality a soup dish with beef and potatoes in it; the above described pörkölt, which is a paprika dish without cream, belonging to the white stew family; and finally paprikasch, which has sour or sweet cream in it. The well-known chicken paprikasch is one of this branch. There are several important points to remember in making goulash or its relatives; one is not to brown the onions too much, but merely to "golden" them in sautéing. It is also better to use lard than butter. It may be sheer imagination, but all goulashes feel happier with half a lump of sugar in them. If you want to get a nice red color, do not add the paprika with the meat, but fifteen minutes after you have put it in the pan. For in the first quarter-hour the meat—beef especially—gives out a lot of blood, and if the meat juices mix with the paprika, the color will be brown. Lastly, do not stir; just agitate the pan gently now and then.)

Game

Game can be cooked in a spick-and-span tiled kitchen, of course, and even exceptionally by some women (who usually are good shots as well); but a log cabin or an open grill is the logical place —and a man's the proper cook. For the nimble Nimrod, then, who would tame his game to the table as well as he tracked and shot it, these pointers:

No furred animal or feathered fowl should ever be fried.

Small game of any sort is best broiled or roasted, except rabbits and squirrels which are stewed like larger game, geese, big ducks and venison, or made into "salmis" and pies. Any game reheated for hash is fine, but it must never be recooked, only warmed up.

In broiling, a strip of salt pork or thick bacon should always be tied tightly over the breast for automatic basting.

Birds, be they tiny teal or tremendous wild turkey, must always be plucked dry. Scalding them kills the flavor: and equally, in cleaning the carcass no water should ever touch the insides. Wipe with a towel dampened in spirits, vinegar or wine, depending upon personal taste.

How "high" game should be or whether the tail of small birds should be eaten is also a private matter, yet it is true that long hanging improves the flavor, gives that gamey taste. So no duck should be cleaned too soon and a rabbit shouldn't be opened short of three days.

[45]

Citrus fruits go best with birds, and tart jellies with furred game, while corn on the cob, as stuffing for quail, or in the luscious form of green corn oysters, is as perfectly suited to all wild flesh as it was when it accompanied the first barbecued hump of buffalo.

Serving diced *croûtons* fried in butter with a wild biddy may seem but an effete, inconsequential detail. But, as a matter of fact, it's the essence of the whole matter; the juices of game are the very life blood of the dish and not one drop can be sacrificed. So serve crunchy toasts and browned crusts always, all sorts and varieties of sippets and soppets, rusks, fried breads and flaky *vol-au-vents*, any kind of crisp dunking bit to sop up the salubrious sauces. Especially is this true with the smaller birds.

Every bit of reed birds, snipe and woodcock are indeed so precious that only the feathers and whistle are discarded. The fact is, their toothsome little bodies are never even opened, but cooked and eaten whole. And those in the know esteem the brains as the most delicate morsel.

BEAR

To be specific: Here's how to handle your next bear: hack off his paws and set them to soak in a salty, winey marinade for two or three days. Then stew with ham trimmings and tasty vegetables for seven or eight hours; cool them, dry them, slice lengthwise in four parts, pepper with cayenne, roll in melted lard and bread crumbs, broil half an hour, serve with red-currant jelly, and who's afraid of the big black bear!

DUCK

You may not feel up to stewing one wild duck in the pressed blood and raw juices of its mate, as they do down in New Orleans where wooden duck presses are as necessary sporting equipment as cork decoys. So instead, stuff one with sage, onion, bread crumbs, butter, salt and pepper; and roast its mate without either seasoning or dressing. This makes a palatable contrast when a little of each bird goes on every plate. But a great way to do a duck is Hunters' Style—*Salmi de Canards Sauvages à la Chasseur* as the menu-makers say. Just clean and wipe a brace of canvasbacks, cut off the legs, wings and breast and set them aside out of reach of the cat while you lightly salt the carcasses and giblets, bake them about the length of time it takes to smoke a cigarette and then hash all together, put even the bones into a stewpan, pour in a couple of glasses of beef or veal broth, add a snugly tied herb bouquet and set to simmering for fifteen minutes or so. In a separate saucepan melt a ball of butter about the size of a tame duck's egg, lightly season the legs, wings and breasts and brown them for a few minutes on each side. Squeeze over them the juice of a lemon and toss in the whole rind, grated. Then put in a cupful of strongly flavored meat broth and strain in all the gravy from the cooked carcass and giblet hash. Sauté for fifteen minutes and serve surrounded by diced butter-fried *croûtons*. A big bowl of sliced oranges makes a swell side dish . . . or try this:

CANVASBACK DUCK

The canvasback duck should be singed, drawn, wiped, trussed and baked in a very quick oven for not over thirty minutes. They should not be stuffed, but should have a small piece of butter put inside of each. Then pieces of bacon may be bound over the breast, and the birds should be dusted at first with pepper, and salted when they are partly done.

MIXED GRILL

Grill or roast cutlets, breasts, filets, tidbits and giblets of anything you have in the bag: rabbit, quail, venison, squirrels, or anything except hell-diver and prairie dog. Meanwhile, toss up a panful of bacon and French fried. Saw a hearty round off a handy hardwood stump, heat it, pile up the murphies and bacon in the center, lay the "scorched" meat all around, remember fingers were made before forks, and have some gherkins concealed in the palm of your hand, a head of celery, salt and pepper hard by to pep up the feast. And drink with it whatever you don't get enough of at home.

POSSUM

It's as fat as the deer is dry. So best skin it, for a good deal of the fat comes off in the process. In true hill-billy style boil it tender in well salted water right in the iron camp kettle. Lift the boiled possum right into the baking pan and go get you a bundle of green sassafras twigs. Tweak off the tip ends to toothpick size and stick them an inch deep into the meat and so thickly you can tell a tenderfoot it's porcupine. Use butter and a little water in the bottom of the pan so it won't burn while baking. Sprinkle well with pepper and dot with butter. Bake to taste, either light or dark brown. Boil sweet potatoes, peel, lay them around the possum and let them finish baking with him. Munch corn bread with the feast to bring out the full sassafras flavor, and it's good enough to make you lick all ten fingers.

PRAIRIE CHICKEN

Yank off the big breasts of dark meat and broil them, with butter for basting. They must be hand-picked of course, wiped clean, never washed and, like all grouse, quail and small birds, dipped in melted butter before they're ready for the fire. A hash can be made of the leftovers, legs, giblets, etc., moistened with claret and lemon and a dozen stoned olives stirred in at the finish. Served with diced *croûtons* fried in butter this specialty of the wheat states is tasty enough to make a prairie pioneer turn on his spit.

[47]

"Ethel! The game warden!"

RABBIT

There are more than a hundred standard recipes for cooking the ubiquitous rabbit—each as tasty as the next. Rather than give you so many succulent styles as to get in your hare, Esky tips you to rabbits roasted with oysters:

Chop a dozen oysters with a good-sized sponge cake to make the stuffing for Brer Rabbit. Add butter and a mere soupcon of cayenne. Roast the stuffed rabbit an hour, eat him in 10 minutes with a sauce of the oyster liquor and butter simmered together with a little flour for thickening, more cayenne and a touch of cinnamon.

Then there's *this* treatment for the rabbit, by a Canadian guide:

Récipé of the Rabbit to the Wine White or the Wine Red

Some slices of lard (salt pork), some butter, some onions, a little oil, and put to fry the all in a pot. Cut then the rabbit into small pieces and put with the rest. When that is afrying add one or two spoonfuls of flour and well rouse (stir) the whole. Next add one quart of the Wine White or the Wine Red, some parsley and a leaf of bay, some salt and pepper. Make it to cook on a fire very slowly. Empty it on a plate hot and then it eats fine. There you have then a Récipé in the true style of Canada Francaise.

SQUIRREL PIE

Even folks who never go hunting with anything more deadly than a kodak should know how to make a squirrel pie. It's easy once they're skinned, cleaned, all hairs and stray ants wiped off with a wet cloth. Save the blood, for the blood of squirrels and rabbits is as precious as those last drops of any game gravy caught by the *croûtons.* To keep the blood from curdling pour a little vinegar or lemon juice into it. Use the heart, liver and kidneys too. Cut the rest up in joints. Mix a pound of finely chopped beef suet with a pound and a half of flour, lots of salt and plenty of pepper. Stir in cold water to make a pie crust dough. Then butter an earthenware dish and line it with the dough, almost an inch thick. Lay in the meat and giblets, pour the blood over and enough water to fill the pie-dish half way. More salt and pepper, much more. Then put a dough cover over all, exactly as you

would with a wood-pigeon pie; wet the edges and make them stick tight so not a bubbling drop of gravy can get out, but leave a little safety valve in the middle for the steam. Bake about two hours in a moderate oven. When the top crust is yellow-brown put on buttered paper to protect its complexion. Take it to the table in the dish that made it.

VENISON

It's best when killed in autumn after fattening on fall berries. And of course it should be young, but even if it's old, it is still the quickest cooking flesh there is. You roast a haunch the same as you do beef, only not so long, and moistened with a whole cup of water. Garnish with watercress and serve with currant jelly or, better still, wild grape. Ten minutes to the pound is the rule, although a doe cooks faster than a buck.

A venison steak is cooked to perfection when covered thickly with damp salt. Broil it, then crack off the crust of salt and you've really got something. But most folks choose the saddle, which must be well larded before roasting. Steaks and cutlets are fine for broiling and the rougher parts are stewed with mushrooms, herbs and a clove of garlic.

Continental Cooking

FOREIGN FLAVORS TO WIN
GUESTS' FAVORS

Ham 'n' eggs, roast beef, fried chicken—your guests can get those wholesome American standbys anywhere. But where, except at the candle-lit table of a true man of the world, can they hope to find the romance of far-away places: the heavy-scented mystery of the East, the sensuous palate-pleasures of France, the rich splendor of old Russia, the earthy warmth of Hungary, the lyric lust-for-life of Italy?

All these, and "glamour" too, rest in the unusual dishes described on the following pages. You'll find "food with a mood" here: abet it with heady wine, serve it wisely and well, and you'll know the double value of being a clever host-cook.

But remember: generations, even centuries, have gone into the development of these unique dishes; you can't expect to master them in 10 minutes. In case of kitchen-casualty, remind yourself that if everyone could do it, everyone would—and Beef Stroganoff would be just another Blue Plate Special.

There *are* "quick studies" in this section—Biftek Bercy, for example: just the thing to back you up when you say, "But, darling, you can't leave in all this rain. Let me fix you something to eat: it won't take five minutes." But for the most part the recipes desire practice and forethought. They're worth it, as you'll know when finally you serve forth your favorite dish to your favored miss. Mood music, firelight, a good wine, an exotic meal: your Special Guest will respond to the flattery implied in your Special Dish.

ARMENIAN

DOMATESLI PILAFF

(Pilaff with Tomato Juice)

Braise three cups dry rice in melted butter till butter bubbles. Boil three cups of broth with three cups tomato juice and pour this over the rice. Salt and pepper, mix well, and bake half hour in oven (375°F.). Take out again, mix well, bake twenty minutes more. "It's wonderful!" says *George Mardikian*, owner of Omar Khayyam's in San Francisco.

SHISH KABAB

Put four or five inch-square chunks of lamb, from which fat and muscle have been thoroughly trimmed, on a skewer with a thick slice of tomato and a piece of onion. Broil under the flame until well done, and then season to taste.

PILAFF

Salt and pepper a cupful of tomato juice and a cupful of stock and boil together. Then add a cupful of rice, and cook without a lid. Agitate the pan occasionally. The liquid has to be completely absorbed by the rice, and when this has been done, add a lump of butter; to melt the latter, shake the pan vigorously.

Now you may add and mix your meat, usually lamb, which should have been cooked separately, and if you own a form, fashion the *pilaf* into a pyramid, for that is the appropriate way for it to be brought to the table.

FRENCH

BIFTEK BERCY A LA PERE FRANCOIS

Fry the filet of beef in butter on a hot range, after having seasoned it on both sides with a pinch of salt and half a pinch of pepper. Some people hold that steaks should not be salted before cooking because they get tough; it ain't necessarily so. Cook the filet well on both sides. It is advisable first to brown one side for just a minute, turn it over and do the other side also for a minute, and then turn it again and give each side two and a half minutes. This way the natural juices of the meat will not escape. Now take the meat out of the pan and put it on a hot plate. In the sauce which remains in the pan put some flour to brown it and pour some red wine into the browned sauce. This red wine may be the "pinard" of the French poorer classes or the fine Bordeaux of the Princes de Polignac. Put in also a finely chopped-up shallot, a bit of parsley, salt and pepper. This whole operation—of course you had the onion and parsley chopped up in advance—must not take longer than a very few minutes. Do not overcook the sauce; the less it cooks (on a very hot range) the tastier it will be, and the meat on the hot plate is impatient for you to pour that marvelous sauce over it and serve it. Remember, the whole thing must be done very quickly. If you want to be very ultra-ultra, fry an individual piece of bread in butter while you are preparing the sauce, place it on a hot plate, place the steak on it, and pour the sauce over.

BRAINS PIQUANTE

Scald the brains in boiling water. Boil them after this with two slices of ham, slices of beet-root and onion, a bayleaf, a little parsley, salt and pepper, in three small glasses of white wine. To make sauce piquante, chop up a carrot, two onions, two shallots, a sprig of thyme, parsley, two cloves, a bayleaf, and chives; put them with an ounce of butter into a double saucepan. When the butter is melting and turning brown on the fire, sift in a tablespoonful of flour, a very little hot water, and a tablespoonful of good vinegar; season with salt and pepper. Boil slowly and strain in through a sieve.

CALVES' LIVER SAUTE PROVENCALE

Cut two pounds of fresh calves' liver into small pieces. Put them with clarified butter into a pan on the hot range, with a peeled and finely chopped onion, two crushed cloves of garlic, and the juice of half a lemon. Season with salt and pepper. Cook for five minutes, shuffling the pan all the time, then moisten with a glass of white wine. Add six chopped mushrooms, some very finely chopped parsley, and cook for three minutes longer.

COQ AU VIN
(For Four)

Take about four pounds of broilers if two broilers are used; cut into quarters, and season with salt and pepper. Place a quarter-pound of butter in a casserole, allow the butter to melt, and when this is very hot, place the chicken in the casserole and cook on hot fire. When the chicken is well browned, add to it some chopped onions, and some mushrooms cut in two. Let this cook five minutes, and then add one tablespoon of flour and a glass of red Burgundy wine. Allow this to cook for ten minutes. Season to taste.

Cut some bacon into rectangles, and sauté it in a pan, but do not crisp. Add the bacon to the chicken before serving. If the sauce is too thick, add some consommé.

CREPES NICOLE

Have some legs and wings of chicken poached with carrots, onion, and a bouquet of thyme, parsley, and a bayleaf. When they are cooked, cut them in small cubes, toss them lightly in butter, season, and sprinkle well with paprika. Add a few mushrooms previously cooked, cut in pieces and mix with a little cream, just enough to moisten the mixture, and keep hot. Prepare a good bechamel sauce and a few thin unsweetened pancakes. Place on each pancake some of the mixture, roll it, and arrange all the pancakes in a long fireproof dish. Add a yolk of egg to the bechamel sauce, a little cream, pour over the pancakes, sprinkle with grated cheese and brown under the grill. Serve at once.

The dish can be garnished with asparagus tops or slices of truffles according to the season.

DUCKLING BIGARADE
(For Four)

Cook a five-pound duck in an oven at 400 degrees, for one hour, and remove from fire. Pour the fat out of the pan, add a glass of sherry and allow it to simmer. Add a few spoonfuls of tomato sauce and a pint of veal stock. Let it boil for fifteen minutes. In the meanwhile, take two oranges and a lemon, remove the outer skin with a knife, and cut the rest up very finely, boiling it in water for five minutes, and adding it to the sauce. Cut two other oranges in slices, put them on the top of the duck, press another orange and add the juice to the sauce. When ready to serve, strain the sauce and add two spoonfuls of currant jelly, pouring it over the duck.

CHICKEN A LA KING MARCHISIO

Mince some green peppers and mushrooms and cook them in a pan with butter for a few minutes. Now add the sliced white meat of a boiled chicken. Season with salt and a bit of red pepper, and a wineglassful of sherry. Let it evaporate; that is to say, let the wine cook away. Add heavy cream to cover. Cook fifteen minutes longer. When ready to serve, add the yolks of two eggs mixed with butter, but after this addition do not let it boil again.

MARINERS CHICKEN

(From the Café of the Mariners along the quai on the Ile Saint Louis)

Take a fat fowl, the size being determined by the number you serve, and prepare it for boiling. Heat about one quart of soup stock (the French prefer veal) and then put in the chicken with several small onions and a bouquet of herbs, tied in a bag so they can be removed. Cook until tender. Toward the last add one pint of good white wine, Chablis preferred. You will get something delicious if not equal to the original. Perhaps it was in the herbs which were grown in the cook's own garden in Brittany.

NOISETTE OF BEEF TENDERLOIN ROSSINI

Trim a tenderloin of beef, cut in slices and beat these, flattening them to a third of an inch in thickness. Then trim them until they are round, like a twig. Each should weigh about three ounces. Salt them on both sides, put in a saucepan a mixture half butter and half oil, and set on a hot fire; now add the meat and let it cook quickly. It will require about 5 minutes to have the meat rare, 7 minutes for medium, and 8 minutes if one wishes it well done. After cooking, remove and lay the pieces on small slices of toast ¼ inch thick. Now select a number of very large chicken livers, cut them in thick slices, sauté them in butter, set a slice on each noisette, and on the top of this a fine piece of truffle. Mask the whole with Madeira sauce. To make this sauce, reduce half a pint of Madeira or sherry, add some brown gravy, thicken with butter mixed with a little flour, and season with salt, pepper and truffle sauce. Serve with a good Burgundy.

PORK CHOPS ORLENA

Take six pork chops about an inch thick. Fry them slowly in a tablespoon of butter and their own fat. Turn often and fry twenty minutes. Meanwhile in a saucepan melt a tablespoon of butter, add a chopped onion and a teaspoon of brown sugar. Fry until brown. Add one-half cup boiling water, one grated carrot, a couple of cloves and a peppercorn, parsley, thyme, salt and pepper and let simmer. When done, take chops out of pan and keep warm, pouring off all fat except one tablespoonful in which you melt one tablespoon of flour. Pour one and one-half cups boiling water into the pan with the onions, then pour into the pan with the flour and stir until it thickens. Put the chops back into the empty saucepan, strain the gravy over them, add one-half cup dry white wine and cook, under the boiling point, for ten minutes.

POULARDE A L'ESTRAGON

Put into a chicken some fine tarragon; truss it and wrap it in bacon. Cook it in butter in a casserole, and when it's done, place the chicken on a platter near the stove. Into the sauce that remains in the casserole pour a good glass of brandy, a glass of Madeira wine, and some veal stock. Add a teaspoonful of chopped tarragon. Strain the sauce through a very fine sieve, and pour it over the fowl, and serve.

RABBIT BOURGUIGNONNE

Cut a rabbit in pieces, put in a pot, and add carrots, onions, leeks, celery, and parsley, cover with Burgundy and leave it in this pickle overnight. Take the pieces of rabbit from the pot the next morning, or whenever you are ready to cook the dish, and put the rabbit in another vessel with another battery of carrots, small onions, celery and parsley; cook until brown—about twenty minutes. Now add some flour, stir until brown, add the contents of the first pot, together with garlic and clove crushed, thyme and laurel, and place over small flame until cooked. Before serving, add diced bacon and mushrooms that have been separately cooked.

RAGOUT OF VEAL FIRUSKI

Cut veal in squares, rather thick. Brown in butter on both sides, then dredge lightly with flour and cook again a few minutes. Add one glass of water and one of claret. Add a bouquet of salt, pepper, thyme, parsley, bayleaf and rosemary. Add a few small onions and a few small mushrooms. Cook until meat is tender, skim off fat and serve.

"I wish my husband could see how suave you are"

SQUAB A LA RUSSE
(For Four)

Split one squab per person as for broiling. Put four ounces (one bar) of sweet butter in a large skillet and cook the birds on both sides. Salt and pepper to taste. When cooked, remove the birds and put them on a hot platter. Add to the butter left in the skillet one tablespoonful of finely chopped shallots, two ripe tomatoes that have been skinned, seeded and chopped very fine, and simmer for a few moments. Then add a pinch of thyme, finely chopped parsley and chives, and when the herbs have been well blended with the mixture in the skillet, add half a pint of cream (sour cream if preferred), stirring slowly. Pour very hot over the squab.

TIPSY DUCK

Put a jointed duck in an earthenware crock, season with salt and pepper, and add 4 ounces brandy, 2 large glasses of claret wine, 2 large chopped onions, a little thyme, bayleaf, allspice, a sprig of parsley, and let stand 4 or 5 hours. Put 4 ounces fresh pork fat and 1 tablespoon olive oil in earthenware casserole, and when hot put in pieces of duck. Brown them for about 20 minutes. Add the wine in which they were soaked, also 1 clove of garlic and ½ pound fresh mushrooms. Simmer gently for 1 or 1¼ hours. Serve in casserole in which cooked. Serve duck on slices of brown toast and with noodles. *La Mission, Haut-Brion*, 1929, is a rare treat with this delicacy.

HUNGARIAN

CHICKEN PAPRIKASCH

(Two spring chickens for four persons.)
Chop three large onions up fine, put in a pan with a tablespoonful of lard, and simmer over very slow fire for about an hour, until it becomes almost a jelly. Be sure that it does not burn. Add one tablespoon of paprika; let the paprika and the jelly simmer another ten minutes. Now put in the cut-up chicken and let it stew, well covered, for a half-hour; then put in two green peppers, all cut up, and salt to taste. Let it stew another half-hour, then mix in a teaspoonful of flour and six teaspoons of sweet cream. Boil it for a split second; if you boil it longer it will become watery. Serve with dumplings or boiled rice.

GOULASH, PEASANT STYLE

Select four or five different cuts of beef and have the butcher dice the meat. Put the meat just as it is into, preferably, an iron pot, without any seasoning, and sear it a little in a bit of fat. Add water to cover meat; add very finely chopped raw onions (six large heads to about five pounds of meat), and put in some pork fat. Let it simmer until almost all liquid is gone (about an hour and a half). Now, only now, add the paprika, and occasionally add very little water. When the meat is soft, pour in as much water as you want sauce. If you want to cook potatoes with this simple but delicious goulash, add the quarter-diced potatoes a half-hour before you wish to serve the dish. Season to taste.

POTTED STEAK, HUNGARIAN STYLE

Pound the chop-shaped and larded steak pieces well, salt and pepper them, and sear them quickly in hot butter on both sides. Transfer the meat into a pan, add a little hot water or bouillon, and cover the pan. When the meat starts to get tender, add some shallot, cut round, and simmer until the meat is wholly tender and the shallot browns; if some of the liquid evaporates, add a little more from time to time. Add a bit of paprika, and lemon, and some cream just before the end, and serve with potatoes broken into very small pieces, or boiled rice.

BAYRISCH KRAUT MIT KARTOFFELN

For eight people dice a quarter pound of bacon. Fry slowly. Mix in three or four tablespoons of flour, add water, vinegar and salt, making a thin sauce, strongly peppered. Shred two to four heads of white cabbage (according to size). Also peel and cut into quarters a pound and one-half of potatoes. Now place the potatoes in a stew pot, spread the cabbage on top and cover with the bacon sauce. Simmer with a tight lid on the pot till the cabbage and potatoes are tender and the sauce has completely amalgamated. Serve with sausages (*bratwurst* is the real thing), fried or cooked in beer.

STUFFED CABBAGE

Take a healthy head of cabbage. Put it in hot water and separate the leaves in it. This process is important because if the leaves are not softened in warm water, they crack and do not remain whole.

Get a half pound of pork tenderloin, half pound of beef (round steak), half pound of smoked pork tenderloin, and ask the butcher to grind these meats for you. Mix the ground meat with two heads of chopped onions, pepper and salt, and a half cup of uncooked rice, adding to this mixture a half cupful of water. Now place the meat mixture in the leaves of the cabbage, rolling the leaves carefully and folding in the ends so they won't come apart in the cooking.

Place in the bottom of a big pot one pound of sauerkraut, two large sliced tomatoes, also 1 pound beef (boiling), 1 sheet spare ribs, and ox tail. Put the stuffed cabbage leaves on top of this, together with two cupfuls of water. Cover the pot, and simmer very slowly. It will be ready in three hours. When finished, add sour cream to the sauce, but be careful to work it away, so the cream and the sauce will amalgamate. Serves 6 to 8.

INDIAN CURRIES

CHICKEN CURRY (1)
(For Eight)

Two five-pound fowls, each boiled and minced.

Sauce Curry:

  2 medium-sized chopped onions
  2 cloves of garlic
  2 celery stalks, diced
  1 bayleaf
  1 teaspoonful powdered mace
  2½ teaspoonfuls powdered curry
  1 quart chicken broth
  Few sprigs of parsley
  ½ teaspoonful mustard powder
  4 tablespoonfuls flour
  2 green apples, diced
  ½ lb. sweet butter
  ½ lb. chopped raw ham
  ½ pint coconut milk
  1 pint heavy sweet cream
  2 tablespoonfuls chopped chutney

Place the sauce ingredients (except flour, mace, curry powder and liquid) in a large saucepan. Mix thoroughly. Cook vigorously for eight minutes. Add flour, mace and curry powder and cook again four more minutes, add chicken broth, coconut milk and cream; bring it to a boil and let it cook slowly for one hour. Then strain into another pan. Place the minced chicken in a saucepan, pour the sauce over, let it boil about ten minutes and serve hot with boiled rice separately. A tray of condiments should accompany chicken curry; this should consist of shredded cooked bacon, chutney, shredded coconut, Bombay duck, roasted peanuts, and chopped hard-boiled eggs. The best chutneys are Ahmuty's or Daw Sens of Calcutta; the chutney absolutely *hors concours* is Vencatachellen, but there is difficulty obtaining it in this country.

CHICKEN CURRY (2)

Chop and fry 4 onions, 3 tomatoes, 2 large cooking apples, 2 bananas, add 3 tsps. raisins and place mixture in large pot. Add 6 cupfuls of chicken stock or water and simmer for 2 hours, then add ½ cupful of chutney and 2 to 3 tsps. curry powder. In the meantime 2 chickens have been fried to a nice brown, but not thoroughly cooked. Add to curry mixture and simmer another hour. Add dash of lemon juice before serving. Accompanied, of course, by rice. If you want your rice to emerge in dry, separate, fluffy grains, put it in a sieve and pour *cold* water over it (after you've boiled it 13 minutes), then let it drain well.

CURRIED EGGS WITH BANANAS

Sauté chopped apple and onion, then add to curry sauce (see recipe this page). Hard-boiled eggs, dice them, and add to curry sauce. Serve on boiled rice, surrounded with fried bananas which have been sprinkled with coconut.

CURRIED PINEAPPLE

(The touch elegant when served with almost any meat.) One can Hawaiian pineapple, 2 tbsp. curry powder, 3 tbsp. butter, ½ tsp. salt. Melt butter, add curry powder and salt. Cut up pineapple in small bits, add pineapple and juice to curry mixture, simmer 15 minutes.

CURRY OF LAMB

Brown lightly four pounds lamb (cut in half-inch squares) in hot saucepan with two tbsp. oil and a chopped onion. Add two tbsp. curry powder and two tbsp. bread flour. Stir well, add a sliced apple, a quart lamb stock, a half cup ketchup, a tsp. salt, and bring to boil. Let simmer for 90 minutes. Remove meat from gravy, strain, add a cup cream and cup of mixed candied fruits, including raisins. (Boil raisins for ten minutes and wash sugar from fruits first.) Pour over meat and serve with boiled rice.

CURRY SAUCE

2 slices onion, 2 tbsp. butter, 2 tbsp. flour, celery salt, ⅛ tsp. pepper, 1-2 tbsp. curry powder, 1 tbsp. *bitters* (optional), 1 cup scalded milk. Cook onion in butter 5 minutes, remove. Add flour, salt, pepper, curry and bitters. Then add milk. Stir and cook until thickened.

SEAFOOD CURRY
(For Six)

One large tomato, two medium-size onions, one clove garlic—chop fine and sauté in two tablespoons butter; add two tablespoons curry powder, one tablespoon paprika, three cloves, a bayleaf, small stick of cinnamon bark crumbled, one tablespoon salt, a half lemon, and sauté ten minutes; add two pounds (in all) shrimps, crabs, scallops, or other sea food, and cook three minutes. Cover with water and cook until shrimps turn pink. A half cup of sour or sweet cream will make a smoother curry and bring out the flavor. Serve with rice and condiments, such as grated coconut, India relish, Bombay duck as well as nuts, bananas, raisins, French fried onions and hard-boiled eggs.

VEAL CURRY WITH MOLASSES
(For Eight)

2½ lbs. veal, 1 tsp. salt, 3 medium size onions, 6 stalks celery and 2 apples . . . all minced; ¼ cup curry powder, ¼ tsp. pepper, ½ tsp. ginger, 1 lb. rice, ½ tsp. tabasco sauce, 1 tbsp. Worcestershire sauce, ⅓ cup cold water, 2 egg yolks, well beaten, 2 tbsp. butter, ½ cup pure New Orleans molasses, 2 cups meat stock or 2 bouillon cubes. Cook veal, onions, celery and apples. In frying pan, pour meat stock and stir in curry powder. Simmer 5 minutes. Add molasses, other seasoning and meat, cook 20 minutes. Pour in water and cook 5 minutes, stirring until thickened. When ready to serve, add egg yolks and heat to boiling, stirring constantly. Serve in hot rice ring.

ITALIAN

CHICKEN ALLA CACCIOTORA

(*Alla Cacciotora* means hunter style, and a hunter has no time or place to get pickled sweet peppers, tomatoes and champignons, and all the other condiments Americans add. This is the real Italian way to prepare it, according to Mons. Raymond of the Passy Restaurant in New York:)

Cut up a chicken into eight or ten pieces and fry the pieces in a little boiling olive oil. When they are nice and brown (in about twenty minutes), salt and pepper them, and after a few minutes more cooking, squeeze the juice of a lemon over them.

FLORENTINE TURKEY

Make a stuffing of three prunes, a quarter of a pound of sausage meat, three tablespoonfuls of chestnut purée, three slices of bacon, and a cooked pear. Fry these for a few minutes in butter. Chop up the gizzard and the liver, and add them, in company of a glass of Marsala. Stuff the turkey and braise it for an hour, with salt, butter, bacon, a blade of rosemary, one onion, one carrot, three cloves, one turnip, and a clove of garlic cut in half.

After having braised it, roast it in the oven, and either pour the sauce over it, or serve the sauce separately. The garlic should be removed after ten minutes of braising.

MILANESE RISOTTO
(For Four)

Wash a cup of rice well. Cook the rice in a cup of chicken broth under a lid, until all the liquid disappears. Put the rice aside, and brown a well-chopped onion in a little butter. Now add the rice to this, and stir constantly, adding a cup of hot water, salt and pepper, and after a couple of minutes stirring, add more butter. Dissolve a little saffron in a quarter of a cup of broth or hot water, and add to the rice to make it a nice yellow color. Sprinkle grated Parmigiano cheese over it and serve piping hot.

PICATA DI VITELLO

Pound small pieces of veal medallions cut from veal steaks until they are quite flat and put in a pan with hot butter, brown them well, add a little thinly sliced ham, salt and pepper and a little fresh sage. A couple of minutes before it is ready to serve, add a few drops of white wine.

SPAGHETTI—AND OTHER PASTA

Pasta is, of course, a collective word for macaroni and its myriad relatives. Spaghetti is the most widely used pasta in this country. Spaghettini is finer than spaghetti; vermicelli is still finer and used mainly in soups; vermicellini is about half the width of vermicelli; capellini is as thin as hair; tagliatelli is a wide noodle; ziti is a fat pasta and has a hole in it; and so on endlessly to cravatte which is shaped like a bow-tie, to gnocchi which are tiny balls made of dough, to ravioli, which you know. In any case, pasta should be dropped into great quantities of rapidly boiling, salted water, then boiled only until barely tender—8 to 10 minutes for spaghetti, unless you like it soft rather than *alledente*. Stir occasionally during cooking to prevent sticking. Drain thoroughly and serve immediately. The Italian way is to pour the sauce over the spaghetti on the plate rather than to mix sauce and spaghetti together.

Here are a few sauce suggestions, equally good on any pasta:

ALLA MARINARA SAUCE
(For Six)

Take a half cup of olive oil, three cloves of garlic chopped finely and a sprig of chopped parsley and fry together for a few minutes, stirring the mixture but not allowing it to get brown. Add a large can of tomatoes, salt and pepper, and a kind of sage, called oregano, that you can get in any Italian grocery store, and cook for three quarters of an hour over a low flame. After it's ready, mix it together with your pasta and use grated cheese on top. Any kind of pasta is good with *marinara* but the best is spaghetti. If you cook your *marinara* sauce together with your meat, the dish is called *pizzaiola*. Of course, your pasta must cook separately.

BUTTER SAUCE

Melt butter in a pan with a bud of garlic. Pour over and toss with spaghetti. Serve with grated Parmesan cheese.

CARUSO SAUCE

Add chicken livers and mushrooms, sauted separately, to marinara sauce.

CLAM SAUCE

Dress spaghetti with clams, minced and steamed; or clams may be added to tomato sauce, along with some of their liquor.

MEAT SAUCE

Brown ground beef in olive oil, or butter, then continue as for marinara sauce. Tomato juice plus tomato paste may be used in place of canned tomatoes (or, for larger quantities, in addition); in such case, cook until the sauce is thick: 2 or more hours. May be made in advance, keep on hand for quick reheating.

SAUCE ORIENTALE

Hash one small onion, cook in a little butter; add 3 medium mushrooms finely hashed; add 2 medium tomatoes, hashed, reduce. Add ½ pint of a dry white wine; add ½ pint of heavy cream. Hash 6 leaves of fresh mint, same amount of parsley, add 2 tablespoons sweet butter, away from the fire; season. Special for au gratin dishes, noodles, spaghetti, etc.

"While you were out, your Mr. Drake called—let's just call him
our Mr. Drake from now on"

RUSSIAN

BEEF STROGANOFF (1)

Pare and trim well all the fat and nerves from a nice tenderloin, cut the latter lengthwise, and *en julienne*, about two inches long and half an inch thick. Put ¼ of a pound of butter in a sautoir and, when very hot, add the tenderloin. Cook over a quick fire, and season with salt and pepper. Now smother some finely chopped onions, add minced mushrooms. When the moisture has evaporated from the mushrooms, wet them with thick, sour cream, and heat for 10 minutes, but without boiling. Dress the beef on a hot dish, and pour the sauce over.

(Joseph, maître d'hôtel of the Sherry-Netherlands, suggests as the best wine accompaniment: a bottle of *Chambertin*—say, *Leon Grevelet Cusset*, 1929.)

BEEF STROGANOFF (2)

Clean two pounds of filet of beef. Slice into very thin little bits and mix this with salt, pepper and a dash of flour. Chop an onion finely and fry it in a saucepan in two and a half tablespoonfuls of butter. Add the bits of meat, fry altogether, and add a quarter of a cup of bouillon (chicken broth will do if you don't have stocks), one tablespoon of Worcestershire sauce, and one cup of sour cream. Mix well and cook until deep yellow-brown, but do not keep on fire long enough to dry the sauce. Put into deep dish and sprinkle with a little chopped parsley. Ten mushrooms cut into small pieces and fried separately in butter may also be added.

This is a good he-man dish and very easy to make. The Poles took their Stroganoffs seriously, and the Európejski's was especially excellent.

BORSTCH A LA RUSSE
(For Six)

Take eight onions, one stalk of celery, three carrots, four big beets and one white turnip. All these are cut in very small pieces. Add to them fresh cream and a little butter, three leaves of laurel, some unground pepper, a small can of tomato paste and some strong beef bouillon (which has been previously prepared), and boil for one hour over a low flame. While this is boiling, add to it one and one-half pounds of cabbage, also salt and a quarter of a glass of sugar. When the vegetables become soft, add five fresh cut tomatoes.

COTELETTE KIEV IMPERIALE

(Its history tracing from the gypsy fires of wandering Cossack bands to the Czar's New Year table, this dish traditionally is swan stuffed with chestnuts and truffles, roasted over a slow fire, with a gravy of red wine and oranges. But here's a simpler form, more suitable for the wolf-sky at homesky.)

Slice cooked breast of fowl—turkey or chicken—and lay the slices on a layer of liver paste in a serving dish. Heat, then pour hot drawn butter over the "cutlets." Serve with hearts of artichokes. Moselle or Graves is indicated —or any dry white wine.

ESCALOPS OF VEAL
(As Prince Obolensky makes them)

Pare and cut two pounds of veal (from the hip preferably) into six even slices, and give them a terrific pounding. Season with a pinch of garlic salt and a pinch of pepper. Brown in a saucepan in pure olive oil on a very hot range, adding a small chopped onion, some chopped mushrooms, chopped parsley, and a glass of sherry. Cook the meat about five minutes on each side.

MUSHROOMS WITH SOUR CREAM

Wash, drain, and slice a pound of fresh mushrooms, but don't peel them. Heat two tablespoonfuls of butter in a saucepan, add a small onion chopped fine and the mushrooms and sauté together for five minutes. Season with salt and pepper, then sprinkle with two teaspoonfuls of flour. Mix well and simmer for a few minutes under lid. Now stir in—a little at a time—a cupful of sour cream, but do not let it come to a boil. Add a few drops of lemon juice or a few drops of Worcestershire sauce.

SHASHLIK

Take some choice rib part of mutton and cut it into roundish little pieces, about the size of the palm of a small girl's hand. Cut some bacon into about the same pattern. Salt and pepper the mutton and bacon pieces slightly, and put them on wooden sticks—in some stylish Polish or Russian households or restaurants they keep silver sticks for this purpose—but they should be thin and round, and about five inches long. First put on a piece of mutton, then a piece of bacon, then a whole small tomato, a piece of bacon, a small onion, again a piece of mutton, bacon, tomato, onion, mutton and so on, close to one another, until the wooden stick can hold no more pieces. Cook—don't take off the stick!—in a saucepan, and when it is about half-done, pour off the fat, add a tablespoonful of butter, together with leaves of green onion, chopped fine. Baste all the time and when it is ready, grab the ends of the sticks and lay them on a bed of boiled rice, and pour the gravy over. Shashlik must be served very hot.

SOUTH OF THE BORDER

VINHADALHOS

From the Portuguese in our midst, mainly those known as "the Islanders," comes a dish that is quite unknown to most of us but which deserves wider circulation. The name, even on Portuguese tongues, sounds as though it were pronounced *vinya die,* and though these people use it in many forms I have met it only in fish and pork chops.

Take a spoonful of pepper and another of allspice and dissolve it, rather mix it, in as small amount of water as you can. Add several cloves of crushed garlic, a few cloves and a bayleaf. Add enough white wine to cover the fish or chops to be treated and set it in the icebox for at least twenty-four hours; three days would be better.

Bring the dish close to the stove and as soon as you lift the fish or chops from the liquid throw them at once into an already heated skillet and fry as usual.

CARIBBEAN DISH

Sauté a few sliced onions and 1 clove garlic in butter till slightly brown. Boil a pound of rice, grate 1/5 coconut. Get a large can of kidney beans. Add a peppercorn to the onions, then add the milk from the coconut, then mix rice, beans, grated coconut and sauce. Serve with Riesling, dry white or a seasonal fruit cup.

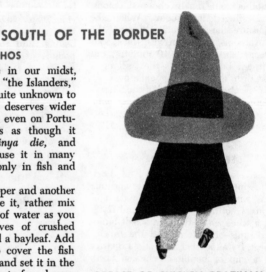

BREAST OF CHICKEN BRAZILIAN

Split the breast of a large chicken in two. Then proceed to make a stuffing of two ounces of butter, a tablespoonful of Chili powder, and some shredded coconut. Mix this and roll it into the shape of a football, and put it in the breast and fold the latter around the stuffing. Now dip the breast into flour, and then in whipped-up yolk of egg, and finally into breadcrumbs. Put some shortening in a pan, and fry the breast in this for five minutes; take it out and put it in oven for another five minutes. Now garnish: fry slices of pineapple, sweet potatoes, slices of bananas; make a rich curry sauce and serve separately.

TURKISH

EGGS A LA CONSTANTINOPLE

(An odd Turkish dish little known elsewhere.)

Mix in equal proportions olive oil and Turkish coffee. (To make Turkish coffee: mix finely pulverized coffee with equal amount of granulated sugar; add the coffee to boiling water and boil three times.) Put in this mixture as many eggs as required, in their shells, and cook them on very low fire for twelve hours. The mixture will penetrate the shells, give the whites an amber color, the yolks the color of saffron, and the eggs will have the taste of the most delicious chestnuts you have ever eaten.

IMARU BAYELDI

Take five eggplants, cut off the stems and skin them thoroughly, but don't forget to leave about an inch of skin all round lengthwise to hold the eggplants together. Chop very finely one pound of onions, sautéing them in olive oil to a golden brown. Add to this three chopped-up tomatoes, a little chopped parsley, and a clove of garlic. Put the eggplants in a pan with the fried vegetables, and cover with water. When cooked remove the eggplants carefully, place them on a dish, and cut their bodies in half, lengthwise, leaving the strip of skin intact, and in between the two halves put the onion mixture.

A TURKISH HORS D'OEUVRE

(Said to have been brought from the East by Anatole France.)

Slice oranges crossways, peel the slices, and remove the pips and the white in the middle of the oranges. Put the slices in the bottom of a dish and cover the oranges with chopped onion, placing on the bed of oranges and onion stoned black olives. Season with salt, pepper, red pepper, and olive oil.

AND ... THE MELTING POT

You may not be able to put your finger on the exact national origin of these dishes, but you'll have no trouble putting your teeth into them. Just unusual enough to rate your adoption . . . just clever enough in their flavor combinations to set apart the host-cook who serves them . . . these concoctions may be hybrid in the begetting but they're pure delight in the eating:

BAKED BEANS WITH WINE

Chop an onion and fry it in butter and add to it diced smoked ham, and fry it some more. Add a large can of kidney beans and pour in a pint of red wine, salt and pepper. Mix thoroughly and heat well but do not boil. Then put the beans in a baking dish and bake it in a moderate oven for twenty minutes.

BARBECUED PORK CHOPS

4 pork chops of 1½-inch thickness, 3 tsps. chili sauce, 3 tsps. lemon juice, 2 tsps. grated onion, ⅓ cup water, 18 prunes, 4 halves of potatoes, ¼ tsp. dry mustard, salt, pepper, cloves, 2 tsps. Worcestershire sauce. Mix chili sauce, lemon juice, grated onion, mustard, Worcestershire and seasoning. Pour mixture over pork chops and let stand 1 hour, turning chops occasionally. Drain and brown in small amount of fat. When brown, put in baking pan, add the water and remainder of mixture. Pit the prunes and insert a clove in each. Add to baking dish together with potato halves. Cover and bake for about an hour.

BEEF TONGUE A LA NOEL

Blanch the tongue by boiling it for twenty minutes; then skin it by scraping off the outside skin; saùté two small onions and a crushed clove of garlic in butter until brown. Add a half pint of beef stock. Place tongue in a roasting pan, pour over the onion-garlic sauce and put it in a medium hot oven. After it has cooked for an hour, add a half pint of California Burgundy. Cook for another two hours. Fifteen minutes before it is ready add another glassful of wine. Skim the fat and strain the sauce. Thicken with roux. Serve tongue and gravy separately.

BRAISED CAPON—TAVERN STYLE

A nice capon of 7 pounds—cleaned and ready to roast—well seasoned. Place it in a speical deep braise pan with 2 carrots and 2 onions sliced. Add some lard and braise for 1 hour and 30 minutes in medium hot oven—basting from time to time with the pan grease.
When ready—remove the capon and ⅔ of the pan grease. Add 3 tablespoons of flour and 4 cups of excellent beer. Put the capon back in the braise pan —braise again for 20 minutes.
Dress capon—strain the sauce—rectify seasoning.
Serve very hot.

BROILED DEVILED SPRING CHICKEN

Split a chicken lengthwise, flatten it out and remove as many bones as possible. Salt and pepper, baste with melted butter and half-cook it in the oven.
Then coat with mustard, cover with breadcrumbs, add a little melted butter, and finish cooking on a grill. Serve with slices of lemon and Escoffier sauce (bottled).

CHICKEN DIVAN

Slice white meat of cooked chicken on a plate and garnish each side with freshly cooked broccoli. Beat some whipped cream into Hollandaise sauce, then spread sauce over food. Sprinkle with Parmesan cheese, then put under the broiler and cook until the sauce is a golden brown. Serve on the plate in which it is cooked.

SAILOR'S POTATOES

Boil potatoes, peel them and cut them into slices. Put them in a saucepan with butter, salt and pepper, parsley and chopped onions, also a little flour. Add two glasses of white wine, or *pinard,* the ordinary red wine.

SMOKED TURKEY CASSEROLE

Cook some wild rice and place it in the bottom of a casserole. Put on top of this a layer of thinly sliced smoked turkey. Cover with a layer of sautéed mushrooms. Pour a sauce over this, made from the stock of legs and bones of the turkey, butter, flour and cream. Serve with currant jelly.

SMOKED TURKEY COLEMAN

Put a layer of seasoned cream sauce in a shallow baking pan. Cover with ½ lb. mushrooms sautéed with 1 tbsp. finely chopped onion. Add layer of finely chopped steamed spinach (wash spinach and leave washing water on leaves; place in saucepan, dot with ½ tsp. grated nutmeg, cover and allow to steam for about 25 minutes). Pour over this slices of smoked turkey breast that have been poached in half the cream sauce. Over all, pour ¼ cup cooking sherry. Garnish with Permesan cheese, fresh black pepper and slivers of pimiento. Bake in moderate oven 15 minutes.

SMOKED TURKEY VENDOME

(For Twelve)

(As served at the Caviar Restaurant, New York.)

½ cup butter
⅓ cup flour
3 egg yolks
½ cup heavy cream
2 bunches broccoli, cooked

Slice a smoked turkey in very thin slices. Place neck, drum sticks, wings, skin and any other trimmings in kettle, cover with water and let simmer, covered, for six hours or more. Strain, reduce to 3 cups of stock to use in making sauce, or add water to make three cups if necessary. Melt butter, add flour, stirring while mixture browns.

Add stock gradually, stirring until smooth and the mixture thickens. Let cook slowly for five minutes. Blend egg yolks with a little of hot sauce and add. Fold in whipped cream. Cover bottom of casserole with broccoli, add turkey slices, cover with sauce and top with grated cheese. Place under broiler flame until cheese melts and browns slightly.

SPINACH SUPREME

(For Four)

Add to two cups of drained, chopped spinach (fresh-cooked or canned) two tablespoonfuls butter, a quarter cup Chablis or Hock Wine, two tablespoonfuls lemon juice, and one teaspoonful Worcestershire sauce, flavor with salt and pepper, heat well and serve.

VEAL CHOPS IN APPLEJACK A LA ELVIA

Fry chops in butter till golden brown. Pour over them glass of applejack, add seasoning, the usual herbs and cover with a lid, letting simmer for a few minutes. Do not let sauce boil. Mix in some very thick cream and serve.

VEAL WITH BRANDY

Take some exceedingly thin pieces of veal. Melt a little butter in a chafing dish, put the veal slices in it, together with chopped parsley, salt and pepper and a few drops of California brandy. Ignite the brandy, and allow the veal slices to burn. Then pour some sweet cream on them. This dish takes seven minutes to make at the table, and it is beautiful on account of the brandy's bluish flame.

VINTNER'S CHICKEN

Cut a broiler as though to fricassee. Brown well in four tablespoonfuls of olive oil over low fire for about twenty minutes. Sprinkle a chopped clove of garlic over the chicken, also two tablespoonfuls of chopped parsley. Cook two minutes and add a small can of tomato sauce. Cook five minutes longer, or until the chicken is tender, and add one third cup white wine to which one teaspoonful lemon juice has been added. Cook another two minutes and serve.

"Try not to notice him. They pride themselves on their unobtrusive service"

"Think of me as being a Yale boy, and just forget which class"

Sauces
TOPPING TOPPERS

Dr. Johnson defined sauce as simply: "Something eaten with food to improve its taste." What's sauce for the goose is not always sauce for the gander, however. That's why the following recipes for a few excellent sauces include suggestions for their most sauce-picious use.

SAUCES

There are only two basic sauces known to culinary art; brown sauce and white sauce, or in professional parlance, *Espagnole* and *Allemande*. The basis of brown sauce is a good stock that may be very easily made of left-over meats or gravy. An excellent stock can be made of some raw bones baked in a hot oven until brown and then cooked in water with onions and carrots and garlic for a couple of hours. If you have this stock you need only to add your various ingredients in order to get a certain definite side sauce. All brown sauces keep well in the refrigerator, differing from white sauces.

The bases of white sauces are milk, cream, butter, or white stock, or their combination. White stock is made by extracting the fluid from a chicken carcass, or feet of fowl, thrown-away necks and even heads of fowl, veal bones or inexpensive cuts of veal. But if you want to make a sauce for fish, use as a base some of the liquid in which your fish cooks.

BECHAMEL

Named after the maître d'hôtel of Louis XIV—is the father of all white sauces, and is exceedingly simple to prepare: Melt two tablespoonfuls of butter in a saucepan, adding to it two tablespoonfuls of flour, mixing well and cooking until a nice brown. Add a pint of boiling milk gradually, stirring constantly, and add a small onion as well. Season to taste and cook for an hour over very low flame. Strain and serve.

BASIC BROWN SAUCE

(The recipes below can be varied to make any number of lesser sauces.) Melt two tablespoonfuls of butter in a saucepan, and brown two carrots and two onions in it, whole or sliced if you like. Mix two tablespoonfuls of flour in it and cook until a nice brown. Add a good pint of your stock, bayleaves, thyme, tomatoes, peppercorns, garlic, celery, parsley, and simmer for two hours. Season to taste. Strain thoroughly, and add a glass of red wine or sherry, and cook a little longer before serving.

BUTTER SAUCE

(Fine with fish and vegetables)

Melt butter, brown it, then add a little lemon juice just before serving.

HOLLANDAISE SAUCE

(Fish, asparagus, broccoli, cauliflower, etc.)

Stir 3 egg yolks in a tablespoonful of water in a double boiler until this takes on a creamy consistency. Then take off the top of the double boiler containing the egg yolks, and move to a warm place. Add a half pound of melted butter to the egg yolks little by little, stirring constantly. Now add another tablespoonful of water. Salt it, and if it is to be served with fish, add a little lemon juice. Strain through cheesecloth.

HORS D'OEUVRES SAUCE

(For Four)

Slice three large mushrooms and squeeze the juice of a half lemon over them; mix thoroughly with a half pint of sour cream, the yolk of a raw egg, two teaspoonfuls of mustard, a pinch of sugar, and salt and pepper to taste. Now mix a glass of milk with a tablespoonful of flour and make this very smooth by stirring with a spatula,

add to the above concoction, and mix well. Put it in the icebox and leave it there for three hours. This sauce is marvelous with all hors d'oeuvres, cold meats, from meat loaf to turkey, and most cold vegetables. If you want it hot, heat it in a double boiler, but don't allow it to boil; keep it just simmering and stir constantly; if the sauce appears too thick, add a little more milk. It takes less than ten minutes to make this sauce.

MARCHAND DE VIN SAUCE

(Excellent with steaks)

Cook 2 finely chopped shallots in a generous glass of claret until the liquid is reduced by half, then add 2 tablespoonfuls of butter, salt and pepper to taste and finely chopped parsley.

MAYONNAISE

This thick sauce, so good with fish, hardboiled eggs, veal; cold chicken, and vegetables, calls for efficiency and undivided attention.

Mix the yolks of two raw eggs with a little dry mustard, salt, and pepper with a spatula. Add a teaspoon of lemon juice, and mix. Now add *very slowly*, drop by drop, and stirring all the time, a cupful of olive oil. Taste frequently and correct the seasoning.

MORNAY SAUCE

See page 39

OYSTER COCKTAIL SAUCE

For a dozen oysters or little necks, put two tablespoons of tomato ketchup into a small glass, add a full teaspoon of grated horse-radish, three or four drops of tabasco sauce, a bit of salt, a pinch of onion salt (or a quarter teaspoon of onion juice). Thin with white wine vinegar (or lemon juice), mixing thoroughly. Place all the oysters or clams in the glass, being careful to pour in any juice from the shells. Serve ice cold, of course.

PARSLEY SAUCE

Chop up some parsley very fine—the more parsley, the better the sauce. Add a little lemon juice or vinegar, and salt and pepper. Also add a little chopped onion or garlic to taste. Saturate this with salad oil, mix thoroughly and pour over your dish. Goes very well with cold boiled fish, boiled meats or boiled potatoes. Makes royal fare out of last night's leftovers.

SAVOY SAUCE

Boil 1 pint domestic Claret till it is reduced by half. Add a little lemon peel, 2 cloves, 4 grains of whole black pepper. Simmer for 5 minutes and add a tablespoonful of butter. Simmer and stir constantly for another 5 minutes; now remove the lemon peel, the cloves and the peppers. Crush the *raw* liver of a fowl, pass it through a sieve and add it to the wine. Stir until sauce thickens to the consistency of mayonnaise. Add just a few drops of lemon juice. A little cream makes this sauce more mellow, but it is very good even without cream. Pour it over your meat. (NOTE: With 2 chicken livers the sauce is much better, while 1 turkey, goose or duck liver is ample to a pint of wine. Use on any kind of meat—roast, boiled or broiled. Fowl, pork, beef or lamb. Makes a fine dish out of tired leftovers.)

WHITE WINE SAUCE

Reduce white wine and vinegar of the same proportions to two thirds by cooking. Add a glass of Bordeaux wine, and a finely chopped shallot, also some pepper, and a bit of thyme and laurel, crushed. Add a large spoonful of veal stock. Let it boil for a few minutes; taste it and adjust the seasoning. Pass it through a fine sieve, and finish it up by adding a little finely chopped parsley.

SAUCE FOR BOILED FISH

Melt a half-pound of table butter and mix in with it four hard-boiled eggs chopped very fine. Season with salt and pepper.

"How many times have I told you t'soive from d'left!"

Salads

TOSSED-UP, NOT FLOSSED-UP

Old French dictionaries said that salads are a *"réunion de choses confusément assemblées."* The trouble in the United States with this definition, that salads are "a union of things confusedly assembled," is that hostesses and tearooms take the definition too seriously—they marry pineapple to cream cheese, nuts to marshmallow, mayonnaise to onions, and so on. American women go berserk when it comes to salads; they try so hard to be unique that in their zeal they really confuse things.

A purist in gastronomy acclaims only one category of salads: green leaves, as, for instance, lettuce, romaine, chicory, dandelion, etc., whichever happens to be in season, well washed and dried, seasoned with salt, pepper, oil, vinegar and mustard. It was about such salads Brillat-Savarin said that they "refresh, invigorate, comfort, and it is my habit to say that they even rejuvenate." In these uncomplicated but marvelous salads the most important thing is that the leaves should be fresh, crisp and vivid in color, the pepper

[71]

freshly ground, the salt preferably sea salt, the oil real olive oil, the vinegar wine vinegar and mustard in powder form.

The proportions are a matter of taste, although here, too, there are some established rules as, for instance, that the measure should be one spoonful of vinegar to two of oil. And first the salt must be dissolved in the vinegar, then the mustard powder, then the oil added, and finally the pepper. Observing this order is important, for the salt and the mustard do not easily dissolve in the oil. If you like garlic, smear a small piece of dry bread (from the heel of the loaf) with it, and mix it in with the leaves. And if you have some herbs, a sprinkle of tarragon, chives, or chervil helps after having tossed and turned the salad forty times.

But there are other formulae as, for instance, this advice from an 18th century cleric:

Two large potatoes pass'd through kitchen sieve
Smoothness and softness to the salad give;
Of mordent mustard add a single spoon,
Distrust the condiment that bites too soon;
But deem it not, thou man of herbs, a fault,
To add a double quantity of salt;
Four times the spoon with oil of Lucca crown,
And twice with wine vinegar procured from 'town';
True flavor needs it, and your poet begs,
The pounded yellow of two well-boiled eggs.
Let onion's atoms lurk within the bowl,
And, scarce suspected, animate the whole;
And, lastly, in the flavor'd compound toss
A magic spoonful of anchovy sauce.
Oh! Great and glorious, and herbaceous treat,
'Twould tempt the dying anchorite to eat,
Back to the world he'd turn his weary soul,
And plunge his fingers in the salad bowl.

BEER CABBAGE SLAW
(For Six)
1 medium sized head of cabbage
1 green pepper, shredded
2 tablespoons celery seed
1 teaspoon salt
1 teaspoon minced onion
1 cup mayonnaise
½ cup beer
¼ teaspoon pepper

Shred cabbage. Add green pepper, celery seed, onion and seasonings. Thin mayonnaise with beer. Add to cabbage. Toss thoroughly. Chill.

CRANBERRY CASHEW SALAD
(For Turkey Times)
Cook 2 cups crans with 1 cup water and 1 cup sugar. When they pop, add 1½ tablespoons unflavored gelatin which has been soaked in ¼ cup cold water, to the hot mixture. When cooked, throw in ¼ cup ground, salted cashew nuts, ½ cup chopped apples, ½ cup diced celery. Turn into molds and chill. Serve on lettuce.

FINGER SALAD
Wash a head of romaine, and dry each leaf separately and well with a napkin. Toast a piece of bread, stroke it gently with garlic, cut the toast into small squares and place them in a salad bowl; put the leaves of romaine over the toast. Soft-boil two eggs, and spread them over the leaves. Add three tablespoonfuls of olive oil, lemon instead of vinegar, salt, pepper, a bit of Worcestershire sauce, mix very well, and finally sprinkle grated Parmesan cheese on top.
Romaine is the only salad that may be eaten with the fingers.

MUSHROOM SALAD
Mix in equal proportions, canned mushrooms sliced into strips, cold cooked potatoes cut into rounds, and strips of raw celery. Season with salt, pepper, olive oil and wine vinegar.

POTATO SALAD—BEER DRESSING
(For Six)
6 medium sized potatoes
1 tablespoon vinegar
2 tablespoons olive oil
1 teaspoon salt
½ teaspoon pepper
1 tablespoon finely chopped onion
½ cup finely diced celery
lettuce

1 cup milk
1 tablespoon butter
3 tablespoons cornstarch
3 tablespoons cold water
2 teaspoons dry mustard
1 teaspoon salt
Dash of cayenne
½ cup cold beer

Cook potatoes in rapidly boiling salted water until tender. Drain and peel. Cut into small cubes. Make a marinade of remaining ingredients. Turn over warm potatoes and let stand until thoroughly cooled. Heap in lettuce cups. Heat milk with butter. Mix cornstarch to paste with cold water. Add to milk with seasonings. Cook over hot water, stirring constantly until thick. Cool. Add beer slowly, beating until smooth. Force through a sieve if necessary. Serve on potato salad.

SALADE MELANGEE
Rub salad bowl with a cut clove of garlic. Then cut into chunks and slices and drop into the bowl: lettuce, cucumber, radishes, tomatoes, celery, carrots, watercress, chicory. Then mash ¼ lb. cream cheese with 2 tablespoons cream. Add and mix in 1½ tablespoons anchovy paste, 1 tablespoon caviar (optional) and 4 tablespoons French dressing. Mix thoroughly, then pour this dressing over the salad. Toss and serve.

THOUSAND ISLAND DRESSING
Mix together very well two tablespoonfuls of chili sauce, one cup of mayonnaise, a half teaspoonful of Worcestershire sauce, the same amount of chopped chives and chopped pimientos.

"Boy! There's nothing like a cool dip in the morning
to start the day right!"

Desserts

SWEET FINALES

A bit of fruit and cheese, a cup of coffee, perhaps a little brandy —that's just desserts for the finest meal. But even so, as your sweet tooth tells you, there'll be times when you'll want to serve something more elaborate. Here are your best bets, ranging from homely to elegant but carefully skirting the trite territory of ice-cream-and-cake. The fact that it does not appear among these dessert recipes is not to indicate that a good deep-dish apple pie, say, floating with syrup and shot full of cinnamon, is not a proper topping for your favorite dinner—even if it *should* be served on a hot-water bag and garnished with digestive tablets. Rather, pie's absence is due to the exhaustive (and exhausting) instructions for piemaking to be found in any ladies' cookbook. Besides, as George Ade wrote in Esquire many years ago, "Pies develop character as well as heartburn. Pie eaters are rugged characters. When they make up their minds to anything their opinions cannot be altered, not even by the use of bicarbonate of soda."

[75]

APPLE DITLER

Quarter and core four eating apples. Boil in a half cup of water and one-half cup sugar to which add the grated rind and juice of a half lemon. When apples are tender remove to a plate, then add one cup of good white wine. Cook for ten minutes more and serve the apples with the hot sauce poured over the fruit.

APPLE TODDY

Roast 6 apples that have been covered with molasses, butter, brown sugar and cinnamon. Add water to cover bottom of pan and after they are tender, pour brandy over. Should be piping hot before serving.

BABA AU RHUM

Cool ½ cup scalded milk to lukewarm. Add 1 cake compressed yeast, crumbled, ½ cup flour and 2 tablespoons sugar. Stir until smooth. Cover and let rise in a warm place about 1 hour. Cream ½ cup butter, gradually adding 6 tablespoons sugar. Beat until light. Add ½ teaspoon salt, 2 teaspoons grated lemon rind, 3 eggs, well beaten, 1½ cups flour and yeast mixture. Beat well, about 15 minutes. Half fill special molds which are well buttered both on the bottom and on the sides. Cover, and let rise until doubled in bulk, about 1 hour. Cook 40 minutes in a moderate oven (350 degrees).

Syrup for the Baba: Boil ½ cup sugar and 1 cup water together 5 minutes. Cool and add ¼ cup rum. Pour syrup over Babas, and let soak in. When ready to serve, add some apricot jam on the top of the Babas.

For Savarin the preparations are exactly the same, the mold only being of different shape.

BAKED ALASKA

On a board place a layer of sponge-cake; lay on vanilla ice cream. On top place a dry, well-beaten mixture of four egg whites and one half cup of powdered sugar. Brown in hot oven for a moment and serve immediately.

BAKED GRAPEFRUIT, HAWAIIAN

Slice the fruit in half and score. Drop spoonfuls of pure molasses between the slices and in the center. Sprinkle with cinnamon and bake under broiler for 5 minutes.

BRANDIED APRICOT PIE

Drain 1 can peeled apricot halves thoroughly. Cover them with ½ cup sugar. Let stand 20 minutes. Dissolve 1 package orange gelatin with 1½ cups boiling apricot juice and water. Pour over apricot halves. Add ¼ cup of brandy. Mix carefully so apricots will remain intact. When mixture is the consistency of jelly, put into a 9-inch baked cracker crumb pie shell. Put into refrigerator at least 2 hours before cutting. Serve with brandy-flavored whipped cream.

BEER CHEESE CAKE

1 pound cream cheese

4 eggs, beaten

¼ cup melted butter

½ cup sugar

2 tbsp. flour

3 ounces currants—raisins

1 cup beer

grated rind of 1 lemon

Rub the cheese through a sieve—add the eggs, sugar and other ingredients. Line an 8 x 3 pan with ordinary pie dough. Spread the mixture evenly in the pan and bake in a medium hot oven for 1½ hours.

BROUSSARD'S ORANGE BRULOT

Cut a thin-skinned orange through the skin, around the circumference, carefully so as not to touch the fruit. With a teaspoon handle, turn the skin back until it forms a cup. Do this at both ends and you have a peeled orange with a cup at each end. Place one cup on your plate, pour some brandy in upper cup, put lump of sugar in the brandy, light the brandy, stir gently as it burns. Drink it when the flame dies. She'll say, "Heavenly."

CAFE BRULOT

In a bowl put a glass of brandy. Then add two lumps of sugar, a half-dozen cloves, one stick of cinnamon, one piece of vanilla bean, a few pieces of dried orange and dried lemon peel. Stir these ingredients for a few moments, then add one pint of boiling coffee. Place a brandy-soaked lump of sugar on a spoon and ignite, then allow the flame to convey itself to the liquid in the bowl. Serve while still hot.

CAFE ROYALE

Take a cup of hot coffee, black, without sugar. Place a lump of sugar on the spoon across the top of the cup and then pour a pony of bourbon across the sugar into the cup. Touch a match to the sugar and when it has burned out, drink the coffee.

CANTALOUPE OBOLENSKY

Make a round incision about 3 inches in diameter at the stalk of a cantaloupe, take out the plug, and remove the seeds with a spoon through the hole in the melon. Then pour 2 wineglasses of sherry into the melon, replace the plug, and place the melon in cracked ice for an hour. Finally, cut into halves and serve in soup plates.

CREPES SUZETTE

First of all make plain French pancakes. Like this: sift a half pound of wheat flour in a bowl and break into this three eggs. Add one ounce of powdered sugar, mix it well; pour in half a pint of cold milk very gradually, mixing constantly for about five minutes. Gently butter a frying pan and put it on the range; when it is hot, pour in about two ounces of the batter and after two minutes of cooking, turn it over and bake it on the other side, also, for two minutes. Place the pancakes (you should have about a dozen) on a hot plate and cover them up and prepare your Crepes Suzette sauce. Make a syrup with powdered sugar and water, not too thick, not too light. Add to this some Cointreau, Curaçao, Cherry Brandy, Anisette, Maraschino. One—for instance, Cointreau—is sufficient, but you may add four or five liqueurs as well. The mixture, the proportions, the strength of the Crepes Suzette sauce is entirely up to you. Now take a pan, if possible silver. Pour into it two or three tablespoonfuls of the mixture. Heat it on a hot fire, and when it is hot, place the pancakes in it one by one, turning them for a few seconds from one side to the other. Then place them on a heated dessert plate and pour the sauce over them.
It is not difficult, but it does require some care.

FUDGE

Melt two ounces of butter in a saucepan, add three-quarters quart of milk, two pounds sugar, four ounces chocolate and stir gently till chocolate melts. Boil without stirring to 238 degrees F. or until sample forms soft ball in cold water. Allow to cool, add vanilla flavor or chopped nuts, and beat with a wooden spoon until it begins to stiffen. Pour into buttered pan to three-quarters of an inch thickness, mark into squares at once.

GRAPE SAUCE

Squeeze bunches of grapes in your hands, strain the juice, boil for half an hour together with a tablespoonful of flour to each quart of grape juice. Stir constantly in the same direction with a spatula till the concoction has a custard consistency. Do not add sugar. Ladle into small individual dishes, and serve it hot, with cream if desired. Or put it in the icebox for an unexpected guest. This marvelous light dessert keeps literally for years in the icebox! The longer it stands the better it becomes.

KIRSCH BANANAS A LA PETE

A quickie dessert can be made in three minutes by slicing some bananas lengthwise and cooking for a few seconds in butter. Then sprinkle with sugar, add kirsch (or brandy if other not available), light and let burn for a few minutes, then serve.

THE POOR KNIGHTS OF WINDSOR

Cut some slices of bread about half an inch thick; soak the slices for a while in white wine and sugar. Cast two or three yolks of eggs. Take the bread out of the wine and dip it in the egg yolks. Heat a little butter in a pan; put in the bread and fry brown. Place the bread slices on a dish and sprinkle cinnamon and sugar over them. Drink a glass or two of white wine with it.

PREACHERS' DELIGHT

Legend has it that a Methodist parson, partaking of a synod banquet in a nearby Babylon, was noted to be pushing watermelon seeds into his Bible. The mystery turned on the dessert: a fine ripe watermelon into which had been poured one quart of good old Bourbon. The minister had hoped to plant such seeds in his garden.
Try it this summer, putting the melon in the icebox overnight.

PRUNEAUX AU VIN

Cover a pound of large prunes with cold water, and soak them for eight hours. Pour the prunes, together with the water they soaked in, into a saucepan where there is a vanilla pod broken in half. Sprinkle in half a cupful of brown sugar and stew on a slow fire for twenty minutes. Remove from the fire, add a cupful of good red wine, and simmer again slowly for ten minutes. Now cool the dish, but do not cool it in an icebox, do not take the vanilla pod out, and serve with sponge cakes.

RED WINE FRUIT JELLY
(For Six)

1 envelope sparkling powdered gelatin
1 pint Red Wine (Burgundy type)
4 tablespoons granulated sugar
1 teaspoon lemon juice
3 sliced peaches—or other fresh fruit

Soften gelatin in ½ cup water until dissolved. Bring Red Wine and sugar to heat, not boil, over a slow fire. Add gelatin and lemon juice. Stir well and pour half the mixture in cup glasses—half full. Add the fruit and put in icebox to chill. When firm enough fill the cups with the rest of the jelly so fruit will not float on top. Serve with sweetened whipped cream.

RICE PUDDING WITH APPLES

Cook a pound of rice in a quart of milk. Stir a quarter of a pound of butter until nearly liquid, with six teaspoonfuls of granulated sugar, six yolks of eggs; mix this with the cooled milky rice, and add to this the egg whites which you have beaten to a froth. Pour half of this mixture into a vessel that has been smeared with butter lightly on the bottom, placing on top six peeled apples from which the cores have been removed and in their stead apricot jam introduced, together with a half lump of sugar soaked in rum. Pour the remaining half of the rice mixture on top and bake in a moderately hot oven for forty-five minutes to one hour.

RUM ICE CREAM

Beat three eggs and add four tablespoons of sugar. Add one pint warm milk and boil the mixture. Allow to cool and add one-half pint cream and two tablespoons of rum. Stir well and freeze.

SABAYON SAUCE

Mix two ounces of sugar and four egg yolks in a mixing bowl, and beat very hard. Add a wineglassful of Marsala or sherry, the juice of half an orange, pour into a double boiler and cook until it binds. Serve with sponge cake.

ZABAGLIONE
(For Four)

Beat 6 egg yolks, then add 1 teaspoon of vanilla extract or 1 vanilla stick, 6 tablespoons of brandy or white wine, 6 tablespoons of granulated sugar and place in a double boiler. Increase the heat gradually and stir constantly until it thickens. Pour into glasses and serve warm or chilled if preferred.

If desired cold: Let get cold and then place in refrigerator; decorate with pistachios. If in a bowl, place lady-fingers around the bowl, and sprinkle with wine, then pour the zabaglione into it and decorate.

(NOTE: This is darned hard to make and takes much patience and slow cooking—which is probably one of the reasons it's so expensive in restaurants.)

Cheese

HIGH "C" OF THE MEAL

"Dessert without cheese is like a pretty girl with only one eye," wrote Brillat-Savarin, French gourmet of the 18th and 19th centuries. A high C of the meal, cheese is not only gifted as a topper-offer and tumtum tranquilizer, but also as an amplifier of the accompanying wine. Professional wine-tasters, in fact, use cheese to sharpen their keenness; it coaxes shy wine subtleties out into the open.

As to which species of cheese is greatest, opinions are so personal, so controversial, that the only way to avoid bad blood is the Assortment System: serve a platter, of cartwheel format, so your guests may choose their favorites. Here are some of the most popular cheeses:

Mold-mottled *Roquefort* gets its impetuousness from outwardly placid sheep's milk. But it doesn't come direct from ewe to you: there's an elaborate business of interpolating specially treated breadcrumbs, followed by protracted curing in cold, naturally drafty caves and grottos.

The imported stuff is bound to be expensive; the American version is Bleu cheese.

Italy's *Gorgonzola,* similarly mottled but made of cow's milk, is larger, crumblier, and even less timid. After a salad whose dresser didn't spare the garlic this cheese can be faced and exterminated with surprising facility. On the bland side there's creamy, discus-shaped *Bel Paese*—soft and self-controlled.

Tricky to deal with are those sob-sisters-under-their-skins, *Camembert, Brie* (larger), and *Pont l'Eveque* (square), hailing from regions west and east of Paris. Yet it's a case of the weepier the better. You show your ecstasy over their luscious dishevelment by the expertness with which you peel, not squash. No fair—and no flavor—if operated on while still firm and unripened, the way they come from the store; the cheese code of honor stipulates that, before sacrifice, they be given their due chance to mellow on the pantry shelf (refrigerator is too cold) till ready to swoon at touch. In that delicate condition any of the trio is cracker fodder of the first order, no matter how untidy the wreckage.

Some people with a zeal for after-dinner dabbling jobs complicate the situation by mixing butter with the cry-baby and then adding Worcestershire sauce (always a safe bet with cheese). Authentic *Switzerland Cheese,* tattooed with the name, gets its delectable ping from the milk of special cows that in summer pasture high up near the edelweiss. The holes are mementos of natural carbon dioxide gas, spontaneously generated as in champagne.

Low pastures have their good points too, the Dutch insist—backing the claim with cannonball *Edams* and fishcake-shaped *Goudas,* and now also long delicatessen store loaves, coated with the same protective wax.

England's flaky, golden *Cheshire* and purple-veined *Stilton* are nice work if you can get them. And if you can get Stilton-in-Port— ummm! America's patented creations include *Liederkranz,* buddy of beer.

For crunching and conveying, split and toasted *Bent's,* swaddled in a napkin, are the traditional. Or try any of the various crackers from the crispies bearing their own butter to the everyday and ever-good "soda cracker."

Coffee
THE CUP THAT CHEERS

When coffee was introduced to Europe in the 16th century, people thought that it rendered women frigid and even barren; a law was promptly passed in Constantinople giving husbands the right to prevent the use of coffee by their wives. Maybe that's why the average woman, to this day, can't make a good cup of coffee. It must be that, basically, coffee is a man's drink. When subjected to the economies of drugstore waitresses or the casual inattention of wives, the cup that cheers but does not inebriate is apt to become a mean, thin liquid with almost unlimited capacities for discouraging real coffee lovers.

So know ye this: no aspect of your cooking skill will bring you greater or more lasting pleasure than the ability to prepare the drink that stimulates wit and digestion. Coffee splices all loose ends, greets the cheese gladly, and spreads a mantle of aromatic warmth.

Here are some of the basic rules for making it properly:

1. Use only freshly roasted, freshly ground coffee.

2. Start with cold, fresh water—and if it is to be poured over the coffee when boiling be sure to pour it *as soon as it boils,* lest the oxygen be dispelled and the water be made tasteless by long boiling.

3. Make sure your equipment is spotlessly clean.

4. Always measure ingredients carefully and time the brewing-period exactly—so you can be sure to duplicate your method time after time once you have settled on the proper combination of water, coffee and time.

[81]

Beyond that, your own taste is boss. Using one of the following systems, experiment until you've reached coffee of the proper strength to match your memory of the best cup of coffee you ever sipped. The proportion usually recommended is 1 tablespoon of coffee to each cup of water, with an extra tablespoon of coffee "for the pot." With men who ken coffee, 2 tablespoons to 1 cup is a more favored strength. And some, to avoid long perking or simmering and the consequent bitter taste, use even a greater proportion of coffee. But there's as much variation in the strength of different coffee blends as there is in the tastes of coffee-drinkers, so suit yourself.

DRIP COFFEE

Coffee is put into the top part of the drip coffeemaker. Water is brought to a boil separately, then poured over the coffee—to drip through to the bottom part of the coffeemaker. Some fanatics insist that the water be poured over the coffee a mere spoonful at a time; others run the water through the coffee 2 or 3 times for added strength. The only certain rules are: preheat the coffee pot with hot water; use drip-grind coffee; stand pot in a warm place so coffee won't cool during the drip process.

GLASSMAKER COFFEE

Water is put into the lower bowl, upper bowl is fitted in, complete with filter or rod, then coffee is placed in the upper bowl. When water is hot, it rises through the tube into the upper bowl. Then as soon as steam comes up through the tube and agitates the mixture, the fire is turned off. Gradually, then, the coffee filters into the lower bowl—from which you serve it. Or—you may prefer to allow the coffee to simmer in the upper bowl for 2 to 5 minutes, for a stronger brew. Or—you may put only an inch or so of water in the lower bowl (enough to create a vacuum when it boils) and heat the remainder of the required water separately, to be poured over the coffee grounds as for drip coffee. In any case, pulverized coffee is used.

OLD FASHIONED COFFEE POT

For this method, favored of our forbears, coffee should be coarsely ground. Dry coffee goes into the pot (or ordinary saucepan) first, then cold water. Bring to a boil, simmer 5-8 minutes, then take it off the stove. A dash of cold water will settle the grounds—or an eggshell thrown into the brew at the outset will have the same effect. Even so, you need a strainer for pouring.

PERCOLATOR COFFEE

Use same proportions as for pot coffee, but use medium-ground coffee—halfway between drip grind and pot grind. Coffee goes into the basket in the percolator, water into the pot; then the water "perks" through the coffee until it is the strength you like: about 8 minutes. With a glass percolator, you can see how you're doing throughout the process; others have a glass piece on top so you can get a glimpse of the brew as it perks.

Whatever the method used, coffee is best when freshly made. Once you've got your own coffeemaking timed, you'll know just when to fade from your dinner table in order to have fresh coffee ready by dessert-time or maybe you'll latch onto an electric coffeemaker that can do its fragrant work right at the table. Ben Jonson said, "As he brews, so shall he drink." Good drinking!

MIDNIGHT SNACKS

The man who can ask his friends in after the theater or other late function, not just to raid the icebox or "have a drink," is a man who is going somewhere—to his cupboard and his chafing dish, of course, but also to the top of his friends' hit parade. Develop *your* snack-knack with:

CHEESE FONDUE

Heat 1 cup of White Wine in an earthen chafing dish rubbed with garlic. Then add, stirring with a fork, 1 pound of methodically hacked-up Switzerland openwork cheese, alias Emmenthaler.

On the side, mix 1 tablespoonful of flour in 3 tablespoonfuls of Kirsch. Add this to the main show, which is still cooking and must still be stirred.

Hunklets of crusty French-type bread, about the size of lemon quarters, now come into play: one of these *brod micken*, impaled on a fork, is used as a stirrer till sopped with Fondue; then seized lightly with the teeth as though it were a toasted marshmallow. But what a morsel! Whereupon the other player takes over, pronto, because if stirring were allowed to lapse, even briefly, things would get stringy. With one participant working while the other eats, the alternation is kept up, punctuated by as many sips of Kirsch as can be crowded in, till no more Fondue is discoverable.

No wine or beer should be partaken of with a Fondue, as either, even at room temperature, would chill it into ropiness inside its consumers. Afterwards, coffee with Kirsch puts a seal of safety on the situation, and from then on one may eat or drink anything with serenity of assimilation. First and last, Fondue is Kirsch's private dish.

MASSOLETTI'S CHEESE FONDUE

Beat together one cup scalded milk, one cup soft stale breadcrumbs, a quarter of a cup mild cheese cut in small pieces, one tablespoonful butter, half a teaspoonful of salt, three eggs. Pour into a buttered baking dish and bake twenty minutes in a moderate oven.

OYSTERS AND CELERY FROM BILLY THE OYSTERMAN

Chop some celery and sauté in butter and, when tender, add to this the oysters (two dozen to three branches of celery) with their liquor, and simmer until the edges of the oysters curl. Add a glass of white wine on the sweet side, season and serve in its own sauce.

WAFFLES

Equipped with a waffle iron, a package of biscuit or pancake mix and a lubricated imagination, you're a cinch for a successful snack session. Here are a few variations on the standard-but-still-good waffles and syrup routine:

Cheese waffles: sprinkle grated cheese atop your regular waffle mixture.

Ham waffles: sprinkle ¼ cup diced, uncooked ham over the batter before closing the iron. Especially good with scrambled eggs.

[83]

Pecan waffles: sprinkle ¼ cup broken nutmeats over batter before closing iron. Good with brown sugar as a change from syrup.

Chocolate waffles (for the ladies): Add a couple of squares of melted chocolate to your standard mixture. Serve with ice cream or whipped cream.

Corn waffles: use prepared corn-muffin mix on your waffle iron, and you'll have so'thun waffles, sho nuff.

Or, for *really* different waffles:

FLEMISH WAFFLES

Put ¼ lb. of flour in a bowl and mix with it ½ oz. of yeast, dissolved in a little warm water. Work well and set to rise. Then work in ¾ lb. flour, with a pinch of salt, a pinch of sugar, 8 eggs, slightly beaten, ½ pint of cream, which should have been boiled, and to which 4 tablespoons of butter and ½ glass of brandy have been added. Work well and let stand for 2½ hours in a cool oven. The batter should now be sufficiently liquid to spread of itself over the well-greased waffle irons. When evenly browned on both sides sprinkle with sugar and serve very hot.

WELSH RABBIT (1)
(For Six)

Place 1 tablespoon butter and ½ cup ale or beer (which may be stale) in a chafing dish or double boiler. When hot, put in 1 pound chopped or grated Cheddar cheese and melt unhurriedly, stirring the while, till smooth. Then add 2 egg yolks which have been intermingled with ¼ cup milk, dash of salt, and 2 teaspoons Worcestershire Sauce. Stir these newcomers into the cheese-scape a moment or two, till thickened.

Serve upon slices of bread whose downsides have been toasted. Sprinkle with paprika. Side issues: celery, olives, salted nuts.

WELSH RABBIT (2)

Cut one-half pound of store cheese into small pieces and place them in the top of a double boiler. Pour over the cheese a half cup of beer, a pinch of cayenne and three pinches of salt. Stir constantly with a stick or wooden spoon and serve on pieces of toast. Now, bring out your bottled beer.

RAREBIT WITH BEER

1 pound good American cheese
1 cup light beer
1 egg
Dash of cayenne
1 tablespoon English mustard
½ teaspoon Worcestershire
Salt
2 tablespoons of butter

Melt butter in chafing dish or thick frying pan. Grate cheese, add, and melt very slowly. Mix seasonings in a cup with a tablespoon of beer; add egg and beat together. As the cheese melts add the beer, a little at a time, stopping when the mixture has the consistency of thick cream. Stir constantly in the same direction. The melting and stirring in of the beer should take at least half an hour. Be careful that it never bubbles. When perfectly smooth, stir in the egg. The cheese mixture should be hot enough so that the egg thickens it slightly. Pour over toasted crackers or slices of thin toast on very hot plates.

Picnic Supper

AN EASY BUFFET MENU

Particularly in the early stages of your cookery experiments, you might do well to plan something simple and deliberately devoid of the delicate touches. A buffet supper, after a cocktail or evening party in your apartment . . . or a picnic sort of meal on your terrace . . . is an easy way to entertain large groups without fuss. Baked ham and beans form a popular menu for just occasions. Add a big green salad, gobs of French and/or brown bread, beer or red wine and you can count on a successful evening.

BAKED BEANS

1 pound pea beans
½ pound salt pork
⅛ teaspoon celery salt
1 tablespoon brown sugar
¼ tablespoon dry mustard
1 clove garlic
2 tablespoons molasses
½ cup tomato juice
½ teaspoon Worcestershire
1 large onion
Pinch cayene pepper
½ cup beer

Pick over the beans, cover with cold water and soak for 24 hours. Drain, cover with fresh water, heat slowly, keeping water below the boiling point at all times. Cook until the skins begin to burst. Test by taking a few beans on a spoon and blowing on them—if sufficiently cooked, the skins will burst. Drain beans and place in bean pot. Scald and scrape pork. Put one strip in the bottom of the bean pot and save the remainder for the top. Mash the garlic clove—mix with the brown sugar, molasses, mustard, Worcestershire, celery salt and cayenne pepper; add the tomato juice and pour over the beans. Cover bean pot and bake 8 hours—375° F. When the beans have been baking for 4 hours, add ½ cup of beer. Uncover the last hour of baking, that rind may become brown and crisp.

HAM IN BEER

1 8-pound ham
Cloves
½ cup brown sugar firmly packed
1 tablespoon dry mustard
2 tablespoons vinegar
2 glasses of beer

Cover ham with cold water. Bring slowly to a boiling point. Simmer for three hours. Remove from water. Skin. Score fat in diamond shapes, and stud with cloves. Make a paste of brown sugar, mustard and vinegar. Pour over ham. Bake in moderate oven (350 degrees F.) 1½ hours, basting frequently with beer. Approximate yield: 24 portions. The juice of the basting on the ham can be made into a delicious sauce to be served on the ham when sliced. (Variation: Put garlic in the water when boiling ham. Bake surrounded by apples, cored but not peeled, the center of each filled with currants. Baste with wine instead of beer.)

[85]

You wouldn't set them before a dainty damsel you hoped to impress, but these homely foods may hit the spot when you're alone and in a shirtsleeve mood . . . or when your bowling team admits a yen for simple, beersy food. They won't set any gourmets on fire, these hamburger-frankfurter-type dishes, but maybe they'll brighten the corner where you are catching a solo dinner.

HAMBURGER SANDWICH

½ pound ground raw beef
1 teaspoon salt
2 tablespoons minced onion
Butter or drippings
1 tablespoon Worcestershire
   sauce

Mix the beef with the salt, onion and Worcestershire sauce. Make into thin cakes and brown on both sides in a hot frying pan containing drippings or melted butter. Turn often, sprinkling with salt each time. When cooked, place between slices of buttered bread or toast and serve very hot.

HOT DOG "STEW"

Chop finely two onions, and brown them in butter to a golden color. Add enough paprika to make it a nice red.

Simmer the mixture for fifteen minutes, stirring occasionally with a spatula so that it will not burn. Cut your frankfurters (two to a person) into about eight sections, and add them to the mixture. Simmer for ten minutes. Add a green pepper, a tomato, a small clove of garlic and a little black pepper. Simmer for another fifteen minutes. Now add peeled and quartered raw potatoes, a little salt, and cook over low flame for thirty minutes. When the potatoes are done, serve. With your fork mash the potatoes into the sauce on your plate, and you'll find they taste even better than unmashed.

CORNED BEEF HASH

Mix two parts chopped meat with one part chopped boiled potatoes and a little chopped onions if wanted. Salt carefully, particularly in the case of corned beef. Add a little pepper. Cook it in a frying pan with butter until well browned, and roll as you do an omelet. Decorate with a poached egg on top, and serve very hot.

MEAT LOAF

Take three quarters of a pound of ground beef and three quarters of a pound of lean ground pork (for four or five helpings) and mix them well together. Also take a roll, soak it in cold water for five minutes, and then squeeze it free of water with your hand. Shred and mix this with the meat. Chop up very finely a small onion, beat an egg (both white and yolk), mix these also with the meat, and season with salt and pepper. Mix once more very thoroughly, fashion into a loaf, and spread the white of an egg over it. Heat a tablespoon of fat in a roaster, slide the meat loaf into it, and add a glass of water. Roast in medium oven for about an hour. Peel small potatoes and place them on side of meat in the roaster a half hour before the meat will be ready. (Or if you prefer you can serve with mashed potatoes.) Baste occasionally.

SAUSAGES OR FRANKFURTERS

Try Swiss *gendarme*, flat in shape, Italian Mortadella, enormous in circumference, a Spanish *estramaduran*, an English Cambridge, a Hungarian salami, a truffled French *saucisson royal* or everyday "hot dogs,"

1.

Brown the sausage slightly in butter. Add a glass of white wine, simmer for ten minutes. Now take the franks out and place them on slices of stale bread fried previously in butter. Go on simmering the sauce, add to it a few drops of lemon juice, the yolk of an egg, a little gravy, a little butter, and season to taste. Pour the sauce over the frankfurters.

2.

Skin the sausages, cut them in half, lengthwise, and place half of them in a buttered pie dish. On top of the sausages lay sliced onions which were slightly browned in butter, slices of raw tomatoes, and season. Lay on top the remaining sausages, cover with consommé (canned), and a thick layer of mashed potatoes. Place butter on top and brown in moderate oven.

BROILED PIGS' FEET

Soak them for 8 hours in water. Drain. Place them in a saucepan with cold water, seasoning, and some raw vegetables. Boil for 5 to 6 hours. Remove and cut each foot in two parts. Wet the surface with a brush dipped in melted butter. Roll in very fine bread crumbs and broil them for 15 to 20 minutes over a moderate fire, preferably a charcoal fire.

CASSEROLE MEAL

4 tablespoons chopped onion
4 tablespoons cooking oil
1 green pepper finely chopped
3 cups leftover meat ground (or ground raw beef)
1½ teaspoons salt
1 cup beer
¼ teaspoon pepper
¼ cup fine breadcrumbs
2 eggs
1 can whole kernel corn
3 tomatoes, peeled and sliced

Brown the onion, green pepper and meat in the cooking oil. Add salt and pepper. When cool add beaten eggs. Oil a casserole; arrange above ingredients in layers with half the corn, the meat, the sliced tomatoes, the other half of the corn. Pour the beer over and then cover with the breadcrumbs. Bake at 350 degrees F. for 45 minutes. Some grated cheese may be mixed with the crumbs if desired.

SAUSAGES IN WHITE WINE

(For Six)

One cup of consommé and one and one-half cups of white wine in an earthenware casserole. Put one carrot and one stalk of celery, finely chopped, in the wine; when the wine is hot, place one dozen large pork sausages in the casserole, cover and cook over a slow flame. If cooked too quickly the sausages will burst. The length of time for cooking naturally depends on the size of the sausages, so this must be determined by the cook. Serve the sausages in the casserole to keep them very hot; mashed or creamed potatoes will prove the perfect complement.

Breakfast

RISE AND SHINE

Rassling up your own breakfast between dressing operations is a problem of technique. Eventually you'll get to the point where you can fix coffee, eggs and toast by remote control while you're shaving and showering. That's when the corner drugstore will have lost another customer—for no public eatery can match the quiet comfort of breakfast at home.

Here are some of the standbys to snap you out of your bachelor daze of a week-day morning (and to put you in training for a "breakfast for two" performance some day!). And on the next page you'll find a real praise-raiser of a Sunday brunch for entertaining.

Toast—Your best bet is an electric toaster that pops the toast up at you when it's done. Lacking that, put bread slices under the oven-broiler until brown on both sides. For cinnamon toast, spread with butter and sprinkle with a combination of cinnamon and sugar, then replace under broiler flame to melt the yummy topping.

Coffee—See page 81. Breakfast coffee is sometimes less strong than dinner coffee or demi-tasse.

Tea—Swirl some boiling water around in an earthenware pot, to heat it, then dump out the water. Then into the pot put one teaspoonful black tea for each cup of tea wanted. Bring fresh cold water to the boiling point, pour over the tea, then cover and allow tea to "steep" about three minutes, or until it reaches the desired strength.

BOILED EGGS

Place eggs in saucepan of boiling water and boil three minutes. Serve in an egg-cup—English fashion—or dump into a coffee cup in the robust American manner.

POACHED EGGS

Fill frying pan three-quarters full of boiling water, break and slip eggs in and cook over low fire until the whites are firm and a film forms over the yolks: transfer eggs with skimmer to a slice of toast.

SCRAMBLED EGGS

1 tablespoon of milk, ¼ teaspoonful salt, pepper and ⅛ teaspoonful butter to each egg. Break the eggs into a bowl, add seasonings and milk, beat lightly with a fork. Heat butter in omelet pan, add egg mixture. Do not stir but, as the eggs cook, scrape gently from bottom of the dish, drawing the cooked mass to one side. Remove from fire when nearly firm throughout and serve quickly.

A Prize Brunch

A PRAISE-RAISER FOR SUNDAY ENTERTAINING

Here is a Sunday morning breakfast that makes two great nations shake hands across the sea and your gastric juices thumb their noses at La Belle France. It is the kidney of Old England and the clam cake of New England, and what a marriage! Get your clams in the shells, soft-shelled or steamers. Wash them thoroughly to get the sand out of their teeth and place them with a single cup of water in a kettle. Cover tightly and cook until the shells open, no longer. When they are cool, remove clams from the shells, separating the soft from the tough parts, using only the latter, which should be put through a food chopper. All this can be done on Saturday night. Strain the juice and set on ice.

In the morning use any good prepared pancake mix or, if you are so good, make your own, and substitute the clam juice for the indicated milk and water, using a little more than called for in the maker's recipe. Add the chopped clams and fry as for pancakes.

Strip and split your kidneys and soak in hot water for five minutes. Lay several rashers (slices to you) of bacon in a skillet and when they are crisp remove them to the oven. Place the kidneys in the bacon fat and fry until brown, over a slower fire than you used for the bacon. If your timing is good the clam cakes and kidneys should come off at the same time. Serve all three parts on the same plate with a slice of onion. Your breakfast menu should read like this:

Ice cold clam juice
Clam Cakes with Kidneys and Bacon
Coffee

You are already building a reputation as a cook.
You might also include:

BUTTERED TOAST SUPREME

Cut the slices as thick as the toaster will take them. Score the bread across and up and down on one side and toast on both sides as you like it and on the scored side place generous gobs of butter. Place toast in the oven until the butter has melted and *penetrated*. One slice is usually enough but you'd better make an extra one for the lady.

Eggs
WITH A PEDIGREE

Unjustly relegated to the breakfast hour, when sleepy taste buds are ill-prepared to appreciate them, eggs come out of their shy shells into their own in a bachelor's design for living. They're ideal for the solo snack, of course, and for the dawn descent of the drinkers. Dressed up as below, they're fit company, too, for a "lovely," leftover from the cocktail hour. And if preceded by a "soup de maison," followed by your salad specialty and accompanied by a complementary white wine, they're worthy of your planned dinner hour, as well. But we don't mean to egg you on: try these improvements on the boiled-fried-scrambled routine, and see for yourself.

BAKED SPANISH EGGS

Fry 3 tablespoons chopped onion and 3 tablespoons chopped green pepper in 4 tablespoons butter until slightly brown, then pour into a baking dish. Break 6 eggs into this dish, being careful not to break the yolks. Mix ¼ cup breadcrumbs with ½ cup grated cheese and sprinkle over the eggs. Cover each egg with 2 tablespoons of beer over the top. Bake in a moderate oven until the eggs are set but not hard. Serve in the baking dish.

OMELETS

Omelets are easy to make and easy to spoil. It is really child's play to prepare an omelet—but one false move, and you may as well throw it away. You've got to be on the job every moment it is in preparation; but then, slow and lazy men do not make good cooks anyhow.

Crack into a bowl two eggs (for each person) and season them with a pinch of salt and a half pinch of pepper. Beat it unmercifully for five minutes, until the whites and yolks are completely mixed; the more the eggs are beaten, the lighter the omelet will be; and beat it with a silver fork. Do not use fancy kitchen utensils like an egg beater un-less you are callous to the contempt of professional chefs.

Take a frying pan and put into it a teaspoonful of best olive oil; do not use butter as it might burn. Heat the oil in the pan until it becomes terribly hot on the brisk flame. When the oil starts to smoke, fume and crackle, pour the eggs into the pan and agitate them gently for no longer than forty to fifty seconds; never dry them out by leaving them longer on the range, as a dried out or burned omelet is uneatable. Now remove the pan to a somewhat less hot spot on the range and fold the omelet with your fork — the side nearest the handle first—into a half-moon shape. Smear a bit of butter over it; take the handle of the pan in your right hand, a hot plate with a napkin underneath it in your left and with a rapid movement turn the pan right over the center of the plate. If you have done all this properly you may crow like a cock: "Ko-ko-ri-ko!" for that is how the French chefs greet a perfect omelet when it is ready. But do not forget that efficiency and quickness count above all, and that an omelet must always be made to order; it is better that the man wait rather than eggs.

Caviar omelet is made exactly like a plain one, except that the caviar, which has been mixed with some sour cream, must be put onto the omelet before it is turned to the half-moon shape. And the caviar must not come from the ice directly, but should have regular room temperature. When it is made right, it is truly a dish to set before a king— or a duke. Any other filling you fancy may be substituted for the caviar—from herbs to chicken livers, marmalade to chopped meat.

A word about the oil for the omelet: Olive oil, like butter, is one of the chief weapons of a chef, and it can be either good or bad. The best comes from Nice, Portugal, Italy, and most districts around the Mediterranean. *Huile Vierge* means that the oil was made from the first pressing of the oil berries. A good oil should consist of a cloudy stratum and a clear stratum and ought to be green in color. Do not use Arrachide, coconut or palm oils or cottonseed oil for cooking.

EGGS BEURRE NOIR

Fry the eggs in butter in small ramekins. At the same time brown well a little butter in another pan, add finely chopped parsley, a dash of good vinegar, salt and pepper. When very hot pour the sauce over the eggs and serve in the ramekin.

EGGS EN COCOTTE

Slightly warm up individual small earthenware ramekins, and pour in their bottoms a little boiling cream. Gently break the eggs (not more than two in a ramekin) and carefully slide them onto the surface of the cream. Season with salt and pepper, and add a tiny piece of butter. Place the ramekin into a pan of boiling water to reach within half an inch of the brim of the ramekin. Cover (but leave a little opening for the steam to escape), put the pan in the oven for ten minutes, and serve.

EGGS POACHED IN BURGUNDY

Put one ounce of butter in an earthenware casserole; sauté one white onion, finely chopped, and add one pint of Burgundy; salt, pepper, one whole clove, a bayleaf, and a slice of fennel; let it simmer for about ten or twelve minutes. Break one egg per person on the edge of the casserole and slip it gently into the simmering wine. Poach for about two or three minutes—according to taste in cooking. Separate them gently, remove with a skimmer, and put each egg on a piece of toast, ready to receive it on a hot platter. Strain the cooked wine and put it back in the casserole and bring to a boil; thicken it with small balls of butter and flour and pour over the eggs on toast.

Carving

KNIFE WITH FATHER

The fine art of carving was, until recently, as absolutely essential a part of a gentleman's education as a knowledge of horsemanship, swordsmanship, and dancing. In the old days, carving was a rite. With impressive, leisurely dignity, the host set about dismembering the fare, with the result that the first person served was about ready for dessert before the careful carver had lopped off his own meat. These days call for fewer flourishes and more speed.

The first essentials for carving are a good knife and fork. What you want is a knife with a fine steel blade about nine inches long and some depth at the heel: the blade should be slightly curved and should taper to the point. The fork should have large curved prongs, so it will not slip out. A steel and an emery stone are also necessary. The blade can be emeried by laying the heel of the knife across it at about a 30° angle, the edge toward you, then draw the knife across the stone toward you lightly without bearing down on it. Reverse and do the same for the other side for about a dozen strokes. This should be done in the pantry. You may use the steel before going to the table but in order to keep the keen edge essential for successful carving, it will be necessary to whet the blade during the course of carving. When whetting the blade, the edge should be drawn along the steel towards you, rather than away.

BIRDS

First sink the fork at a spot a couple of inches behind the point of the breast bone with one prong on either side of the bone: there is a special place for it, which was apparently designed to accommodate forks, and you will find it readily. Now slip the point of the knife under the far wing and make an upward cut for the joint that holds the wing to the turkey, a straight cut well towards the neck so as not to undershoot the joint. If the wing doesn't drop off, get the knife into the joint and break it if necessary. The leg or drumstick and the second joint should be removed in one piece. Make a straight cut for the joint that holds it to the turkey. Cut an inch or two above the "Pope's nose", going as far as you can; then slip the knife behind the joint and cut to the juncture again. This should separate the whole business from the body of the fowl. Once it is off, put the fork in the second joint and cut for the juncture of the drum stick and the second joint. Now one side of the bird is stripped of its appendages and you are ready to carve the breast. Put the fork in the same position in which you originally inserted it in the bird, and lay the bird on its side, legless side up, so that the slices of breast, as you carve them, will remain in position until you lift them off. If you permit the bird to remain upright, the slices would fall off to the side and, while this is all right with ham and certain other joints, it will not do with turkey: the breast will crumble and the slices be difficult and unappetizing to handle. So, lay the bird on the side and cut the slices with firm, even strokes. Slices should not be thick.

DUCK

Young duck or duckling is carved in a similar manner to chicken or turkey. First, the wings are removed and then the breast is either sliced or, if it be a small bird, it is removed in one piece. Next the leg and second joint are removed, divided or served in one piece if it is small.

GOOSE

If you ever have to tackle a roast goose, remember that the breast of a goose, more than that of any other bird, is most highly esteemed, and the carver may not have to give much attention to any other part, though some people find the legs excellent.

WILD DUCK, TEAL, ETC.

Epicures consider only the breast of wild fowl worth eating and usually only this is served.

FOWL

Roast and boiled fowl (chickens, capon, etc.) are cut in a manner similar to roast turkey.

PHEASANT

The choicest parts of the pheasant are the breast and the wings, as is true of most fowl. Pheasant is carved exactly as turkey.

PARTRIDGE

There are several ways of carving a partridge. The usual method is to cut the bird along the top of the breast bone and divide it into two equal parts: a half partridge is a fair portion for one person. If it is necessary to make the partridge do for three people, the legs and wings may be easily severed and a leg and a wing will provide a helping, while the breast will provide a third helping. The partridge may also be cut into four equal portions if necessary. Woodcock and pigeon are carved in the same manner—in either two, three or four portions.

GROUSE

Grouse may be carved in the same way as partridge. It is well to know that the backbone of the grouse is highly esteemed by many and considered, along with the same portion of many game birds, to possess the finest flavor.

SNIPE

Snipe are served whole as these tiny birds make but a single helping.

MEAT

Meat should always be cut across the grain, the one exception to this rule being the saddle of mutton which is always carved at right angles to the rib bones, in slices running parallel with the fibers or grain of the meat. Ham and beef should be cut in very thin slices and lamb, mutton and pork in fairly thick ones.

A round of beef, or ribs rolled, are not so easy to carve as some joints. A thin-bladed knife is recommended. First, cut a thick slice off the outside of the joint at its top, so as to leave the surface smooth, then thin and even slices should be carved.

A calf's head is nearly always boned before serving, and is then cut in slices like any other boned or rolled joint. If it is not boned, you should carve the head in strips from the ear to the nose. With each of these should be served a piece of what is called the throat sweetbread, cut in semi-circular form from the throat part. (The eye and the flesh around it are favorite morsels with many: they should be given to those guests who are known to be connoisseurs.)

[94]

VEAL

Breast of veal consists of two parts: the rib bones and the gristly brisket. These two parts should be separated: then the rib bones may be detached separately and served.

MUTTON

Leg of mutton is comparatively simple to carve. The knife should be carried sharply down and slices taken from either side, as the guests may desire.

The saddle of mutton is a fine old English dish: it consists of two loins connected by the spinal bone. The meat is generally carved across the ribs in slices running parallel with the backbone and the grain of the meat, and with each portion is usually served a small piece of fat cut from the bottom of the ribs. Plenty of good gravy and red currant jelly should be served with this.

In carving a shoulder of mutton the joint should be raised from the dish and as many slices cut away as can be managed. After this the meat lying on either side of the blade bone should be served by carving it from the knuckle end. The joint can then be turned and slices taken off along its whole length.

PORK

A leg of pork is carved as a leg of mutton: the knife should be carried sharply down to the bone right through to the crackling. A loin of pork, if it is properly prepared at the butcher's, may be divided into neat and even chops and presents no particular carving problems.

HAM

Here the carver must be guided by whether he desires to practice economy or to serve immediately from the best part. Under the first supposition, he will commence at the knuckle and cut thin slices toward the thick part of the ham. If he prefers to serve the finest part first, he will cut across and down to the bone at the center of the ham.

LAMB

A leg or shoulder of lamb is carved as a leg or shoulder of mutton.

SUCKLING PIG

If you should ever have occasion to carve a suckling pig, don't be alarmed: it is not a very difficult feat. The pig should be served with the head separated from the body, and it is usually sent to the table with the body separated in half. The first point to be attended to is the separation of the shoulder from the carcass. The next step is to remove the leg; then the ribs remain fairly open to the knife. The other half of the pig may be served in the same manner. All parts of a suckling pig make delicious eating but, in serving it, you should consult the preferences of your guests.

FISH

A steel knife and fork should never be used for fish because contact with this metal is apt to spoil its flavor, particularly with certain choice varieties which owe their excellence almost entirely to a delicate characteristic flavor. A silver or plated slicer and fork should be provided for carving and serving fish. Be careful not to break the flakes which ought to be served as entirely as possible, although short grained fish, such as salmon, should be cut lengthwise.

LOBSTER

To dress a lobster properly, insert a knife at the center of the back and cut through towards the tail. Then turn the lobster around and cut through towards the nose. (Be careful to cut towards the tail first, otherwise the shell will most certainly break.) After the lobster is cut, remove the brains. These are usually of a greenish color and are found at either side of the lobster head. The claw shells should be cracked open with a hammer or nutcracker and are sometimes served as a separate dish.

CRAB

In preparing a crab for consumption, place it on its back and insert your fingers between the shell and the meat. Using your thumbs as levers, push the body away from the shell: then break off the claws, remove the poisonous "fingers" and cut away the sides of the back shell.

Drink

LIQUOR IS QUICKER

"There is much to indicate that in our civilization alcohol has a very useful function to perform and may be a source of increased happiness and decreased hostilities."—KARL MENNINGER

"Let us drink for the replenishment of our strength, not for our sorrow."—CICERO

"Here's how!"—ESQUIRE

Tips on Technique

If you would build perfection potables that recondition the human system in three cool sips . . . if you would cast the spell of friendly hospitality over every gathering, be it planned or spontaneous, around your bar . . . you'd best capitalize on the years (even centuries) of taste-and-tell experiments made by your predecessors in the world of whistle-whetting. Previous palates have picked out the spirits which blend with each other to banish the dispirited from your hearth, so even though a new drink will be born every second whenever good fellows get together, it will take a long time to cap the classics included in this book.

[99]

But, more than that, artful Ph.D.'s (philosophers of drinkology) have discovered make-or-break secrets you'll seldom find in recipes. Take this advice—whether you're a novice in the down-the-hatch field, starting from scratch, or an amateur in good standing at the bar—and you'll be spared the cocktail that doesn't quite come off, the highball that stoops too low, the cooler that fails to warm the heart. The result will be thirst-quenchers such as money cannot buy in a crowded bar, where the cash register is king. They'll be drinks as you like 'em, when you like 'em and where you like 'em—at home.

Here, then, are the open secrets of drink-making:

1. Use only the best ingredients—and show them proudly, full face, on your bar, not anonymously in suspicious-looking decanters.

Selecting "the best" is a matter for your own taste, but if you can't personally spot a raw whisky or a sad Scotch at first sip, you'll have to trust a reliable dealer, brand-names and indicative price-tags. A drink is, of course, no better than its ingredients—from liquor all the way down to lemon juice.

When the budget rears its ugly head, use *your* head: a good blended whisky will do very nicely in mixed drinks, so save that 8-year-old straight bourbon for "neat" drinks, highballs, and Old-fashioneds. If you're stuck with a cloudy gin and can't bring yourself to break it over the head of the guy who sold it to you, try it in fizzes or Collinses but never in a Martini. If you can't afford a really good cognac, serve a lesser liqueur; use the cheap brandy for a blue flame on the pudding but not for a give-away inhaler.

2. Use *exact*—not hit-or-miss—measurements.

If you'd like to vie with the professionals and rely entirely upon your eye, then spend 48 hours a week manipulating a mixing glass so that it acquires invisible level marks, comparable to the tone spacings that a violinist's fingers deal with on his fiddle strings. Otherwise wield a jigger carefully, not only to arrive at the result intended by the recipe but also to be able to repeat that result again and again.

3. In mixing, stick to the shake or stir technique prescribed by the recipe.

Martinis and Manhattans are stirred in a pitcher of ice, not only to make them icy cold and to blend their ingredients but also to prevent their clouding up as would be the case were they man-handled in a shaker. Drinks which include sugar, eggs, cream, fruit juice, etc. will be cloudy anyway, so shaking is in order for best mixing. When in doubt, use your noggin: pure liquors are not shaken unless that method is specifically prescribed; seltzer water is never under any circumstances meant to be flattened in a shaker. But when you *do* shake, *shake!* A Ramos Gin Fizz takes the extreme —12 minutes of shaking—but it follows that any drink which needs a shaker to blend it needs a *good* job of blending (and chilling) done on it.

4. Use plenty of ice—and wherever possible pour your liquor *over* ice rather than adding ice to already-poured liquor. Don't use the same ice twice.

Except to a Britisher, nothing is more depressing than a warm drink. If you're worried about over-dilution of highballs, use less soda rather than less ice. Ice *cubes* are used for stirred drinks, but cracked ice is the order for shaker-drinks. That makes sense when you think about it, and a bar gadget (p. 104) makes it easy. The main thing is that it be *ice only*, not a pool of ice and water. When crushed ice is called for, as in juleps and frozen daiquiris, you'll pound it in a bag (p. 104)—but, again, make sure it's *dry* before you put it in the glass.

5. Use prechilled glasses. When you haven't time to cool them in advance in the refrigerator, fill them with crushed ice and let them shiver while you mix the drinks. Then dump out the ice, *wipe out the glasses* and pour in the drink. That way your cold drink will stay cold, or that ice in the drink won't immediately begin to dribble.

6. Match your service to your mixing, or attention will be distracted from your good deeds at the bar. Pour smoothly, cutting off the flow from pitcher or shaker with a sharp uplift or a quick twist to prevent sloppy dripping. Don't fill glasses so full that they spill over at first clutch, provide coasters or cocktail napkins, spear olives or drink-fruit on toothpicks so they can be easily gobbled or removed. Keep the bar clean, and be sure glasses are spotless—and dry. Always recap bottles as soon as you've finished with them.

"I see you've forgotten the glasses again"

What the Well=Dressed Bar Will Wear

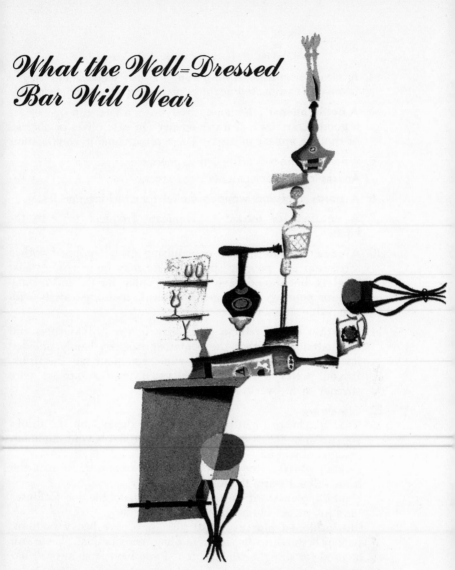

If you were to collect all the bar gadgets on the market, as interesting a hobby as that might be, you'd probably have to build a new wing on your barroom. You'd have a Waring Mixer for frappes, a Hamilton Beach for flips, an electrical unit for hot toddies, a midget refrigerator for ice-cubes and beer and mixes, special racks for wines and, no doubt, a constant hangover. Fun is fun, but so are funds—so here's a basic list of bar accessories.

1. **A jigger measure.** Especially practical is the four-jigger, its quartet of capacities ranging from ¾ oz. (½ jigger) to 1 oz. (a pony) to 1½ oz. (1 jigger; standard cocktail slug) to 2 oz. (enough for a Collins, fizz or generous highball). There are also patented pourers which, installed in bottle necks, dole out precise doses; and some jiggers are built in combination with bar spoons, corkscrews or bottle-openers.

2. **A long bar spoon**—for use both in measuring teaspoons of sugar, etc., and in stirring cocktails.

3. **A muddler-round-based wooden stick**—for mashing sugar and bitters, as in the Old-fashioned.

4. **A glass or plastic stirring rod,** for use whenever seltzer is involved (carbonated mixtures may collapse at touch of metal).

5. **A bottle opener** (the hook variety) . . . a beer-can opener . . . a good corkscrew . . . a can-opener (in case olives or cherries or the like appear in cans). These often come in combination.

6. **A paring knife** for cutting lemon peels, etc.

7. **An icepick** and/or a patented ice shaver.

8. **A sturdy bag** and **wooden mallet** for crushing fine ice.

9. **A vacuum ice bucket**—to eliminate frequent trips to the kitchen.

10. **A good cocktail shaker**—or a mixing glass equipped with a screw top and pouring spout. Shaker may be of either metal or glass, but should have a large opening for ice and a small one for pouring. Try to get a non-leak, non-drip variety with removable strainer.

11. **A pitcher** or **tall mixing glass** in which to stir Martinis and Manhattans. See that the container has the handy, molded lip which holds back the ice while you pour out the drink. If you prefer a mixing glass, you'll need a circular wire strainer to fit over the top for pouring.

12. **Glassware**
Your glassware repertoire will largely depend on the drinks you are most accustomed to serve; but probably your minimum equipment will be:
cocktail glasses: they should be solid-stemmed, so that the hand will not warm the drink.
highball glasses: if you want them to double for Collinses and Juleps, get 14-ouncers with straight sides.
Old-fashioned glasses: make sure they have heavy bottoms, so they'll stand up to your muddling machinations. These can be used for straight-drinkers, too, if you haven't shot- or drink-glasses.
sherry glasses: they can be pressed into extra service for liqueurs.
goblets: these can be used for wine, sours, flips.

Never one to put a horse-blanket on a beautiful girl, Esky puts thumbs down on colored glasses which disguise the good looks of the drink itself. Only clear glass is in the clear with everyone but the camouflage experts.

13. **Trays**—If you haven't an official bar—whether it be a portable tucked into a corner of the living room or a real bar you can sip up to—you'll want an oversized tray to use for the purpose. Load it with liquor, bitters, fruit, necessary glasses and gadgets, ice bucket and carry it into the midst of the guests where you can make the drinks in plain sight. In any case, you'll want at least one tray for passing drinks, and collecting empties.

Parties call for planned purchases, but for your own elbow-bending as well as for whatever impromptu imbibing is occasioned by drop-in guests, you'll want a supply of the makings. Here's Esquire's "progressive" cellar, based on the needs for building best-liked drinks. If you've room for reserves, have at least one spare bottle of the liquors you use most. If not (or if you live above a liquor store!), buy as the spirits move.

Cellar #1

1 bottle dry gin
1 bottle French Vermouth

Mainly Martini-minded, this spare stock affords you a surprising range—through the orange blossoms, the rickeys and fizzes and Collinses. And if you have foreign guests the vermouth can be served straight or with carbonated water and a slice of lemon peel.

When you're ready to expand, add:

Cellar #2

1 bottle rye, bourbon or blended
  whisky

1 bottle Italian Vermouth
1 bottle orange bitters
1 bottle Angostura bitters

Now you're all set for the Manhattan, the second choice in America, as well as for Old-fashioneds, whisky sours, highballs, juleps and a zing-string of other whisky-based drinks. Then, to almost double your potential for quick hospitality, add:

Cellar #3
Martini and Manhattan makings
PLUS 1 bottle of good Scotch

Nobody can now take you aback—nobody, that is, except an unexpected aunt. So to be prepared for the "middle-man" between hard and soft drinking, have in reserve:

Cellar #4
1 bottle dry sherry
(and, while you're at it, include 1
bottle of port, for after-dinner callers
as well as your own good-book evenings)

Next in line, for pleasant sipping, we recommend:

Cellar #5
1 bottle good cognac
1 bottle white Crème de Menthe

Now you're not only equipped to serve up the popular stinger, but you can play the lavish host with an offer of brandy in an inhaler, or brandy and soda—or, for the ladies, a menthe frappe. (If she says, "I thought it was supposed to be green!" assume your lordly air and she'll soon conclude that white is much, much smahter.)

Cellar #6
1 bottle best rum

Let your favorite drinks decide the type of rum to buy; there's light and dark, Jamaican and Puerto Rican and Cuban and New England and Bacardi. There is seldom any great damage done by substitution, except in the case of a Bacardi cocktail, but maybe when you're flush you'll flush a sample of each. There are so many popular rum drinks that you may want to move our Cellar 6 up to first or second place, particularly in summertime.

Cellar #7
1 bottle Pernod
1 bottle Peychaud Bitters

Reaching down to New Orleans, you lift up the makings for Sazeracs—and discover as well that a few drops of Pernod pick up a Martini, give a new twist to the long gin drinks, and cast a sophisticated air over any bachelor's bar. You'll probably discover the long, innocent-tasting absinthe frappe, too, but try not to drink them before breakfast!

Now, if not sooner, add the trimmings:

Cellar #8
Champagne, ready to celebrate the day you got married or didn't
Your choice of liqueurs
Irish whisky
Vodka
Applejack

Dubonnet and/or Byrrh
Sloe Gin
Curacao, Cointreau, Benedictine and Crème de Cacao seem to be most versatile — adding their interest to cocktails as well as to after-dinner relaxation.

And there you are—loaded!

But we should warn you (if your vibrating wallet has not already done the job) that this method of being prepared for anything is expensive. We refer not so much to the original outlay as to the ever-present temptation of such a well-stocked bar. So don't cry in your cocktail if you're "stuck" with only the makings of Martinis, Manhattans, Old-fashioneds and highballs. They furnish enough good cheer for any ordinary occasion!

THE CELLAR'S JUNIOR PARTNERS

Keep on hand as many of the following accessories as you find uses for:

cold beer

cold soda, mineral water and ginger ale

maraschino cherries

pitted olives or cocktail onions

oranges, lemons and limes (for peel, juice and garnish)

sugar: lump, superfine and powdered

nutmeg for flips, punches, hot drinks

cinnamon sticks

Grenadine (for the ladies' pink drinks)

Orange Flower Water (for Ramos Gin Fizz, etc.)

cream and eggs for the flips and fancy drinks

BARTENDER'S BOX SCORE
—a jack-up for the mixer's memory

"And for you, my dear, a vermouth cassis, of course." Smile something like that in the direction of a new friend and she's sure to be (a) flattered that you remembered to provide her top tipple and (b) pleased to know she won't have to pretend she likes Scotch.

It's the wise host who knows his guests' preferences in potables. Rather than trusting to your memory or your friends' patience, "put it in writing," right here, whenever you pick up a clue about your guests' likes and dislikes in the drink department. Rum and coke, only, for Janet? No bitters in any drink for John? Plain water, always, in Mary's highballs? Note it here, on the sly—then note how your host-stock rises when you unfailingly trot out the favorite drink for everyone.

GUEST	HIT-DRINK	HATE-DRINK

GUEST	HIT-DRINK	HATE-DRINK

"Hi- Old Sourpuss—I just had four Martinis!"

Cocktails

THE FIVE O'CLOCK WHISTLE WHETTERS

Of the thousands of concoctions which slide down unsuspecting gullets in the fair name of cocktails, there are only a few which—year in, year out—rate encores and re-pours. Since you'll stir up a hundred Martinis, Manhattans or Old-fashioneds to every fancy-handled "drip drink," we've arranged these aristocrats of good cheer—together with the companion-classic Daiquiri, Stinger and Champagne Cocktail—in Esky's Goodtime Sip Parade, a compact section for your handy quick-reference.

Worthy of almost equal if less frequent respect are such good cocktails as the Sazerac, the Toddy, Ward Eight, Rum and Scotch Old-fashioneds, Sours and the least-repulsive of the Fizzes. These, "Good for a Change," invite your experimentation on page 114.

But there'll be times (your bartender should have told you) when you must steel yourself to mix up one of those fluffy, multi-colored abominations which, for some mysterious reason relating to iron-insides and paralyzed palates, the "ladies" insist upon downing. The habitual-offenders of these unmanly drinks are segregated under "Something for the Girls," confined to page 117 where they can't interfere with your own tasteful toasting.

And then, for those occasions when you're possessed of a particular bottle of spirits and a random spirit of adventure, we've included a selected, alphabetized list of additional cocktails "Something for the Boys." No need to splash through pages of Caribbean cocktails when your cellar is down to its sole bottle of gin; just turn to the gin section (page 123) and run your barspoon down the list until something strikes your fancy.

[111]

Esky's Good-Time Sip Parade

MANHATTAN

2-1 MANHATTAN

3 dashes Orange Bitters
⅓ Italian Vermouth
⅔ Rye or Bourbon

Pour over ice cubes in tall glass, stir clockwise, chuck in a square piece of lemon rind, stir some more, then pour into chilled glass — with or without maraschino cherry.

4-1 MANHATTAN

4 parts Rye or Bourbon
1 part Italian Vermouth
Stir, don't shake, with ice and pour into glass holding the proverbial cherry or, preferably, a twist of lemon peel.

DRY MANHATTAN

2 parts Rye or Bourbon
1 part French Vermouth
Stir gently with ice and pour into chilled cocktail glass. No cherry with this one.

THE OLD-FASHIONED

Them what likes their Old-fashioneds without sugar, without bitters, without water or seltzer, without ice and certainly without fruit are just too old fashioned to name their drink as "straight whisky, please." Actually, the only debatable part of an Old-fashioned is the fruit garnish—the cherry, orange-slice and sometime stick of pineapple which serious drinkers claim interfere with their Old-fashioned elbow-bending. Here's how!

OLD-FASHIONED

In a squatty, robust-bottomed tumbler of the type designed for and dedicated to this drink, place a lump of sugar. Wet this down with 3 dashes of Angostura bitters. (Some use 2 teaspoons of water, as well. Many prefer only 1 or 2 dashes bitters.) Crush the sugar with a wooden muddler, preferably one which has never been washed nor used for any less worthy purpose. Rotate glass so that sugar grains and bitters give it a lining, then add a crystal-clear lump of ice. Now pour in 1½ oz. bourbon or rye. Twist a bit of lemon peel over the top.

A Maraschino cherry, a slice of orange and a chunk of fresh or canned pine-

apple may be added; the drink may be given a final stir . . . but in both cases fall back for criticism from Old-fashioned addicts.

VARIATION: add a dash of Curacao. Try reducing sugar to ¼ lump. Equal amount of granulated sugar may be used, but be sure to muddle.

ECCENTRIC OLD-FASHIONED

1 complete lemon peel
squeezed into glass
½ teaspoon sugar
½ teaspoon curacao
2 ounces whisky
Shake well but do not strain and serve in glass garnished with slices of pineapple, orange and cherries.

MARTINI

VERY DRY MARTINI
French method
1 part French Vermouth
5 parts Gin

Stir gently in tall glass with ice, strain into cocktail glass, add pitted green olive, twist piece of lemon peel over each glass then drop peel into martini.

DRY MARTINI I
1 part French Vermouth
3 parts Gin
Dash of Orange Bitters

Stir without great heat in tall glass half-filled with broken ice, then pour into cocktail glass. Twist a small segment of lemon peel (1 inch by ¼ inch) over the top then drop into glass.

DRY MARTINI II
1 part French Vermouth
2 parts Gin

Stir with ice in tall glass, until chilled. Serve in cocktail glass with green olive or pearl onion. Twist piece of lemon peel on top.

MEDIUM MARTINI
1 part French Vermouth
1 part Italian Vermouth
2 parts Gin

Stir with ice in tall glass; strain into cocktail glass containing green olive.

SWEET MARTINI
Ladies Only
1 part Italian Vermouth
1 part Tom Gin
Dash of Orange Bitters

Stir with ice; serve with green olive. Twist piece of lemon peel on top.

VARIATIONS: For spirited occasions a few drops of Pernod, Oxygene or the local absinthe adds just the right touch to the dry Martini. Sticklers insist that a small pickled onion be used in lieu of the olive when absinthe is used. Maraschino, Benedictine, sprigs of mint, Creme de Menthe, orange peel and Angostura bitters are occasional "third rails" for the gin-vermouth combination.

THE DAIQUIRI

Lime-and-rum of a Cuban sort was put on our social map by the Spanish-American War. A landing was made at Daiquiri near Santiago (the home of Bacardi), and the soldiers "refreshed" themselves as though this were Ticonderoga—the glad news of their all-round success spreading through the Army and Navy; since when our alliance with *Ron de Cuba* has been continuous and active. Thus:

DAIQUIRI COCKTAIL
Edition of 1898
Juice of half a lime
1 jigger (1½ oz.) Bacardi rum, White
1 barspoon powdered sugar

Shake vimfully with cracked ice till shaker frosts; strain into cocktail glass.

FROZEN DAIQUIRI COCKTAIL
Modern Arctic-Tropic Edition
Juice of entire lime
2 oz. Puerto Rican rum, white
1 teaspoon sugar

Assemble in an electric mixer, which is thereupon filled up with puffed-wheat-size ice. When almost frappéd,
pour through large-meshed strainer into a "saucer" champagne glass, allowing enough of the fine ice to tumble through to form a floe that would tempt a penguin. A dash (about 20 drops) of Cointreau is a crafty touch sometimes applied.

VARIATIONS ON THE THEME: Some insist they form a more perfect union by adding a dash of white Maraschino liqueur; others interpolate a squirt of Triple Sec. Still others pink the whole situation up with Grenadine, in which case we are out of the Daiquiri category entirely but by no means in the bleak wilderness if bright eyes have anything to say about it. A particular cult even make beige Daiquiris with Jamaica.

THE CHAMPAGNE COCKTAIL

Not a tipple to tender as a prelude to hamburgers and onions, the champagne cocktail is nonetheless such a lasting favorite with a certain genre of gals that you should have it in your collection. To make an impression (to say nothing of a dent in your budget), use a fine grade of dry champagne.

CHAMPAGNE COCKTAIL

Take a nice full-blown lemon and from it scrape off as much of the yellow as you can with a cube of sugar. Place the sweet in a champagne glass with a small lump of ice, add a dash of Angostura bitters and slowly fill the glass with champagne, stirring it only enough to dissolve the sugar. Serve with a twist of lemon peel.

THE STINGER

Formerly a quiet member of the "horsey" set, an also-ran in the cocktail derby, the Stinger buzzed into popularity when wartime pilots discovered how well it lives up to its name. Even though Army-Navy plane clothes have been doffed for plain clothes, the ex-fliers still like to check out on the Stinger. Flight Plan below:

STINGER

2 parts brandy
1 part white Crème de Menthe
Stir with cracked ice in tall mixing glass; strain into cocktail glass. The Stinger is sometimes served with a pair of short straws.

Good for a Change
GIMLET
A gimlet is a bore—not so the Gimlet

The connection between the Gimlet (cocktail) and a gimlet (carpenter's boring tool) is obscure—and who cares? Anyway, the Gimlet is a sharp thirst-quencher and a mainstay of the British Empire in high-temperature lands East of Suez. You can also get a very decent Gimlet in London. At the Savoy it's made like so: 3 parts dry gin to 1 part Rose's lime juice. Shake with ice and strain into a large 4 oz. cocktail glass. Add a dash of soda water for zip. A true Gimlet must be made with Rose's bottled lime juice, which vanished like nylons during the war but is now seen around again. Rose's has a distinct flavor—like lime candy drops. You can make a pseudo-Gimlet with fresh limes (jigger of gin, juice of 1 lime, 1 tsp. sugar), but it won't taste like a Calcutta or Singapore Gimlet.

SILVER FIZZ

1 oz. lemon juice
1½ oz. gin
1 teaspoonful sugar
1 egg white

Shake furiously with cracked ice, strain into highball glass, fill up with sparkling water. Give stirring rod a couple of twirls in it.

RAMOS, or NEW ORLEANS FIZZ

Juices of ½ lime and ½ lemon
1 oz. sweet cream
2 oz. dry gin
White of one egg
3 dashes Orange Flower Water

Shake with vim and vigor amid cracked ice. Pour into tallish glass, which has been dunked upside down in a saucer of lemon juice and then in powdered sugar, add seltzer stingily (or none at all) lest there be too much dilution. (*Note:* Another recipe calls for ½ teaspoon powdered sugar. In any case, the secret is in long shaking. Twelve minutes is stated as the proper time.)

[114]

THE SAZERAC

For this New Orleans powerhouse, the glass *must* be thoroughly chilled. Put a few drops of Pernod (absinthe without the illegal wormwood) into a large Old-fashioned glass, then tile and roll the glass until its inside is thoroughly coated. In a tall mixing glass with several cubes of ice, stir until well-chilled:

    2 oz. bourbon or rye
    3 dashes Peychaud bitters

Then pour, without the ice, into the chilled glass. A lemon peel is sometimes twisted over the top. (Some recipes call for a dash of Italian Vermouth, in addition.)

COLD TODDY

In the bottom of an Old-fashioned glass, crush:

    ½ teaspoon sugar
    1 strip lemon peel, about 1" long
    1 teaspoon water

Add 1 or 2 cubes ice. Pour in 1½-2 oz. your favorite whisky, give it a quick stir, and there you are. You may add a bit of water or seltzer if you want to last longer.

SCOTCH OLD-FASHIONED

Substitute Scotch whisky for bourbon or rye in the Old-fashioned recipe, page 112. Occasional Scotch drinkers like it, but an earnest Scotch-lover's reaction will be, "You've ruined some mighty fine Scotch."

THIS WARD EIGHT

Into a bar glass half filled with broken ice, put

    1 teaspoon Grenadine
    1 oz. rye or bourbon
    Juice of ¼ lemon or ½ lime

Shake briskly and strain into cocktail glass. (Some use ½ lemon plus ½ teaspoon sugar. ½ pony of water is sometimes added.)

or . . . THIS ONE

    Juice of 1 lemon
    1 barspoon powdered sugar
    ¾ large whisky glass bourbon

Dissolve sugar in juice and whisky. Pour in large glass with a large piece of ice and add:

    3 to 4 dashes Orange Bitters
    3 dashes Crème de Menthe
    ½ jigger Grenadine

Fill glass with seltzer, add

    2 slices orange
    1 stick pineapple
    1 or 2 cherries

WHISKY SOUR

This is simply a species of fortified lemonade in concentrated form:

    1 part lemon juice
    1 spoonful sugar
    3 parts bourbon or rye

Ice, stir and pour into short glass. Women like it decorated with fruit.

EL PRESIDENTE

The vanguard of Manhattan cognoscenti has discovered what regulars of El Chico in the Village have known for many a moon: the El Presidente cocktail is elixir for jaded gullets. Here's how George Stadelman makes it at El Chico:

Over ice in a tall mixing glass, pour:

    1 oz. white Cuban rum
    ½ oz. orange curacao
    ½ oz. dry vermouth
    dash of Grenadine

Shake or stir well, then strain into cocktail glass. (When stirred instead of shaken, it will pour a delightfully clear, deep orange color.) A twist of orange peel may be added.

RUM SOUR
(As served in Cristobal, Panama)

    1 teaspoon plain syrup
    Juice of one-half lime
    Half cocktail glass of rum

Ice and shake and pour into small glass. Decorate with fruit if wanted and/or with a few drops of egg white.

BACARDI COCKTAIL

There used to be a club in Chicago where you could down one of these free if you asked for *Bac'*-ardi instead of Ba-*car'*-di, but no matter how you splice it, this rum drink is a favorite—particularly with the ladies.

1. *As served at the Bacardi Distillery, Santiago*

    Juice of ½ lime
    1 teaspoon sugar
    1½ oz. Bacardi rum

Shake with very fine ice; strain into cocktail glass.

2. *The pink kind*

    Juice of 1 lime
    ½ teaspoon sugar

    1½ oz. Bacardi rum
    dash of Grenadine

Shake well with fine ice; strain into cocktail glass.

3. *Variations on the theme*

    Juice of half a lime
    1 teaspoonful of Grenadine
    1 part gin
    2 parts Bacardi

RUM OLD-FASHIONED

Substitute light or dark rum for bourbon or rye in the Old-fashioned, page 112. This new-fashioned Old-fashioned is especially tasty on a hot summer's day.

BRANDY

THE SIDECAR
    ⅔ brandy
    ⅓ Cointreau
    Dash of lime juice

Shake with very fine ice; strain into frosty cocktail glass.

SIDECAR 2
(50 Million Frenchmen . . .)
    ⅓ lemon juice
    ⅓ Cointreau
    ⅓ cognac

Shake with cracked ice; strain.

Something for the Girls

ALEXANDER (1)

½ jigger of gin
¼ jigger of Crème de Cacao
¼ jigger of cream
Ice, shake and serve in cocktail glass.

ALEXANDER (2)

⅓ Gin
⅓ Crème de Cacao
⅓ Cream

BRONX

⅔ jigger of gin
1/6 jigger French Vermouth
1/6 jigger Italian Vermouth
Dash of orange juice. Ice, shake well and serve in cocktail glass.

BRONX (W)

⅔ Gin
⅓ Orange Juice
2 slices fresh pineapple in glass (new way requires ⅓ gin, ⅓ Italian Vermouth)

CLOVER CLUB

Squeeze juice of one lime into shaker
Add white of one egg
Two dashes of Grenadine
1½ jiggers of gin
Shake thoroughly and serve in cocktail glass.

CLOVER CLUB

Juice ½ lemon
½ spoon sugar
½ pony raspberry syrup
¼ pony white of egg
1 jigger gin (star glass)

ORANGE BLOSSOM

⅓ orange juice
⅓ Tom gin
⅓ Italian Vermouth

PINK LADY

1 oz. gin
½ oz. applejack
White of one egg
Juice of ½ lime
Couple dashes of Grenadine, strawberry syrup or raspberry syrup
Shake vigorously with cracked ice. Strain. Sprig of mint optional decoration.

or PINK LADY

¼ oz. apple brandy
¾ oz. dry gin
½ oz. lemon juice
½ oz. of Grenadine
White of one egg
Shake valiantly with cracked ice; strain.

SLOE GIN FIZZ

1 jigger sloe gin
Juice one-half lemon
1 teaspoon powdered sugar
Shake well with ice, strain into highball glass and fill with soda.
(Its hunting pink color and fruity opulence are topped with a handsome collar of natural foam which, if the sloe gin be of first quality, is gladsome aplenty.)

GREEN FIZZ

2 oz. gin
1 teaspoon sugar
1 teaspoon green Crème de Menthe
Juice 1 lemon
White of egg
Cracked ice
Shake well and serve

Perfect for the "young innocent," pseudo or otherwise, the flip may be made with sherry or port in place of the brandy in this version:

THE FLIP

1 fresh egg yolk
1 teaspoon sugar
1 jigger brandy
Shake well. Serve in small wineglass. Sprinkle with nutmeg.
And for the slightly less timid, try:

RYE FLIP

1 egg
½ spoon sugar
1 jigger rye whisky
Shake, strain and sprinkle nutmeg on top.

BRANDY FLIP

2 oz. brandy
1 dash bitters
½ teaspoon Curacao
1 sprig of mint
½ teaspoon sugar
Lemon peel
Shake well and strain into wineglass.

"She ordered it because it had a cute name"

Something for the Boys

BOURBON AND RYE

Either bourbon or rye may be used in any of these cocktails, depending on your taste and oftentimes your locale. Rye is favored in the East, bourbon in Middle and Far West.

ALGONQUIN

2 parts rye
1 part French Vermouth
1 part pineapple juice

AMARANTH

1 dash of Abbott's Bitters
⅔ jigger rye whiskey
Stir, add powdered sugar and fill with carbonated water .

BRAINSTORM

¼ French Vermouth
¼ benedictine
½ best rye whiskey
Stir well with ice and float orange peel on top.

BROWN UNIVERSITY

½ Bourbon whiskey
½ French Vermouth
2 dashes orange bitters

CHAUNCEY

¼ rye whiskey
¼ gin
¼ Italian Vermouth
¼ brandy
Dash of orange bitters.

CLIQUET

1 jigger Bourbon whiskey
Juice of one orange
1 lump of ice
1 dash of rum
Stir instead of shaking

COMMODORE

⅓ bourbon whiskey
⅓ Crème de Cacao
⅓ lemon juice
Dash of Grenadine syrup, serve in champagne glass. Tradition can be improved by the use of an electric mixer, with the resultant ice-floe similar to that of an Arctic-Tropic Daiquiri.

COLUMBIA

1 jigger rye whiskey
1 piece lemon peel
½ lump sugar
Fill with hot water.

DOOLITTLE SPECIAL

½ lemon, muddled
3 dashes syrup
1 jigger whiskey

EWING

1 jigger rye whiskey
1 dash of bitters
Stir.

FANCIULLI

½ bourbon whiskey
¼ Italian Vermouth
¼ Fernet Branca Frappé

FLORIDITA SPECIAL

⅓ rye whiskey
½ sweet vermouth
1 teaspoonful Amer Picon
½ teaspoonful Curacao
½ teaspoonful sugar
1 dash bitters
Lemon peel
Cracked ice
Shake well and serve.

GLOOM LIFTER

Juice one-half lemon
½ spoon sugar
½ pony raspberry syrup
¼ pony white of egg
1 jigger whiskey
½ teaspoon brandy

HARRITY

Dash of bitters
1 dash gin
1 jigger whiskey

HEARNS

⅓ bourbon whiskey
⅓ Italian Vermouth
⅓ absinthe (or legal variant), dash of bitters (Hold your hat)

HONOLULU

⅓ bourbon whiskey
⅓ French Vermouth
⅓ Italian Vermouth

JAPALAC

1 jigger rye whiskey
1 jigger French Vermouth
Juice of one-quarter orange
Dash of raspberry syrup

JUMBO

⅓ Italian Vermouth
⅓ French Vermouth
⅓ Whiskey

[119]

JUNIOR
⅔ rye
Equal parts of lime juice and Benedictine make up balance, with dash of bitters.

LIBERAL
½ rye whiskey
½ Italian Vermouth
3 dashes Amer Picon
Dash of orange bitters

LIBERAL
Dash of orange bitters
3 dashes Amer Picon
½ whiskey
½ Italian Vermouth (stir)

McCRORY
1 dash bitters
⅔ jigger whiskey
Stir; fill from siphon
Add powdered sugar

McKINLEY'S DELIGHT
1 dash absinthe
2 dashes cherry brandy
⅔ whiskey
⅓ Italian Vermouth

MILLIONAIRE COCKTAIL
1½ oz. whiskey
½ oz. Curacao
1 dash Grenadine
White of 1 egg
Shake with ice as though 7 demons were goading you to it; strain into non-stingy cocktail glass.

MONAHAN
Dash of Amer Picon
⅔ Whiskey
⅓ Italian Vermouth (stir)

NARRAGANSETT
⅓ Italian Vermouth
⅔ whiskey
1 dash anisette (stir)

PAN AMERICAN
1 jigger rye whiskey
½ lemon, muddle
3 dashes syrup

PRINCE
2 dashes orange bitters
Whiskey
2 dashes Crème de Menthe on top

ROSEMARY
½ French Vermouth
½ Whiskey

SHERMAN
Dash of bitters
Dash of orange bitters
3 dashes absinthe
⅔ Italian Vermouth
⅓ jigger whiskey

SKY CLUB
Juice one orange
1 jigger whiskey; flavored with heavy rum
1 lump ice (stir)

SOUTHGATE
¼ lump sugar dissolved in one-half pony water
Dash of bitters
1 jigger whiskey
1 piece twisted lemon peel

SUBURBAN
Dash of orange bitters
Dash of bitters
1/5 port wine
1/5 Jamaica rum
3/5 whiskey

TEXSUN COCKTAIL
2 parts rye whiskey
1 part French Vermouth
1 part Texsun grapefruit juice
Shake well with ice and serve with cherry.

THOMPSON
⅓ Italian Vermouth
⅔ whiskey
1 piece each of orange peel, pineapple, lemon peel

VOLSTEAD
⅓ Swedish punch
⅓ rye whiskey
1/6 orange juice
1/6 raspberry syrup
1 dash of anisette

WALDORF
Dash of bitters
⅓ whiskey
⅓ absinthe
⅓ Italian Vermouth

WHEELER
Juice one-quarter orange
1 jigger French Vermouth
1 jigger whiskey
Dash of raspberry syrup

WHISKEY DAISY 1
1 jigger whiskey
Juice of one-half lemon
3 dashes Cointreau or Curacao
1 teaspoon sugar
Shake with fine ice, strain into 8 oz. highball glass, fizz from siphon. Fruit garnish optical. May be served unstrained, with straws.

WHISKEY DAISY 2
1 jigger whiskey
Juice of one-half lemon
1 oz. raspberry syrup
½ teaspoon sugar
Shake with fine ice, strain into highball glass, fizz from siphon. Garnish with fruit if you like; fine ice may be kept in instead of strained out.

WHISKEY DAISY 3

1 jigger whiskey
Juice of one-half lemon
Shake with fine ice, strain into high-ball glass, fill with sparkling water. Or leave ice in and serve with straw.

WHISKEY AND MINT

3 sprigs of mint
½ lump sugar; dissolved
Press mint lightly
1 jigger whiskey
Ice

WHISKEY AND TANSY

3 leaves Tansy, or
1 pony of Tansy mixture
1 jigger whiskey

WRIGHT SPECIAL

6 jiggers of rye
6 jiggers of port wine
Juice of three lemons
4 teaspoons of sugar
Shake in a shaker with cracked ice, then add the beaten whites of 3 eggs. Shake for another few moments, then pour into cocktail glass in which a cube of pineapple has been placed.

SCOTCH

In answer to the old plaint that there are not many ways of downing the gentleman's drink except with water or soda, here are several satisfactory Scotch cocktails. It takes a Scotch drinker to appreciate them, though; they're not for the average cocktail taste.

ARTISTS' SPECIAL

(As served at Artist Bar, Rue Pigalle, Paris)
⅓ Scotch whisky
⅓ sherry
1/6 lemon juice
1/6 Groseille syrup

THE BAIRN

⅔ Scotch whisky
⅓ Cointreau
1 dash orange bitters

BENEDICT

⅓ Scotch whisky
⅓ Benedictine
⅓ ginger ale

BILL ORR

2 jiggers Scotch whisky
Juice of small orange
1 dash of orange bitters

BORDEN CHASE

¾ Scotch whisky
¼ Italian Vermouth
1 dash of orange bitters
1 dash of Pernod or oxygene

BUNNY HUG

(A dance of the post-war period)
⅓ gin
⅓ Scotch whisky
⅓ absinthe

BYRRH COCKTAIL

⅓ French Vermouth
⅓ Scotch whisky
⅓ Byrrh

CAMERON'S KICK

⅓ Scotch whisky
⅓ Irish whiskey
1/6 lemon juice
1/6 Orgeat (almond) syrup

CHANCELLOR COCKTAIL

⅔ Scotch whisky
1/6 French Vermouth
1/6 port wine
1 dash of bitters.

GENTLE JOHN

1 jigger Scotch whisky
1 dash of orange bitters, French Vermouth and Cointreau

GLAMIS

(pronounced Glarms)
½ Scotch whisky
½ Calisaya bitters

GLASGOW

½ Scotch whisky
½ French Vermouth
3 dashes absinthe
3 dashes bitters
Ice and shake well.

THE HEATHER

⅔ Scotch whisky
2 dashes of French Vermouth
1 dash of Angostura bitters

HIGHLAND BITTERS

One of the most famous of the authentic Scotch mixtures is called "Highland Bitters" and is almost as old as the industry itself.

Grind in a mortar the following:
1¾ oz. gentian root
½ oz. orange peel
1 oz. coriander seed
¼ oz. camomile flowers
½ oz. cloves
¼ oz. cinnamon.
Add this to two bottles of Scotch. Let it stand two weeks, sealed, in a crocker jar. Then drink.

HIGHLAND COCKTAIL

½ Italian Vermouth
½ Scotch whisky
1 dash of bitters

JOHN McCLAIN

1 jigger Scotch
1 teaspoon syrup
2 dashes of bitters

L. G. COCKTAIL

(Favored by Scot Labor M.P.'s)
1 glass Scotch whisky
Followed by one glass beer

MODERN COCKTAIL

⅓ Scotch whisky
½ sloe gin
1 dash orange bitters
1 dash absinthe
4 dashes gum syrup

MORNING GLORY FIZZ

1 white of egg
1 teaspoon of sugar
1 juice of lemon
1 glass of Scotch whisky
1 teaspoon of oxygene
Shake well and pour into large glass, fill to top with soda.

REMSEN COOLER

Put peel of whole lemon in large glass with two lumps of ice. Add glass of Scotch whisky and fill with soda.

ROB ROY

2 parts Scotch whisky
1 part Italian Vermouth
1 dash of bitters

ROBBER COCKTAIL

⅔ Scotch whisky
⅓ Italian Vermouth
Dash of bitters
Serve in cocktail glass with cherry

SCOTCH SAZERAC

1 jigger Scotch whisky
1 teaspoon Italian Vermouth
1 dash of absinthe or oxygene

STONE FENCE

1 jigger of Scotch whiskey in large glass
1 lump of ice
Fill with cider

TOM JOHNSTONE

½ Scotch whisky
1/6 lime juice
1/6 Italian Vermouth
1/6 Cointreau

TRILBY COCKTAIL

⅓ Scotch whisky
⅓ Parfait d'Amour
⅓ Italian Vermouth
2 dashes absinthe
2 dashes of orange bitters

TRINITY

½ Scotch whisky
⅓ French Vermouth
1 dash of Crème de Menthe
1 dash of orange bitters
1 dash of apricot brandy

WALTERS

½ Scotch whisky
¼ orange juice
¼ lemon juice

WOODWARD

⅓ Scotch whisky
⅓ grapefruit juice
⅓ French Vermouth

GIN

ASYLUM COCKTAIL

1 part gin
1 part Pernod
Dash of Grenadine
Pour over large lumps of ice
Do not shake

BLACKTHORN

⅔ sloe gin
⅓ Italian Vermouth
Dash of Angostura
Twist of lemon peel, or dash of
  lemon juice
Stir with ice; strain into cocktail glass.

CHINA CLIPPER COCKTAIL

Conspicuous passenger:
  1 Chinese golden lime
(These kumquats, preserved in syrup
and put up in earthenware jars are
obtainable at any Chinese shop or restaurant.)
  ⅔ gin (yellow dry gin jibes best
    with the color scheme)
  1/6 dry vermouth
  1/6 grapefruit juice
  2 shots orange bitters
  1 or 2 drops of the syrup of the
    kumquat
The liquid ingredients are stirred in a
mixing glass with ice cubes and
poured onto Miss Golden Lime, already in her glass cabin. Pleasant take-
off!

CHOCOLATE SOLDIER

⅓ Dubonnet
⅔ gin
Dash of lime juice

THE CONNECTICUT BULLFROG

The ingredients are awful but the result does have something.
  4 parts gin
  1 part New England rum
  1 part lemon juice
  1 part maple syrup
Shake these ingredients together until
your arms ache. Then have someone
else do the same thing with about ten
times the usual amount of ice.
  Serve frappé. All your guests will
gratefully swear that they are at the
Waldorf-Astoria.

CORNELL

½ French Vermouth
½ gin

PALE DEACON

3 jiggers grapefruit juice
2 jiggers dry gin
1 dash of powdered sugar
Shake with cracked ice, serve in
frosted glass.

ROSY DEACON

2 jiggers grapefruit juice
1 jigger sloe gin
1 jigger dry gin
1 dash powdered sugar
Shake with cracked ice, serve in frosted
glass.
  Jack F. Zimmerman, Akron, O.

DELMONICO 1

¾ oz. gin
½ oz. of French Vermouth
¼ oz. Italian Vermouth
½ oz. cognac
2 dashes Angostura
Twist of orange peel

DELMONICO 2

Dash of orange bitters
½ French Vermouth
½ gin
2 slices orange peel

DEWEY

Dash of orange bitters
½ gin
½ French Vermouth

DIKI-DIKI

1/6 dry gin
1/6 grapefruit juice
⅔ applejack
Ice and shake.

DUBONNET

50-50 gin and Dubonnet
Stirred with a citrus twist

DR. COOK

Juice one-half lemon
White of one egg
Two dashes Maraschino
¾ gin (claret glass)

EMERSON

Juice one-half lime
Small teaspoon Maraschino
⅓ Italian Vermouth
⅔ Tom gin (stir)

FLORADORA

Juice one-half lime
½ teaspoon sugar
½ pony raspberry syrup
1 jigger gin
Frappé, fizz with ginger ale and serve in Tom Collins glass.

FREE SILVER

Juice one-quarter lemon
½ spoon sugar
⅔ Tom gin
⅓ Jamaica rum
½ pony milk
Ice, shake and serve in tall glass, fill up with soda.

GIBSON GIRL

½ French Vermouth
½ dry Tom gin (stir)
Squeeze lemon peel on top
A new one going the rounds is a *"Ginsicle," a variation of Havana style Daiquiri*. Fill a champagne glass with chipped ice, shaved fine. Pour over this half a jigger of fruit juice or prepared syrup, then add a jigger and a half of gin.

GOLDEN DAWN

⅓ apple brandy
⅓ apricot brandy
⅓ dry gin
Dash of orange juice
Shake well, strain into cocktail glass; top with barspoon of Grenadine, which will submarine to the bottom of the glass and there stage a sunrise effect.

HEARST

One dash orange bitters
One dash Angostura bitters
½ jigger Italian Vermouth
½ jigger gin

HOFFMAN HOUSE

Two dashes orange bitters
⅓ French Vermouth
⅔ gin
Squeeze lemon peel on top

KISS THE BOYS GOOD-BYE

½ sloe gin
½ brandy
½ white of egg
Juice of 1 lemon
Shake very well with plenty of ice and strain.

MAIDEN'S PRAYER

(Served on the edge of the couch)
¼ dry gin
¼ Cointreau
¼ lemon juice
Dash of orange bitters
Ice and shake well

MY OWN

(M. L. Burnside, Lake Worth, Florida, claims parenthood to this one)
1 jigger gin
½ jigger French Vermouth
¼ jigger Italian Vermouth
2 dashes bitters
1 spoonful cherry heering
Shake lightly, strain, and add twist of lemon peel.

OPERA

⅓ gin
⅓ Dubonnet
⅓ Crème de Mandarine

PARADISE

⅓ apricot brandy
⅓ dry gin
⅓ orange juice
Dash of lime juice
Ice and shake well.

PENDENNIS COCKTAIL

¾ oz. Hungarian apricot brandy
1½ oz. gin
Add the juice of one lime or lemon
2 dashes of Peychaud bitters
Pour the mixture over cracked ice, strain into cocktail glasses.

POET'S DREAM

⅓ Benedictine
⅓ French Vermouth
⅓ gin
Lemon peel squeezed on top

PRAIRIE CHICKEN

1 pony of gin
1 egg in claret glass
Pepper and salt
Cover top with gin and serve

PRINCETON

Dash of orange bitters
⅔ jigger Tom gin
Stir; fill with seltzer

PRINCETON CLUB GIN DAISY

1½ oz. gin
1 oz. lemon
½ oz. orange
Dash of raspberry syrup
Frappéd and served in a Delmonico glass.

RACQUET CLUB

Dash of orange bitters
½ gin
½ French Vermouth
Orange peel

ROSE

¼ Grand Marnier
¾ gin
Ice, stir and serve

SAN MARTIN

⅓ dry gin
⅓ dry vermouth
⅓ sweet vermouth
1 teaspoon anisette
1 drop bitters
Stir with cracked ice, strain into glass, first wetting the brim with lemon and sugar.

SAVANNAH

Juice of one-half orange
1 jigger of gin
White of egg
Dash of Crème de Cacao

SLOE GIN

Dash of orange bitters
⅔ sloe gin
⅓ Plymouth gin (stir)

SWAN

Juice of one lime
¼ jigger of gin
½ jigger of French Vermouth
2 dashes of Abbott's bitters
2 dashes of absinthe

TEXSUN RANGER

¼ Texsun grapefruit
1 teaspoon Maraschino
⅓ sweet vermouth
⅓ dry vermouth
⅓ dry gin
Shake well with ice, strain and serve with a few almonds.

TEXSUN SPECIAL

2 parts gin
1 part cognac
1 part French Vermouth
Dash of Cointreau
Juice one-half grapefruit
Shake well with ice and serve.

THIRD DEGREE

⅛ French Vermouth
⅞ gin
Several dashes absinthe

TIPPERARY

⅔ sloe gin
⅓ French Vermouth
1 teaspoon lemon juice

TRILBY

Dash of orange bitters
⅓ French Vermouth
⅔ gin
1 dash Crème Yvette

TUXEDO

⅔ gin
⅓ sherry
Dash of orange bitters

UNION LEAGUE

Dash of orange bitters
⅓ port wine
⅔ Tom gin (stir)

VIRGIN

⅓ forbidden fruit
⅓ white Crème de Menthe
⅓ gin
Shake well and strain

WHITE ELEPHANT

⅓ Italian Vermouth
⅔ dry gin
White of one egg

YALE

Dash of orange bitters
½ Tom gin
½ Italian Vermouth (stir)
Little seltzer on top

ZAZA

2 dashes orange bitters
⅓ Tom gin
⅔ Dubonnet (stir)

"It's Pop! And he's holding up a man on each arm again!"

RUM COCKTAILS

BATISTE

⅔ Bacardi rum
⅓ Grand Marnier

BROWN DERBY

2 parts dark rum
1 teaspoon maple sugar
Juice of one lime
Shake well and serve.

CHRISTOPHE

(As served at Cap Haitian)
⅓ gin
⅔ Haitian rum
Dash of sugar
Peel of a lime
Ice and shake well

COMMODORE

½ teaspoon sugar
One dash lemon juice
White of one egg
One drink of Bacardi rum
1 Dash of Grenadine
1 dash of raspberry syrup

COOL O' THE EVENING

Crush thoroughly 1 sprig mint in shaker. Add juice ¼ lemon, ½ teaspoon sugar, 1 jigger white rum, cracked ice. Shake till heavy frost. Strain into cocktail stemmer. (No fresh mint? Then use coupla drops *white* Crème de Menthe.)

CRYSTAL RUM FIZZ

1 dollop of Haitian rum
2 dollops of ginger ale
1 Cryst-O-Mint Life Saver
(The Life Saver is used to take the curse off the rum. It should not be allowed to dissolve, but should be stirred gently and used again for the second, third, and fourth drinks. After that, you won't miss it.)

DESSALINES

½ Haitian rum
¼ clairin
¼ whisky
¼ lime juice, dash of sugar
Ice and shake well.

EYE-OPENER

Liqueur glass old Haitian rum
Teaspoon Grenadine
Yolk of one egg
2 dashes of Curacao
2 dashes apricot brandy
Ice and shake well

FLYING TIGRE COCTEL

½ Bacardi Oro
¼ gin (or more)
¼ Grenadine (or less)
Bitters
Sugar
Shake with fine ice. Then pour without straining into large cocktail glass. (Captain in the U. S. Marines, Amphibious Group 7, S.W.P.A., sends this one, gathered at Santiago de Cuba in 1942. Here's to you, Captain!)

HAITIAN COCKTAIL

1 jigger Haitian rum
1 jigger fresh lime juice
1 spoon powdered sugar
Ice, shake and serve in cocktail glass.

HAITIAN RUM PUNCH

3 parts of Haitian rum
1 part of sugar
Peel of lime
Dash of bitters
Ice and stir a little

HARPO'S SPECIAL

2 oz. rum
1 drop bitters
½ teaspoon Curacao
Juice of one-half lemon
½ teaspoon sugar
Shake well and strain.

HONEY BEE

1 part honey
4 parts Bacardi
1 part lemon juice
Mix well, then add ice and shake.

THE "I DIED GAME, BOYS" MIXTURE

1 dollop Haitian rum
1 dollop apricot brandy
1 splash of drinking water
(Most sincere drinkers do not care for this one as they say the water adds an unfamiliar tang that they can't learn to like.)

NUGENT

2 oz. rum
1 teaspoon sugar
½ white of egg
Juice of one-half lemon
Shake well with ice and strain.

PEG O' MY HEART

½ lime juice
½ Cuban rum
Color with Grenadine

PETION

(Served at the Tourist Bar, Port-au-Prince)

⅓ rum
⅓ Benedictine
⅓ clairin
Lime juice and sugar
Ice and shake well

PRESIDENTE VINCENT

(As served by Paul Cator)

½ rum
¼ French Vermouth
Lime juice and sugar
Ice and shake well

PRINCE GEORGE

⅓ Grand Marnier
⅔ Bacardi
Juice of half lime
Twist of lemon peel

ROOSEVELT

½ Haitian rum
¼ French Vermouth
⅛ orange juice
Dash of sugar syrup
Ice and shake well.

RUM DUBONNET

½ jigger rum
½ jigger Dubonnet
Juice of one-half lime

RUM ORANGE COCKTAIL

¼ orange juice
¼ Italian Vermouth
½ Bacardi
1 pinch powdered cinnamon
Ice, shake well, and serve in cocktail glass.

RUM SIDECAR

(Equal parts rum, lemon juice, Triple Sec.)

RUM SOUR

¾ oz. lemon juice
¼ teaspoon sugar
1¼ golden lightbodied rum
Shake with ice; give glass a "lid" of 151 proof rum.

SUICIDE COCKTAIL

1 dollop of Haitian rum
½ dollop Crème de Cacao
1 dollop White Rock
1 Cryst-O-Mint Life Saver
    dropped from a great height.
(In preparing this drink, the glass is placed on the floor and the mixer stands erect, holding the Life Saver at shoulder height. If he misses the glass three times in a row, he does not need another drink—not very badly, anyway.)

SUNSHINE COCKTAIL

Equal parts pineapple juice, dry vermouth, white rum. Dash of Grenadine. Stir with cracked ice.

Convincing, too, is the **WEST INDIES COCKTAIL** which consists merely of unfruited rum, Angostura, and ice. The estaters use these as doubt-removers

WHAT'S IT?

White of one egg
½ jigger Jamaica rum
½ jigger port wine
Ice, shake, serve in eight-ounce glass, fill up with soda.

WINE COCKTAILS

AMERICAN BEAUTY COCKTAIL

1 part muscatel, 4 parts champagne, thoroughly chilled and garnished with a large grape.

ARISE MY LOVE

Put 1 teaspoon Crème de Menthe in a champagne glass, then fill with champagne.

BAMBOO COCKTAIL

Whose assembly line-up runs: one jigger of sherry, one jigger dry vermouth (both now ably produced in this country), two dashes Angostura (the extension of whose century-old heavy-secret manufacture to certain West Indian islands of Uncle Sam's has won them the name of Embittered Virgins), stirred with ice and strained into stem glass bonused with green olive or pickled onionette.

Ernest Hemingway's
DEATH IN THE AFTERNOON COCKTAIL

Pour 1 jigger of absinthe into a champagne glass.

Add iced champagne until it attains the proper opalescent milkiness.

Drink 3 to 5 of these slowly.

DUBONNET

1 glass Dubonnet
½ glass lemon syrup
Balance soda water

On the blonde side, there's **GOLDEN FRAPPE** constructed with one cup of white port (in case you aren't acquainted with this wine type, now's the time!), one cup of orange juice, two tablespoons lemon juice, two tablespoons sugar; stir till sugar is dissolved, then pour over finely crushed ice in a quartet of tallish tumblers. And how beautifully those bullfrogs are singing this evening. Like parched nightingales.)

MARCONI WIRELESS

Two dashes orange bitters
⅓ Italian Vermouth
⅔ applejack

MERRY WIDOW

½ French Vermouth
½ Dubonnet

Fruit of the hen figures cheerily in the perennially apropos **PORT FLIP** over which country-clubbers cast an appreciative lip. Its formula, as your great grandsire could have told you, calls for the contents of two eggs, cracked on the rim of a shaker, two teaspoons sugar, one cup of port, much, much cracked ice; shaken dementedly. Pour into two Delmonico glasses or fair sized goblets. Freckle with nutmeg.

SENSATION

2 parts port wine
1 part brandy
Twist of lemon peel
Stir well and serve.

SHERRY COCKTAIL

2 parts dry sherry, pre-chilled
2 parts French Vermouth pre-chilled

SHERRY OLD-FASHIONED

With the full trappings of an *Old-Fashioned*—the lump of sugar, thrice shot with Angostura and muddled till dissolved; twist of lemon epidermis, double jigger *sherry*, ice cube or two; Maraschino cherry, orange slice, glass baton; and serve pronto before the melting of the ice undermines authority.

As a greeter, there is the **SUN VALLEY SPECIAL** which meets all new arrivals when they check in—in most cases a wonderful friendship is struck up at first taste, resulting in steady companionship thereafter.

This drink is none other than the old continental standby, vermouth straight, served in a new manner in the distinctive new Italian Vermouth glass—a 4½-inch stemless goblet which rises, four-sided and four-cornered, in a shapely crescendo from a square base.

The inventory discloses 3 oz. of Italian Vermouth, 2 cubes of ice, twist of lemon peel, a straddled slice of orange, and a cherry pierced with a paper-feathered arrow, demonstrating that the William Tell school of fruit shooting has made progress.

VERMOUTH

2 oz. Italian Vermouth
1 teaspoon Amer Picon
½ teaspoon Curaçao
1 dash bitters
1 lemon peel
1 small sprig mint
½ teaspoon sugar
Shake well with cracked ice, and serve with cherry.

VERMOUTH SPECIAL

½ teaspoon sugar
1 lemon peel squeezed into glass
1 dash bitters
1 sprig mint
½ teaspoon Curaçao
1 teaspoon Amer Picon
2 oz. Italian Vermouth
1 oz. whiskey
Shake well with ice, strain, serve.

WALSH'S CHAMPAGNE COCKTAIL

1 lump sugar
1 sprig mint
Lemon peel
Fill glass to brim with champagne
Serve with cherry
Use 10 oz. glass. Fill with cracked
ice

BRANDY AND CORDIALS IN COCKTAILS

BRANDY DAISY

2 oz. brandy
½ oz. Grenadine
Juice of 1 lemon
Shake with finely cracked ice; pour unstrained into ample highball glass; decorate with fruits ad lib. Harpoon with straw.

BRANDY SOUR

1½ oz. brandy
Juice of half a lemon
1 teaspoon sugar
One to three dashes of Angostura.
Shake with cracked ice. Strain into glass, preferably Delmonico. May be cargoed with orange slice and a cherry.

BRANT

¾ brandy
¼ white mint
2 dashes of bitters
1 piece of lemon peel

BYRRH—CASSIS

1 glass Byrrh
½ glass Cassis
Balance soda water

CAFE COCKTAIL

1 black coffee
½ Crème de Cacao
½ cognac
1 teaspoonful sugar
Lemon peel
Shake well, strain and serve

CALEDONIA

⅓ Crème de Cacao
⅓ cognac
⅓ milk
Yolk of egg
1 dash bitters
Lemon peel
Shake well, strain, and serve with cinnamon on top.

CHAMPAGNE DES PAUVRES

1 glass of brandy
½ glass lemon syrup

COFFEE COCKTAIL

1 pony of brandy
2 ponies of port
1 egg yolk
¼ spoon sugar
Serve in claret glass

CUBAN COCKTAIL

⅔ brandy
⅓ apricot brandy
Juice of one-half lime
The use of *cordials in cocktails* has become firmly established. As so much of civilized drinking is in the taste and pleasant afterglow, it is a good variation on the standard mixtures. There follow some of the cocktails using cordials, mainly from France where most of the liqueurs originated.

ANIS DEL OSO

1 glass Anis del Oso
1 glass Grenadine
Soda water in tall glass

APPLE BRANDY COCKTAIL

4 parts apple brandy
1 part Grenadine
1 part juice of lemon or lime
Agitate coolly and sieve.

APPLE BRANDY OLD-FASHIONED

Follow the directions on page 112, substituting apple brandy of reputable make for whiskey in the Old-Fashioned

BETWEEN-SHEETS

⅓ cognac
⅓ Crème de Cacao
⅓ cream
1 dash bitters
1 teaspoon sugar
Lemon peel
Plenty cracked ice
Shake well, strain and serve.

BLACKJACK

1 pony Kirsch
1 dash brandy
1 pony coffee

Frappéed with fine ice. Any of these will bring out the figure-skating-champ instincts in you.

BOSOM CARESSER

1/6 Curaçao
1/6 brandy
⅓ Madeira
1 teaspoon Grenadine
1 yolk of egg

BRANDY COCKTAIL

Use 10 oz. glass
Cracked ice
1 sprig of mint
1 lemon peel, squeezing juice in glass
½ teaspoon sugar
1 drop bitters
½ teaspoon Curacao
2 oz. cognac

Shake lightly, strain and serve.

BRANDY COCKTAIL (1)

1 jigger brandy
1 dash gin
1 dash bitters

BRANDY (2)

½ brandy
½ French Vermouth
1 dash of orange bitters

BRANDY CRUSTAS

(as served at Harry's Bar, Paris)
Take small wine glass, moisten rim with lemon, dip rim of glass into castor sugar. Peel the rind of half a lemon and fit this curl of peel into the contour of your glass. Then in a shaker mix 1 teaspoon of sugar, 3 dashes of Maraschino, 3 dashes of bitters, juice of one-quarter of a lemon, 1 glass of brandy. Shake well and pour into a prepared glass.

BRANDY DAISY

⅔ brandy
1/6 grenadine
Juice of one-half lemon

Shake well, pour into large *cocktail* glass, add cherry and dash of soda.

GIN-AND-CORDIAL COCKTAILS

EAST INDIA COCKTAIL

1½ oz. brandy
1 tsp. pineapple
1 tsp. Curacao, preferably the red
3 dashes Angostura

Ice and shake; strain onto a cherry.
1 teaspoon of Curacao
1 teaspoon pineapple syrup
1 jigger brandy
2 dashes Abbott's bitters

Stir with spoon, serve with cherry in cocktail glass.

FRENCH VERMOUTH AND CURACAO

1 glass French Vermouth
½ glass Curacao
Soda water

FULL HOUSE

Dash of bitters
⅓ yellow chartreuse
⅓ Benedictine
⅓ apple whiskey

GIN WITH COINTREAU
(½ pony)

Gin 1 jigger; juice of ½ lime; white of 1 egg; Grenadine 1 dash. Shake and strain into wine glass whose rim has been sugar-frosted. Identification tag: BOXCAR.

WITH CREME YVETTE
(⅓)

Gin 1 jigger; white of egg. Shake, strain. Handle: BLUE MOON.

WITH MARASCHINO CORDIAL
(¼ oz.)

Gin 1½ oz.; lemon juice ½ oz. Shake, strain. Code word: AVIATION.

WITH GRAND MARNIER
(¾ oz.)

Gin ¾ oz.; juice of ¼ lemon and ¼ orange. Shake, strain. Orderer's cry: RED LION.

WITH BENEDICTINE
(⅓)

Gin ⅔; maraschino ⅓. Shake, strain. Halloo: HONOLULU.

WITH CURACAO
(¼ oz.)

Gin 1½ oz.; unsweetened pineapple juice ½ oz.; orange bitters 3 dashes. Shake, strain, garnish with Maraschino cherry. Dubbage: GIN ALOHA. (L. Mackall inventor. No money refunded.)

HARVARD

Dash of orange bitters
2/5 jigger brandy
3/5 Italian Vermouth (stir)
Fill from chilled siphon

HOP FROG

⅓ brandy
⅔ lime juice
Ice and shake

JACK ROSE

Juice of lime
⅓ Grenadine syrup
⅔ applejack

JACK ROSE COCKTAIL

1½ oz. apple brandy
½ oz. grenadine
Juice of one-half lemon or lime

Shake with cracked ice; strain.

JAPANESE

1 jigger of brandy
2 dashes Orgeat syrup
1 slice lemon peel

KIRSCH AND CASSIS

1 glass Cassis
½ glass Kirsch
Balance soda water

LIL NAUE

½ cognac
⅓ port wine
⅓ apricot brandy
1 teaspoon sugar
1 lemon peel
Yolk of egg

Shake well with cracked ice and serve with cinnamon on top.

MY SIN COCKTAIL

1 oz. absinthe
1 oz. anisette
1 drop bitters
White of egg

Plenty of ice, shake well and strain.

NETHERLAND COCKTAIL

1 oz. brandy
1 oz. Curacao
Dash orange bitters

Stir amid cracked ice. Strain.

NETHERLAND

⅔ brandy
⅓ Curacao
1 dash orange bitters

PUMPKIN COACH COCKTAIL

2 parts liqueur Cesoriac
1 part vermouth (Italian Cinzano)
1 part cherry juice
3 limes (to each pint)

Slathers of ice (or you will go home in a basket.)

QUEEN ELIZABETH

¼ Benedictine
½ French Vermouth
¼ lime juice

STIRRUP CUP

1 jigger cherry brandy
1 jigger brandy
Juice of half lemon

(Attributed, but not by me, to George Washington)

TRIPLICE

⅓ Benedictine
⅓ French Vermouth
⅓ gin

TROPICAL COCKTAIL

1 dash of bitters
1 dash of orange bitters
⅓ Crème de Cacao
⅓ Maraschino
⅓ French Vermouth

TURF COCKTAIL

2 dashes orange bitters
2 dashes Maraschino
2 dashes absinthe
½ French Vermouth
½ gin

Shake well, ice, and serve with olive.

VALENCIA

⅔ apricot brandy
⅓ orange juice
2 dashes orange bitters

WARDAY'S

1 teaspoon yellow chartreuse
⅓ applejack
⅓ Italian Vermouth
⅓ gin

WEDDING BELLS

1/6 cherry brandy
1/6 orange juice
⅓ gin
⅓ Dubonnet

WHITE LADY

⅔ Cointreau
1/6 Crème de Menthe
1/6 brandy

XANTHIA

⅓ cherry brandy
⅓ yellow chartreuse
⅓ gin

BLUE MOON

⅔ gin
⅓ French Vermouth
1 dash orange bitters
1 dash of Crème Yvette

"It started as a cold, but with his remedies I'd say it's closer to a hang-over now"

CORONATION

⅓ Italian Vermouth
⅓ French Vermouth
⅓ applejack
Dash of apricot brandy

DOLORES

⅓ cherry brandy
⅓ Crème de Cacao
⅓ Spanish brandy
White of one egg

DREAM

⅓ Curacao
⅔ brandy
Dash absinthe

GRENADINE COCKTAIL

1 teaspoon Framboise syrup
⅓ oxygene cusenier
⅓ gin
⅓ white mint
Shake well and strain into cocktail glass.

GYPSY

⅔ vodka
⅓ Benedictine
1 dash of bitters

KRETCHMA COCKTAIL

2/5 vodka
2/5 Crème de Cacao
1/5 lemon juice
1 dash Grenadine

MACKINNON

1 jigger Drambuie
¼ jigger Bacardi
Juice of one-half lime
Juice of one-quarter lemon
Shake well. Serve in tall glass with plenty of ice and seltzer.

MAIDEN'S KISS

1/5 Crème de Roses
1/5 Curacao
1/5 Maraschino
1/5 yellow chartreuse
1/5 Benedictine

MORNING AFTER

1 white of egg
1 teaspoonful anisette syrup
1 glass absinthe
Dash of soda on top

NIGHT CAP

1 yolk egg
⅓ anisette
⅓ Curacao
⅓ brandy

PLUIE D'OR

⅓ gin
⅓ vielle cure
1/6 Curacao
1/6 Kümmel

POUSSE-CAFE

⅓ Crème de Cacao
⅓ Drambuie
⅓ cognac
Pour carefully into liqueur glass:

POUSSE L'AMOUR

⅓ Maraschino
Drop in 1 yolk of egg
⅓ crème vanilla
⅓ brandy
Egg yolk must not run into the liqueur.

PRINCE GEORGE

⅓ Grand Marnier
⅔ Bacardi
Juice of one-half lime—twist of lemon peel

QUELLE VIE COCKTAIL

⅓ Kümmel
⅔ brandy

SIDECAR

½ Cointreau
½ brandy
Juice of one-half lemon

SNOWBALL

1/6 Crème de Violette
1/6 white Crème de Menthe
1/6 anisette
1/6 fresh cream
⅓ gin

ULYSSES

⅓ cherry brandy
⅓ French Vermouth
⅓ brandy
Squeeze orange peel on top

WIDOW'S KISS

¼ Parfait d'Amour
¼ yellow chartreuse
¼ Benedictine
White of egg floated on top

Wines

THE DRINK OF THE GODS

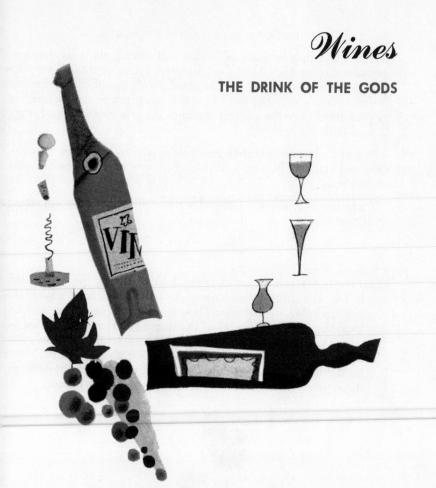

Wine has been a prop for every major love scene since Aeschylus dubbed the gleaming goblet the "mirror of the heart"—why not at *yours?*

Wine has worked its flavor-magic at the tables of the great from time immemorial—making a feast of fine food, adding a welcome pick-up even to dull provender—so why not at *your* table?

Don't be intimidated by wine-lovers' mumbo-jumbo about vintage years, intricate serving rituals, do's and don'ts in dealing with the precious stuff the vintners sell. The "right wine" is simply a matter of opinion; the "rules" are nothing but majority opinion on how best to bring out the flavor of wines and their accompanying foods. Besides, many of those "rules," based on the selection and service of European wines, are just so much excess baggage when it comes to buying and enjoying American wines. "Vintage year," for example, means nothing to a California wine; reliable climate spares the American wine industry those off-years which makes one in three European harvests a dud. State and federal laws combine with American marketing methods to assure standard flavor and character for each brand, thus eliminating another area of margin-of-error guesswork that sometimes plagues the buyer of foreign wines.

[135]

In fact, the whole business of buying and serving wines has become so much simpler since Americans discovered their own back vineyard that no one need quiver at the snobbish shrine of old. Take the "rules" or leave 'em—but don't miss the real pleasure that wine adds to your meal (nor the aura of romance that the wine bottle brings to your table for two!).

But by Lord Chesterfield's gentleman, who by definition is never rude unintentionally, you'd do well to know the rules before you break them.

There are two major classes of wines—table wines and appetizer or dessert wines.

TABLE WINES result when the pure juice of the grape is allowed to ferment naturally and completely; their alcoholic content is less than 14% by volume. They may be red or white, still or sparkling (effervescent), but the natural and complete fermentation uses up most of the grape sugar so they are usually dry.* And there you have the reason for their fine suitability for the table: unless you like Coca-Cola with fish or candy with steak, you wouldn't want a *sweet* wine with your dinner.

APPETIZER AND DESSERT WINES result when the natural fermentation process is stopped before completion by the addition of grape brandy. This not only ups the alcoholic content to 17-21%, but also preserves some of the natural grape sugar, making a sweetish wine. Sherry, muscatel and port are the best-known among these brandy-*fortified* wines.

A third category is made up of aromatized wines like Vermouth, but since they are used mainly in mixed drinks or as aperitifs they concern bartender more than cook.

Within each class, of course, there is a profusion of names and fames. If you have a reliable dealer, you may be able to get along very well, in buying American wines, simply by asking for "a light red wine" or "a dry white wine" or whatever *class* your needs dictate. Within each class you will then learn the various types: claret and burgundy, say, among the still red wines for table use . . . chablis and sauterne among the whites. But those names,

Dry means the opposite of *sweet*.

[136]

which merely indicate wine-*types* in America, all come from Europe, where the name is a virtual birth certificate, thus it's a good idea to know something of European wines, if only to understand what the names on American wines infer.

Here is a run-down on the best known foreign wines, followed by comparable information which may help you in selecting the best native wines.

Wines of France

The most celebrated French wine districts are:

BORDEAUX Wines grown in that section of France surrounding the old Gascon seaport, on the Gironde River, are all called Bordeaux, but they range from the fresh white Graves to the full red St. Emelion or Pomerol. Of the eight wine districts of Bordeaux, the three most famous are Medoc, Graves and Sauternes. Medoc is the home of most of the great clarets—dry, light, delicate red table wines. Chateau Lafite Rothschild and Chateau Margaux are the greatest of these. Graves produces several great red wines (Chateau Haut Brion, for example) as well as pleasant whites which are reasonably dry. Sauternes are medium-sweet white wines recommended for use with dessert; Chateau Y'quem and Chateau Latour Blanche are most honored among sauternes.

Bordeaux wines are shipped to the world under three main types of labels: Chateau bottling, i.e., wine of a definite vintage produced from grapes grown on an estate and bottled there; Monopole or Trade Mark brand of shipper, usually a blend of wines of a number of vineyards and, lastly, the Parish or District label—also wines of several vineyards and often of several vintages.

Except for the great Chateau wines of extraordinary vintages, the Monopole or Parish labels of a reliable shipper are usually a better buy; a shipper's reputation depends wholly on the quality of these wines.

BURGUNDY The ancient Duchy of Burgundy, long famous for its wines, offers both red and white wines. The red wines are dry, full-bodied and fruity. The white wines are very dry and quite thin when compared with those of Bordeaux. Most of the Burgundy wine available in America is shipped under the name of the Parish or district where it was produced, although some wine has come over under the vineyard name as Estate Bottled wine.

Best known names in Burgundy are Chambertin, Romanee-Conti, La Romanee, Corton, Clos de Vougeot, Macon, Beaujolais and Pommard in red wines; and Chablis, Pouilly, Meursault and Montrachet in white wines. A quantity of sparkling wine, red and white, is produced in Burgundy.

CHAMPAGNE The finest sparkling wine in the world is produced from wines made from black grapes grown in a strictly limited area that comprises the old Province of Champagne—in the northeast corner of France, now called the Department of the Marne. Although sparkling wines are made all over the world wherever grapes grow, and many of them are labeled "champagne," none has ever equaled the lightness, delicacy, finesse or character of true champagne. Since it takes 10 to 15 years to prepare the best champagne for market, there is no such thing as a bargain champagne. It is truly the "drink of the gods."

Champagne in its natural state is perfectly dry, but many varieties have a sweet liqueur added in the last stages of preparation. The French labels indicate the amount of sweetness added, like this: Nature (no sweetening added) . . . Brut (up to 1% sweetening) . . . Extra Dry (up to 3% sweetening) . . . Sec or Dry (up to 5% sweetening) . . . Demi-Sec (up to 8% sweetening) . . . Demi-Doux (up to 10% sweetening) . . . Doux (up to 12% sweetening).

Since champagne is usually a blend of several wines from different vineyards, the best buying guide is the blender's reputation. Here are just a few of the finest producers: Charles Heidsieck, Pol Roger, Pommery and Greno, Veuve Clicquot, Louis Roederer, G. H. Mumm and Co., Bouche Fils.

VOUVRAY Light and quite sweet are the wines of the Valley of Loire. They are very delicate and do not always travel well, consequently, they are not well known outside of France. There is a sparkling Vouvray which is like a sweet champagne, and even the still wines are mildly effervescent.

COTE D'OR RHONE Wines from the Rhone Valley—south of Burgundy and toward the Mediterranean—are distant cousins of Burgundies. The reds are of a deeper hue—almost purple—and the whites pack an unexpected punch. The best known are Côte Rotie, red; Hermitage, red, white and straw-colored; Château-Neuf-Du-Pape, red, the traditional beverage of the Avignon Popes; and Tavel, a pinkish wine.

ALSACE Wines produced in this redeemed province on the French side of the Rhine resemble the German more than the French wines; Alsace forms the southern fringe of the Rhine vineyard region. Alsatian Rhine wine is dry, fruity, flowery; other wines of Alsace are named varietally: Riesling, Tokay, Sylvaner, Traminer, etc., after the vines themselves.

Wines of Germany

The two principal wine-producing districts of Germany are the valleys of the Rhine and the Moselle rivers, with their tributary streams, the Main and the Nahe (to the Rhine) and the Saar and the Ruwer (to the Moselle). Although both white and red wines are produced, it is only the whites which are renowned—and they rank almost equal to the French wines. *Rhine* wines are usually very dry and light, with a delicate bouquet. *Moselle* wines are still lighter, have a more flowery bouquet. They also have a tang that gives the impression of a slight sparkling quality on the tongue.

Names of Rhine wines to remember are: Hochheimer, Niersteiner, Rudesheimer, Liebfraumilch and Steinberger. Moselle wines to remember are Zeltinger, Brauneberger, Piesporter, Barnkasteler. Polysyllabic words on labels can be a help in intelligent ordering, if you've the patience to study them out: *auslese* means made from selected bunches of grapes . . . *beerenaulese* means made from selected individual grapes from selected bunches (and it also means the wine is going to be very expensive!) . . . *spatlese* means that the grapes were allowed to hang on the vine until covered with a mold —to make a sweet and alcoholic wine . . . *naturwein* or *Ungezuckerter Wein* means made from ripe but not overripe grapes, thus comparatively dry . . . *edelbeeren* indicates that the grapes were overripe . . . *throckenbeerenauslese* means you're in for the rare

[139]

"The old monastery would be pretty dull without it"

treat; this wine is made only once in 5 or 10 years, from selected semi-dried grapes; it's sweet, and dear . . . *cabinet* is applied to any wine which is the finest of its kind.

Wines of Italy

Italy is said to be one large vineyard. The best known red table wines from Italy are Chianti, Barolo, Barbera, Nebbiolo (sometimes sparkling); whites include Ovrieto, Est! Est!! Est!!, Asti Spumanti. But probably the Italian wine best liked and most used in America is the red Chianti from Tuscany. Chianti is in its prime five or six years after vintage—so look for dust on the familiar straw-covered bottle!

Dessert Wines

SPAIN Sherry from Jerez has never been successfully imitated elsewhere in the world. See page 148 of the "Drink" section for a description of the various types—and remember Oloroso when you want an unusual after-dinner wine.

Spain's second claim to wine fame is Malaga, an 18%-alcohol wine which is very sweet, walnut-colored and sprung from Muscat grapes. The most famous of its three types is Lacrima Christi—for which grapes are dried in the sun, their precious juices captured, and their fortified wine product mixed with another heavy and sweet wine. Another type is Moscato. Malaga gets better and better as it gets older and older; it has been stored for centuries without deterioration!

PORTUGAL Along the upper reaches of the Douro River, the steep banks stretch back on both sides, entirely covered by vineyards that produce the grapes from which true Port is made. Most Port is ruby-red, although a small amount of white Port is made; and most Port is a blended wine, but there *are* "vintage ports" of exceptional years. These are the four general types of Port:

RUBY The gay dog. Red as its name and lusty as it looks. Rich, full-bodied, fruity, slightly astringent. But don't develop into a Three Bottle Man or you'll get gout. Serve at (dining-, drawing- or bed-) room temperature.

TAWNY Older, milder, subtler. Less sweet. The color ranges, according to age, from purplish brown ("medium") to topaz yellow (extremely old). For epicures and invalids. Serve chilled.

WHITE Actually yellow. Made from white grapes. Best when old and dry, to be served chilled to wash down your pre-dinner caviar and rattlesnakes.

VINTAGE Product of a specially declared "Vintage Year," kept separate from wines of ordinary years. Gains its maturity in bottle instead of in cask. Takes a Jeeves to open it. Serve at baronial-hall temperature.

MADEIRA On the little island off Portugal, the famous Madeira wine is grown—rich, nutty, brown-colored and potent. Madeira wines lack standardization. Making it is a business of collecting new wines pressed from a dozen kinds of grapes grown in every conceivable sort of tiny vineyard, subjecting them to hot-storage treatment in an *estufa* (substitute for old-fashioned trip to Indies and back), fortifying them with 10% extra alcohol, toning them with older and different wines, and thereafter touching them up with a bit of this and that during the course of a generation or so.

The nearest one can come to a classification is to say that:

MALMSEY is the most honeyedly luscious and should be served with dessert and after. Also good at tea time with wafers or cake.

BUAL (or **BOAL**) is the medium-sweet; safe choice when you don't know your guests' preferences. Serve any time.

SERCIAL is the distinctly dry one, a bit strange and unaccountable at first sip; but at second sip you begin wondering how much there is in the house. Serve before dinner or with first course.

SOLERAS are very old wines (all types) that have been kept up to their spark by the judicious addition of younger ones.

All Madeira wines are best served *slightly cool, not cold.* The island's winter climate during the duke and duchess season gives you the hint: it's 61° F.

SICILY The island of Sicily produces Marsalla, a Madeira-like wine which is mildly fortified. It tastes a bit like sherry, but is richer, more mellow. Its varieties are designated as:

VIRGIN Not fortified with brandy, but nonetheless 19% or more alcohol by volume

S.O.M.—Superior Old Marsalla

O.P.—Old Particular

L.P.—London Particular

O.S.—Old Solera

An especially sweet Muscatel is also produced in Sicily—a natural sweet wine suitable for dessert use. The Sicilian Malvasia is fortified.

HUNGARY Hungary's most famous wine is Tokay—a sweet, pungent wine which is the product of *natural* fermentation of perfectly dried grapes. The drier is called Szamorodni and the sweet Azzu.

American Wines

. . . And almost every one of those wines is "made in America," too. Here, however, the names are merely clues to the wine's character—not pedigrees, as in Europe. "Sauterne" on a French label means a distinct wine made from three particular grapes and grown only in a particular small section of the Bordeaux district. "Sauterne" on an American label tells nothing but the type of wine.

in the producer's opinion; it may come from any one of the 27 wine-growing states in the U. S., from any one of the countless grape varieties cultivated in this country. And it is generally much drier than the European original—in accordance with the American preference.

That's why it may be helpful, in choosing among the myriad American wines, to know these general facts:

1. Grapes for dessert wines must be ripened to a high sugar content, so hot sunshine is indicated. Interior valleys and southern parts of California provide said hot sunshine in large quantities—so "Fresno Valley," "Southern California," "San Joaquin" or "Sacramento Valley" are good signs on a sherry or port label.

2. Grapes for table wines should be developed to fruit acidity rather than fruit sweetness, so the cooler weather of the northern coast of California or the eastern states is more appropriate. Grapes for dry wines of California seem to attain greater finesse in the northern regions, notably those in the vicinity of San Francisco: the Sonoma, Napa and Santa Clara districts. Such place-names may some day come to mean as much in their way as Bordeaux and Burgundy; in the meantime, their presence on the table-wine label is reassuring.

3. California vineyards are based on transplanted European vines, so California wines bear a close resemblance to the Old World product. But the harsher climes of Ohio, New York and the 24 other wine-producing states of the United States require hardier vines; so wines from states other than California, made from American grapes, are distinctly different from the European; they should be enjoyed as the unique wines they are, not subjected to unfair comparison. The Delaware, the Catawba and the Scuppernong are the best of the native grapes; all produce a wine of tangy, wild flavor. They are, when well made, very clean and sound and pleasant. And the sparkling wines from the East—notably from the Finger Lakes District of New York—have a natural dry zest which is saluted even by those who prefer the subtler European flavor in their still wines.

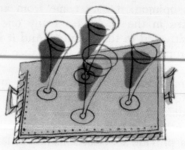

How To Serve Wines

After you've sipped enough wines to be able to form your own judgments, you may decide that wine's at its best when it's drunk from the bottle or watered with ice cubes or taken by injection. But until that time when you can indulge your own preferences on the basis of your own experience, you may want to be guided by the men who know the Bacchus-brew best: the wine experts. Their common-sense advice for uncommon enjoyment of table wines can be boiled down to three:

1. Red wines are best with red meat, white wines with white meats, fish and fowl. Champagne goes with everything. (Practically any good wine goes with practically any good dish, but if you went at it blindly you would probably discover that a light ethereal white seems inadequate for a ruddy roast beef or steak, while an opulent-bodied Burgundy is apt to overpower the delicate flavor of fresh fish. Switched, these combinations would be perfect.)

That color-scheme "rule" makes for easy memory, but if you would be more specific here's a list to ignore:

APERITIF—(Sherry, the foreign aperitifs or standard cocktails. Hence cocktail ingredients)

HORS D'OEUVRE—Dry white, Chablis, Sauterne

OYSTERS—Chablis, Sauterne or Champagne

SOUP—Chablis or Sauterne

FISH—Chablis, Sauterne, Moselle, Alsatian

ENTREE—Light meats, chicken, etc.—White Burgundy; Pouilly or Chablis, Rhine wines

GAME—Red Burgundies: Chambertins, Pommards, etc.

ROASTS—Red Bordeaux; red Burgundies, Claret

DESSERT—Champagne or White Bordeaux, Chateau Y'quem

CHEESE, FRUIT OR NUTS—Burgundy or Claret (Stilton takes port) or fortified wines like Madeira, port, sweet sherry.

COFFEE—Brandy (cordials for women)

2. One table-wine is sufficient for all but a formal dinner, but if more than one wine is to be served during the course of the meal the heavier, fuller-bodied wines should follow the lighter and more delicate—which usually means that reds follow whites. Sweet wines are reserved for last—with the dessert. However, it is perfectly correct to serve champagne as a dessert wine, even though a heavier wine has been previously served during the dinner.

3. Red wines are generally served at room temperature, while whites are chilled—but all sparkling wines are served chilled. To be more explicit:

All chilled.
{
Champagnes
Sparkling Burgundies
Carbonateds
Still Whites
Dry Sherries
Vermouths
Aperitif Wines
}

All still Reds at room temperature. (Or slightly chilled if you prefer.)

Ice is never put into the wine itself, of course. To chill, place in the refrigerator for an hour or so, or set the bottle in a bucket of ice for 20 or 30 minutes. To bring to room temperature, put the wine on the dining table a few hours before dinner. Never warm wine artificially. Beyond that, it's a question of niceties like these:

Preferred wine glasses are colorless, so the wine's color is not obscured, and stemmed, so the hand does not warm the wine. You can get by very nicely with simple 5-6 oz. stemmers to be used for all table wines, plus 3-4 ouncers for dessert and appetizer wines.

Wine should be poured slowly, so that the sediment which may have settled is not disturbed. The host usually pours a little in his own glass before filling his guests' glasses, just in case a bit of cork spills out with the first pour. Wine glasses are customarily filled only partially, so that the full fragrance will gather in the glass between wine-level and brim.

Connoisseurs say that smoking interferes drastically with the enjoyment of wine (as it does with food)—possible exception is sherry. And, of course, wine is meant to be sipped for its own sake, not gulped for thirst's sake.

How To Store Wines

For all wines, avoid sunlight, shock and temperature changes. Fifty-five to sixty degrees is best for wine storage, but if that's not possible, try for a constant temperature in any case.

For table wines: store all wine having 14% alcohol or less on its side, preferably with the bottom of the bottle a bit higher than the mouth, so that the cork will be kept moist by the wine. This keeps the cork expanded, tightly sealing the bottle, and thus eliminates the danger of Invasion by Air. Once opened, table wine should be stored in the refrigerator; left open and at room temperature it will turn to vinegar, sometimes within a day or so.

For fortified wines: store dessert and appetizer wines in an upright position, preferably standing so that one bottle can be removed from the shelf without disturbing the others.

If you have room, it's a good idea to lay down a cellar. Many wines improve (and increase in value) after a lay-away period . . . buying by the case means economy . . . and a handy source of supply is a convenience as well as a connoisseur's delight. The apartment dweller can often manage a "cellar" by way of a sturdy wooden cabinet or a honeycomb of shelves in a closet. The home owner has a natural in his basement, in any even-temperatured, dark spot away from the furnace.

If you are going about accumulating wines that will be a practical adjunct to your living and not merely a hobby to exhibit to friends, it is well to begin with your needs. Take your typical menu to an unimpeachable dealer and let him start you off on your taste tests. Sample a different wine each week and gradually arrive, by elimination, at the types that suit you best. When you hit on a good one, buy in quantity for your cellar.

In addition to the "spirited" appetizer known as a cocktail, there is a wine-based contribution to the cocktail-hour known as the aperitif. A companionable beverage, getting along harmoniously with the various viands to follow, the aperitif rarely exceeds an alcoholic tally of 18-20% by volume, compared to the cocktail's 20-90%. The wise host always has one such "continental cocktail" to offer, along with his more potent potables.

[147]

Although the French consider Pernod and Oxygene aperitifs, the Hungarians drink Szamorodni, and other national groups go in for Aquavit, Lillet, Tequila, Rojena, vodka and so on. The Big Four aperitifs are:

1. SHERRY

True sherries, wines grown in and around Jerez, Spain, fall into four main classes: *palido* (full-bodied, of medium color and dryness); *fino* (very pale, light, dry and delicate); *amontillado* (pale, very dry, a perfect aperitif); and *oloroso* (deeper-colored, nutty-flavored, best for after-dinner use). The other names you will run across include *amoroso,* a pale, golden, medium sherry of the *palido* class; *manzanilla,* thin and dry with a bitter flavor; *vina de pasto,* so dry and light it is used as a table wine; *montilla,* very pale and extremely dry when old, with something of an *amontillado* flavor.

Very dry sherries should be chilled to 50°F.; medium sherries such as *amoroso* should be slightly chilled and rich *olorosos* improve if the bottle is opened and left standing at room temperature. All are served in a pipe-stem, V-shaped 2 oz. glass.

2. VERMOUTH

Italian Vermouth is made from aged and blended white wines infused with some 25 or 30 herbs and fortified with brandy to about 16% alcoholic strength. Of the many varieties, the most seen are the standard (containing a good deal of sugar and about 15% alcohol, usually drunk straight) . . . vermouth bianco (a white vermouth, very sweet, which is a favorite with the fair sex) . . . and the dry (which has about 18% of alcohol by volume). Serve it:

ICED AND WITH SODA

Fill a large goblet ½ or ¾ full of vermouth, add several lumps of ice and a small amount of soda. Good before and during lunch as well as in the cocktail hour.

CHILLED AND STRAIGHT

Blend French and Italian varieties to suit your palate, chill but don't ice, and serve in a regular cocktail glass. Add a twist of lemon if you're in the mood.

THE AMERICANO

3 oz. Italian Vermouth
Dash of bitters
Slice of lemon peel
Seltzer as desired
Serve in a small highball glass or goblet.

French vermouth, a blend of fine white wines fortified with spirits and aromatized with some 40 herbs, is pale and dry, lacking the sweetness of the darker Italian product. Its characteristic taste is due to the fact that its wine-base is aged in much the same way that sherry is treated—left in butts out in the sun and rain for at least 2 years. Here's how:

VERMOUTH CASSIS

3 oz. French Vermouth
½ oz. Crème de Cassis
Seltzer to taste
Serve with ice in a small highball glass or goblet.

THE ENGLISH WAY

½ Italian Vermouth
½ French Vermouth
Serve cold with a twist of lemon peel.

"An apéritif"

3. BYRRH (rhymes with "her")

The juice of sweet and dry grapes is mixed, then passed over a series of aromatic plants and Peruvian bark to produce this aperitif of stimulating taste and aroma. It is served . . .

frappéd, in a cocktail glass
chilled, in a wine glass with ice
and water or soda, in a highball
glass as byrrh-cassis, in same
proportions as vermouth cassis
or as . . .

BYRRH-CITRON

3 oz. byrrh
½ oz. lemon syrup
Soda or plain water to taste
Serve in highball glass with lump of ice.

4. DUBONNET

. . . a blend of carefully selected old "liqueuer" wines to which Peruvian bark or quinine is added. It has a rich, slightly sweet flavor with the qualities of a mild liqueuer. Serve it . . .

. . . well chilled in a small sherry or cocktail glass
. . . with soda or water and ice in a highball glass, or as a

DUBONNET COCKTAIL

½ Dubonnet
½ gin
Slice of lemon
Stir with ice and strain into cocktail glass. (Whisky, sherry, vermouth or rum may be used in place of gin; the combinations are legion.)

P.S.: People who like to make rules say that aperitifs should always be chilled, should never be served with anything more imposing than plain salted crackers or cheese wafers and should always be *sipped*, not gulped. We say: do what you like, so long as you like it!

After-Dinner Drinks

CORDIALLY YOURS

After a good meal, a good liqueur—to aid digestion and conversation as well as to clear the palate for further drinking. Gourmets groan at the thought of following a heavy meal with anything but brandy, others claim almost-equal rights for Crème de Menthe, each country has its favorite cordial—and so the question of an after-dinner tipple turns out to be dealer's choice. Since cordials increase as rapidly as rabbits, it is almost impossible to give a full listing... but here are the sturdy ones which have survived for centuries. Let your palate (and your purse) prevail!

Absinthe Licorice-tasting powerhouse, now illegal but agreeably replaced by Pernod or Oxygene.

Advocaat A thick cordial from Holland, often called "egg brandy," made of eggs, sugar and brandy.

Anisette Made from anise seeds (from France).

Apple of Paradise A native Cuban cordial made from a local fruit.

Apricot Liqueur Choice dried apricots distilled with fine old cognac. Very popular.

Aquavit Danish version of kümmel, caraway seed flavor predominates.

Arrak Flavored with anise (from the Near East).

Benedictine Proprietary formula, from France.

Calisay The national liqueur of Spain, brandy with two per cent quinine, flavored with Peruvian bark.

Calvados French version of our apple-jack.

Cascarilla Favored by South Americans, made from spices and barks on a brandy base.

Cassis Used in France as an aperitif but here mainly for mixing. Made from the French black currant.

Chartreuse Secret formula, made by French monks in Tarragona, Spain.

Cognac The best of brandy, from France.

Cointreau Fine old cognac distilled with orange peel.

Crème de Cacao—Heavy and sweet, made from the beans that supply us with cocoa, distilled with brandy.

Crème de Menthe Peppermint liqueur from France and Holland. Three varieties: green, red and white.

Crème de Rose and **Crème de Violette** Brandy bases flavored with essence of the flowers. Left over from the gay nineties, used mainly in pousse-café.

Curacao Named after the island where the small sweet oranges grow that are used in its composition. Brandy base.

Drambuie A concentration of venerable Scotch whisky flavored with honey and herbs.

Fiori d'Alpi A sweetish liqueur, flavored with Alpine flowers, featuring a branch of the stem encrusted with sugar in each bottle.

Forbidden Fruit American cordial made on a brandy base from citrus fruits.

Goldwasser Brandy base flavored with herbs in which float small specks of gold. Not enough to change the rate of exchange. The old alchemists believed gold was good for internal as well as external disorders.

Grand Marnier A famous version of Curacao with a secret formula.

Grappa Italian version of marc.

Grenadine Made of pomegranates, for flavoring.

Kirschwasser Distilled from the wild cherries that grow in Switzerland and the Black Forest.

Kümmel Especially favored in the colder countries. Distilled from grain, flavored with seed of cumin, a plant resembling fennel (Holland).

Mandarin A brandy base flavored with Mandarin oranges.

Maraschino A sweet liqueur made from the cherries that grow in Dalmatia. The white brand is a swell addition to any bar and can be used in place of a spoon of sugar. Especially good in the Daiquiri, Cuban style.

Marc Distilled from the grape skins left over from winemaking. Strong.

Noyau Made from the crushed seeds of cherries, peaches, plums, apricots on a brandy base.

Oxygene Milder absinthe-substitute from Belgium.

Oyjen Spanish version of absinthe, a little sweeter.

Parfait Amour Another version of Crème Violette.

Peach Brandy An American product.

Pernod—Resembling absinthe (from France).

Pimiento Made on a Jamaica rum base flavored with the essence of the pepper. Spicy and hot.

Pisco Brandy Chilean marc.

Prunelle Brandy base flavored with the pits of wild plums. A swell drink for clearing the palate.

Strega Similar to chartreuse and in great favor among Italians.

Subrouska A green vodka.

Swedish Punch—A rum derivative liked by the Nordics and sailors. Called Caloric because it gives off heat.

Triple Sec Curacao restyled. Colorless, higher-powered, less sweet. One wheel of the Sidecar.

Veille Cure Another version of chartreuse, formula secret.

Vodka An eau de vie from Russia and Poland.

[152]

CORDIAL COMBOS

Here are some of the better known methods of gilding the after-dinner lily:

B & B

1 part cognac
1 part Benedictine

Mix, pour into liqueur glass and serve at room temperature.

LIZARD SKIN

Hollow out half of a large orange
Pour in large jigger brandy
Light flame, extinguish after a moment, then drink.

BRANDY CHAMPARELLE

¼ Curacao
¼ yellow Chartreuse
¼ anisette
¼ brandy

POUSSE-CAFE

1/6 Maraschino
1/6 raspberry syrup
1/6 Crème de Cacao
1/6 Curacao
1/6 Chartreuse
1/6 brandy

BROUSSARD'S ORANGE BRULOT

(As served in the famous New Orleans restaurant)

Cut a thin-skinned orange through skin around circumference, careful not to touch the fruit. With a teaspoon handle, turn the skin back until it forms a cup. Do this on both ends and you have a peeled orange with a cup at each end. Place one cup on your plate. Pour some brandy into upper cup, put a lump of sugar in the brandy, light, stir gently as it burns, then drink it when the flame dies. (Brandy burns more easily if previously warmed; run hot water over the bottle before bringing to table.)

CREME DE CACAO, CREAM FLOAT

Gently pour 1 teaspoon heavy cream onto Crème de Cacao in liqueur glass. Serve without stirring, the cream a clean layer on top.

(The trick is to pour these slowly, one by one, into a liqueur glass so that the colors stay in their strata. This is not governed by law, but specific gravity. You can choose your own colors.) And in the good old summertime, when an ordinary cordial seems forbiddingly heavy, flavor-cravers will favor: *Iced Crème de Café* (rich coffee liqueur, one jigger thereof, in glass of shaved ice, filled up with fizz and topped with sweet cream). And *Iced Crème de Cacao* (voluptuous chocolate liqueur with vanilla aura, similarly coolerized). And short-strawed fragrant verdant *Menthe Frappé* (Crème de Menthe liqueur shaved-iced in a cocktail glass). And *Apricot Delight* (1 part each of orange and lemon juices, 2 parts Apricot Brandy, ice-shaken and strained). And *Pernod Highball* (famous legal version of Absinthe, now made in America, fizzed and cubed). And cetera.

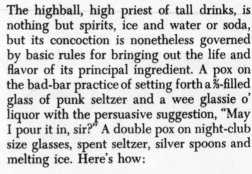

The highball, high priest of tall drinks, is nothing but spirits, ice and water or soda, but its concoction is nonetheless governed by basic rules for bringing out the life and flavor of its principal ingredient. A pox on the bad-bar practice of setting forth a ⅔-filled glass of punk seltzer and a wee glassie o' liquor with the persuasive suggestion, "May I pour it in, sir?" A double pox on night-club size glasses, spent seltzer, silver spoons and melting ice. Here's how:

1. Use a tall glass—at least 12 oz.—preferably uncolored, definitely sparklingly clean, admirably narrow-mouthed so soda will not collapse ahead of schedule.

2. First, put in the ice—one very large or two normal cubes for most Americans; let the no-ice Britishers speak up.

3. Next, pour the liquor over the ice. Scotch, bourbon, rye, brandy as you will. The amount varies with customs-of-the-service, but 1½ oz. is an average stick.

4. Only then pour in the very cold sparkling water to the desired height—usually four times the amount of liquor. Bubbles thrive on coolness, but rapidly melting ice downs them, so the soda must be pre-chilled in a refrigerator. Some prefer plain water rather than fizz in their highballs, but if you would please palates don't try to pass off the chlorine-clogged stuff that comes from the kitchen faucet. Use an alkaline-sided mineral water, or any purified, bottled aqua—but *cold*.

5. Spare the spoon and save the drink. The slightest contact with silverware squelches the bubbles—which do the mixing job unassisted. If one of your guests is stir-crazy, give him a plastic or glass swizzle stick.

6. Serve the drink immediately. Recap and replace in the refrigerator any leftover fizz water.

Here's a good trick to remember when you're entertaining sundry tastes and the bartending business is booming. Divide your serving tray into sections with strips of adhesive tape, on which you write "Scotch and water," "Scotch and soda," "Bourbon and soda," etc. Use clean glasses for each round, place the various combinations in their proper tray-sections, and then simply twist the tray about before each guest as he reminds you of his preference.

GINGER ALE HIGHBALLS

There's no special name for these whiskey-and-ginger ale combinations made by highball rules, except in the case of Scotch which, when coupled with ginger ale, sometimes goes under the heading of "Presbyterian."

COLLINS

Sometimes mistakenly label John Collins (which is really a gin drink), the whisky collins goes like this:

Squeeze the juice of a lemon into a tall glass
Add a heaping teaspoon of sugar
Stir, then add 2 ice cubes or plenty of cracked ice
Pour in a generous jigger of whisky—bourbon or rye
Fill with cold soda water
Stir with glass swizzle

It is well to stir before each sip, to keep sugar mixed and drink effervescing. Some garnish with cherry, orange slice.

RICKEY

Put several ice cubes in fizz or highball glass
Squeeze juice of half a lime over ice, then drop lime skin into glass
Pour in 1 jigger whiskey
Fill with seltzer
Stir with glass rod

WHISKY SHAKE

Juice of 2 limes
¾ teaspoon sugar
2 oz. whisky
Shake with great quantities of fine ice; strain into tall flute glass.

MISSISSIPPI PUNCH

Stir in Collins glass:
2 dashes lemon juice
1 teaspoon sugar
2 dashes Angostura bitters
Add:
1 oz. whisky
1½ oz. rum
1 oz. brandy
Fill with cracked ice; garnish with fruit if desired; attack with straws.

HORSE'S NECK

Strictly speaking, this is a teetotaler's drink, but add whisky to the basic and see how it goes:
Peel the whole rind of a lemon
Place it in a Collins glass, spiraling up from bottom and hooking over edge
Add 2 cubes of ice
Pour in 1 jigger whisky
Fill with cold ginger ale
A dash of bitters is sometimes added to the whisky.

MAMIE TAYLOR

Squeeze ½ lime into Collins glass
Add 2 cubes of ice
Pour in 1 jigger Scotch
Fill with cold ginger ale

MILK PUNCH

Into shaker filled with shaved ice put:
1 teaspoon sugar
1 jigger whisky
Fill glass with milk. Shake. Strain into large goblet or highball glass. Sprinkle with nutmeg.

[155]

MINT JULEP

Creeping gingerly onto the julep battleground, armed with enough formulae to please all violent schools of thought on the subject of creating this classic among long drinks, Esquire takes sides only to the extent of backing these general rules:

1. Use a prechilled, dry 12 or 14 oz. glass, tall and slim, if the traditional silver beaker is not available.
2. *Crush* the ice by puffing it in bag or towel, then hammering it with mallet or banging it against a sturdy sink. Then be sure it is absolutely dry, draining off the water before putting it in the glass.
3. Use only the freshest mint and, of that, the smallest, most tender leaves.
4. Don't handle the glass with bare hands. Use a cloth, or serve with a doily, if you would preserve the frost.
5. The glass will not frost if in the wind, if wet, with undried ice or if excessively handled. You can sometimes speed the frost by twirling the glass or by placing in coldest part of refrigerator for about 30 minutes.

Here, then, is an assortment of recipes, each sworn by (and at) by perfectionists of the wide-apart Virginia, Kentucky and Why-go-to-all-that-trouble-for-a-drink schools:

JULEP

(From Louisville's famous club, The Pendennis.) (This one's anti-crush, anti-sugar.)

Use a 14-oz. or 16-oz. silver julep cup. Dissolve a half or one lump of granulated sugar in clear spring water. Add two or three sprigs of tender mint, place gently (don't bruise the mint). Fill the cup with cracked ice and add 2 full jiggers of Kentucky bourbon whisky. Stir gently and refill the julep cup with cracked ice. Take a full bunch of tender mint, cutting the ends to bleed, and place on top. Let it stand for about five minutes before serving. There should be a small linen doily with each julep, as the frost on the cups makes it uncomfortable to hold.

JULEP

(This is a middle-of-the-roader; slightly crushed, a little sugar)

Place five or six leaves of mint in the bottom of a prechilled, dry twelve-ounce glass or silver beaker; add one teaspoon sugar; crush slightly with a muddler. Pack glass with finely crushed ice (dry, beaten in a bag is the best method); pour one and one-half jiggers of whisky over the ice. Stir briskly until the glass frosts. As this stirring will melt some of the ice, add more ice and stir again before serving. Stick a few sprigs of mint into the ice so that the partaker will get the aroma. Serve on a plate or hold in napkin; the touch of a hand would kill frost.

[156]

MINT JULEP
In the manner of Irvin S. Cobb

Take a clean glass and crush a few sprigs of mint with a spoon. Rub the mint all around the inside of the glass, then throw it away. Now fill the glass with finely cracked ice. *Slowly* pour in a measure of bourbon, then add about 2 tablespoons of water in which a lump of sugar has been dissolved. *Do not stir.* Place sprigs of fresh mint in the mouth of the glass.

VIRGINIA JULEP
(A test of patience!)

Pour a measure of bourbon over several sprigs of mint and allow this to stand for half an hour.

Dissolve a teaspoon of sugar in a little water and place in a glass. When half an hour has passed, remove the mint from the whisky and pour the bourbon into the sugar and water. Pour this mixture back and forth between the two glasses until the liquids are well mixed, then . . .

Fill a glass with finely crushed ice and pour the mixture over it. Stir briskly until the frost forms on the glass, then fill the top of the glass with sprigs of fresh mint.

JULEP
(A more minty variety)

Use about 10 sprigs of mint to the glass. Place in a bowl and dust with enough powdered sugar to cover lightly, then add 1 ounce of water for each julep. Macerate thoroughly and let stand for 10 or 15 minutes. Strain through a fine sieve into a glass filled with crushed ice. Fill the glass with fine bourbon, stir thoroughly. Insert a large sprig of mint in each glass and stow in the refrigerator for 30 minutes before serving.

(NOTE: No matter what form of julep you take to, and particularly if you follow the old-timer's habit of "sweetening" your julep with more bourbon without bothering to build a new base, you might well remember this little tale: A certain Virginian of yore, visiting a friend in Kentucky and offered the customary toddy of those days, turned missionary and showed his host how to make a julep. A year later another acquaintance called to see the Kentuckian and found that he had died. The old butler explained that "a gemmen fro Ferginny done come by and showed the Marster how to eat grass in his whisky and he done et hisself ter death!" A case of half-knowledge, obviously. The impulsive convert had learned the basic art of making, but alas, not the higher art of slow and stately sippage whereby bourbon's soul transmigrates in the manner of Eric, or little by little.)

GIN

CHERRY JULEP

1½ oz. dry gin
1 oz. sloe gin
1 oz. cherry brandy
1 teaspoon Maraschino cherry syrup and 2 or 3 muddled cherries
Juice of one-half lemon
1 teaspoon sugar

Stir well, pour into 12-oz. glass, add cracked ice, and fill glass with seltzer. Garnish with one-half slice of lemon or orange, if desired as a color effect for the aesthetically-inclined.

GIN AND TONIC

(The tonic is a sparkling water containing one grain of quinine. Sounds terrible, but wait until you try it! It's the drink of the tropics from the Sailors' Bar at Cartagena to the cool verandah of the Myrtle Bank Hotel at Kingston, Jamaica, and Christophe's Citadel at Milot, Haiti.)

1 generous jigger of gin
½ fresh lime
1 split of tonic water

Serve in regular highball glass with cube of ice.

FRENCH "75"

2 ounces of gin
1 teaspoon powdered sugar
Juice of one fresh lime or one-fourth lemon

Shake well with ice. Pour into ten-ounce glass, and then fill with champagne. Some add 5 dashes of bitters.

GIN CUP

Take a pint cup, pure silver
Fill it with crushed ice
Put in juice one-half lemon
Put in tablespoonful powdered sugar
Joggle cup *slightly* for five minutes
Add large jigger best gin
Let stand until entire outside heavily frosted
Sit quietly: only a mutt will talk or read
After 15 minutes of sedate joy
Take 15 minutes more of same
The day becomes beautiful!

GIN JULEP

Bruise four sprigs of mint with a spoonful of powdered sugar. Add two ounces of gin. Fill tall glass with crushed ice and stir until frosted.

GIN RICKEY (Dry or Sloe)

Squeeze half a lime into ordinary bar glass, over cubes of ice. Toss in lime-skin, add 1 jigger of gin and fill with soda water. Stir briefly. (Dash of Grenadine sometimes added. For a sweeter drink, when dry gin is used, crush the lime-half with 1 teaspoon sugar before adding ice, gin and sparkly.)

JOHN COLLINS

Follow directions for Tom Collins, below, but use Holland gin, pungently schnappy and a bit unexpected tasting at first sip.

LEE MILLER'S FROBISHER

Use 10-oz. glass
2 ozs. gin
1 dash bitters
1 lemon peel
Plenty cracked ice
Fill glass to brim with champagne
Stir

SINGAPORE SLING

1 jigger sloe gin
½ jigger dry gin
½ jigger apricot brandy
½ jigger cherry brandy
½ lime juice
1 teaspoon sugar

Stir in 12-oz. glass with cracked ice. Fill with seltzer water. Decorate with cherry, slice of orange and stick of fresh pineapple. (Drink will be a deep red in color.)

TEX COLLINS

1 jigger gin
Juice one-half grapefruit
1 tablespoon honey

Stir well, add ice and fill tall glass with soda.

TOM COLLINS

Squeeze the juice of a lemon in a tall glass, add a heaping teaspoon of sugar, a generous jigger of Tom or London gin, plenty of cracked ice, and fill with soda water. It is well to stir before each gulp, as that keeps the sugar mixed and the drink effervescing. Variation: add several lusty shots of Angostura bitters.

RUM

AIR MAIL

Mix in shaker:
Juice of one-half lime
1 teaspoon honey
1 jigger gold rum

Add cracked ice, shake; strain into highball glass and fill with dry champagne.

BACARDI COLLINS

Mix in shaker:
Juice of one lime
1 teaspoon sugar
1 jigger Bacardi

Shake well with ice; strain into Collins glass ballasted with ice cubes. Fill with fizz.

CHARLIE COLLINS

In bottom of large glass, mix:
1 tablespoon fresh lime juice
½ tablespoon sugar
Plunk in a couple of ice cubes;
pour over them:
1 jigger Jamaica rum
Fill with sparkling water.

COCONUT COOLER

Get a coconut, bore out one of the eyes and drain off the milk. Mix half milk and half Jamaica rum, ice, and fill with charged water.

COOPER COOLER

Over plenty of ice in 10-oz. glass, pour:
1 jigger Cuban rum
Fill with ginger ale, then twist over top and drop in:
1 inch piece lime or lemon peel

CUBA LIBRE

Into Collins glass squeeze one-half lime, then drop in the skin. Add cubes of ice, then pour in:
2 oz. Puerto Rican or Cuban rum
Fill with cold Coca-Cola
Serve with a stirring rod.
(NOTE: A Cuba Libre is sometimes made without the lime juice, in which case it is more correctly described as a "Rum 'n' Coke." Serve drink without half-lime skin, if you prefer.)

CUBAN COOLER

Ice cubes in tall glass—measure of favorite rum—fill with ginger ale—decorate with sprig of mint.

FISH HOUSE PUNCH

Juice of one-half lemon
1 barspoon sugar
1 jigger rum
⅓ jigger brandy
Strain into glass filled with shaved ice. Decorate with fruit.

MILK PUNCH

(As served on rolling days at sea and a rainy day in Colon, Panama.)
1 teaspoon of sugar
2 pieces of ice
½ cocktail glass of rum (or brandy or whisky)
Put in shaker and fill with rich milk. Shake well and serve with nutmeg on top.

MOJITO (OR MOHITO)

Juice of one-half lemon
Scant teaspoon sugar
1 jigger rum
Shake, strain into tall glass containing ice cubes, fill with seltzer. Decorate with fresh mint leaves.

PLANTERS PUNCH

There are almost as many versions of this tall cooler as there are planters, but the 1-2-3's go something like this:

One of sour (juice of one lime)
Two of sweet (two teaspoons sugar)
Three of strong (3 oz. redolent old heavy-bodied Jamaica rum)
Four of weak (ice and water)

Lots of shaking and what garnishment you please.

or this, for the less sugar-sold:

"One of Sweet (1 dessert spoon sugar or gum syrup)
Two of sour (2) dessert spoons fresh lime or lemon juice)
Three of weak (3 tablespoons fine ice)
Four of strong (4 tablespoons rum)"

At the conclusion of this aria, add Angostura dashes; stir or shake and strain into tall glass of cracked ice fancied up with ½ slice lemon, ½ slice orange, sliver of pineapple, Maraschino cherry and anything else you may care to contribute. Trinidad's prideful prescription uses a teaspoon of Angostura, is garnished solely with a slice of lemon and is sprinkled with nutmeg.

Here's how Barbados smites the spot:

PLANTER'S PUNCH, UNPULLED

Half fill an 8-oz. glass with chipped ice; add 2-oz. rich-bodied, super-fragrant rum of the ancientest, 1 tablespoon Falernum (a bouquet syrup with overtones of Barbados rum, herbs and essences), 1 flick Angostura; fill up with water or soda; stir like anything; bon-voyage with fruit. Sprinkle nutmeg or a touch of pepper.

And this one uses fizz-water:

Juice of one-half lime
1 teaspoon sugar
1 jigger rum

Shake in shaved ice and pour unstrained, into tall glass. Fizz to brim. Add dash Angostura if wished; fruit decor ad lib, flurry of nutmeg.

And here's a sugarless variation:

Juice of one-half lime
1 oz. Curacao
Dash of Grenadine
¾ oz. rum

Shake or stir with ice. Strain into fruited tall glass half-filled with crushed ice. Sprinkle with red pepper.

RUM COLLINS

Juice of 1 lime or one-half lemon
1 teaspoon sugar
2 oz. rum

Shake with ice, pour unstrained into Collins glass and fill wth sparkling water. Or mix juice and sugar in bottom of glass, add ice cubes, then pour in rum and seltzer. Bottled Collins mix can be used: ice cubes, then rum, then bottled mix.
De luxe version: use 1 tablespoon Falernum in place of sugar. Variation: add a dash of Angostura bitters.

RUM PUNCH

Pour over fine ice in tall glass:
   1½-2 oz. your favorite rum
   Juice of half or whole lime
   1 tsp. or more sugar syrup, to taste

Stir, stick in some mint sprigs and the show is complete. No shaking. No fruiting. Just drinking.

RUNT'S AMBITION

2 oz. rum
2 oz. gin
2 oz. whisky
2 oz. port wine

Shake with ice; strain.

ZOMBIE

After-guesses regarding the composition of this voodoo spook of dynamite are apt to be confused by a forest of lamp posts. There's no knowing what some zealous mixers may load into multi-rummed specimens, but here are a couple of formulae at the right.

ZOMBIE A LA No. 1 BOY

Juice of one lime
1 barspoon brown sugar
1 barspoon passion fruit
¾ oz. Puerto Rican or Cuban, white
¾ oz. Puerto Rican or Cuban, gold
¾ oz. 90-proof Jamaica
1 oz. 151-proof Demerara

Stir together all these ingredients except the last; pour into 14-oz. glass which has been filled three-fourths full of cracked ice; float the 151-proofer as a lid; garnish with mint or fruit. A straw proposition.

ZOMBIE A LA PUERTO RICO

Onto cracked ice in shaker pour:
¾ oz. pineapple juice (unsweetened)
¾ oz. papaya nectar (canned)
Juice of sizable lime
¾ barspoon powdered sugar
⅓ oz. apricot brandy
1 oz. Puerto Rican, white, 86 proof
2 oz. Puerto Rican, gold, 86 proof
1 oz. Jamaican heavy-bodied 90 proof

Shake. Without straining, pour into Zombie glass, adding cubed ice to nearly fill. Bedoll with sprig of mint, small square of pineapple; skewer 2 cherries on toothpick and set so that it bridges the rim. Carefully pour on a shallow float of tropical heavy-bodied 151 proof. Sprinkle a light flurry of powdered sugar. Pair of straws.

BRANDY

BRANDY FIZZ

Juice of one lemon
1 barspoon sugar
1 jigger brandy
2 dashes yellow Chartreuse

Shake well with ice; strain; fill glass with siphon.

BRANDY FIX

Dissolve one teaspoon of sugar in one teaspoon of water in small tumbler. Add juice of half a lemon, 1 jigger of brandy, ½ jigger cherry brandy, fill the glass with chipped ice, stir and serve with a straw.

BRANDY MINT JULEP

3 jiggers cognac brandy
4 sprigs mint (uncrushed)
1 teaspoonful powdered sugar

Place mint in large glass, and then dissolve sugar. Add brandy and shaved ice. Stir well till very cold.

BRANDY PUNCH

Fill wineglass half full shaved ice
Add one teaspoon sugar
1 teaspoon pineapple juice
Juice of one-fourth of a lemon
A few dashes of lime juice
1 larger jigger brandy

Stir well, add a squirt of soda, serve with a dash of rum and fruit on top.

EGG LEMONADE

Fill your shaker half full chopped ice, add one fresh egg, one teaspoon sugar, juice of one lemon, one jigger of brandy. Shake well, strain into large glass and fill with soda.

FRENCH "75" or KING'S PEG

Juice of one lemon
1 teaspoon fine granulated sugar
2 oz. brandy
5 dashes bitters

Shake with cracked ice and pour unstrained into highball glass. Fill with champagne and stir gently.

SANGRIA (Argentinian)

Proportions for this brandy julep vary, so follow the general julep rules (page 156) and follow your taste with these ingredients:

brandy   claret
orange juice   Triple Sec

WHITEHALL PUNCH

(Holiday Drink)
Created by Florida-promoter Henry M. Flagler

Into a mixing glass squeeze the juice of 1 lime. Add 1 jigger brandy, 1 barspoon Grenadine, 1 dash syrup. Fill with cracked ice and shake well. Then strain into a tall glass which has been well frosted and is full of snow ice. After straining the drink into the glass, fill up with more snow ice and top off with seltzer. (For the full treatment, you would place glass in individual silver bowl and pack shaved ice to within 1 inch of brim.) Decorate with a strawberry, slice of orange and pineapple. Serve 2 straws and sip slowly to savor delicate bouquet.

WINE
(And one cider gate-crasher)

CLARET LEMONADE

Fill a tall glass ¾ full of lemonade prepared in the usual manner. Atop this pour claret—carefully—so that it *remains* on top. When the partaker inserts spoon and stirs, it's a pretty sight.

EMPIRE PUNCH

(As served at Casino Bar, Dieppe)

In a large tumbler put three or four lumps of ice, then add:
1 teaspoon Curacao
1 teaspoon Benedictine
1 teaspoon brandy
1 wineglass of claret

Fill to top of glass with champagne, stir well, decorate with fruits.

GENERAL HARRISON'S EGGNOG

Use large tumbler. One egg; one and a half teaspoonfuls of sugar; two or three small lumps of ice. Fill the tumbler with cider and shake well. This is a splendid drink, and is very popular on the Mississippi River. It was General Harrison's favorite drink.

PORT WINE SANGAREE

1 barspoon sugar
1 jigger water
4 oz. port wine

Mix in bottom of tall glass, add ice, then fill with seltzer.

RHINE WINE AND SELTZER

This is ½ Rhine wine, ½ seltzer water in tall glass with 2 or 3 ice-cubes—a perfect drink for the very young or the very cautious.

(Variations: Add 1 jigger dry sherry . . . add 1 tablespoon lemon juice . . . garnish with cucumber slice.)

ROYAL PLUSH

Into a tall glass with ice cubes, pour ½ burgundy, ½ champagne. Stir gently.

"He says he talks to himself and the conversation's so dull
he wants a Mickey Finn"

SAUTERNE CUP

When there's a group thirst to be quenched of an afternoon, put big lumps of ice in a glass pitcher, pour in:

1 quart sauterne
1 pint soda
1 wineglass sherry
1 pony brandy

Add:

Rind of one lemon
3 slices orange
3 slices lemon
1 slice cucumber peel
Any fresh berries available

Stir and serve in tall glasses ornamented with fruit. Or substitute champagne for sauterne, add 1 pony white Curacao and use fresh mint instead of fruit.

SIR CHARLES PUNCH

(Christmas)

Fill a large tumbler half full with shaved ice. Add to this one teaspoon of granulated sugar, one wineglass of port, ½ glass of brandy, ½ glass of Curacao. Stir well with a spoon. Ornament the top with slices of orange, pineapple and split grapes.

SOYER AU CHAMPAGNE

(One of the most popular drinks at Christmas in the continental cafés)

Take a large tumbler and in the bottom put two large tablespoons of vanilla ice cream. Add 2 dashes of Maraschino, 2 dashes of Curacao, 2 dashes of brandy, then fill to the top with champagne. Stir and add a slice of pineapple, a slice of orange, a slice of lemon, 2 cherries and 2 strawberries.

THE SUNSET LIMITED

2 jiggers American muscatel
Juice of half a lemon
Ice cubes
2 dashes Angostura
Couple of squirts of seltzer
Fill glass with American Chablis
Stir lightly—mint sprig trimming, if available

Since muscatel is of the "fortified" group (meaning that like sherry, port, and Angelica it is backboned with brandy), the above Sunset cannot be accused of lack of glow.

WINE COLLINS

Squeeze juice of ½ lemon into Collins glass, fill to half-way mark with any table-wine. Add ice cubes, fill with sparkling water and stir. Sugar may be added to lemon juice if desired.

Beer

THE COOLER WITH
THE COLLAR

There's not much you can "do" with beer, except indulge in the pleasant task of drinking it. But in the interests of justice to the cooler with the collar, Esquire offers this 10-plank platform for handling foam on the range.

1. Bottled beer doesn't thrive on sunlight. Hide it away till you are ready to put it away.

2. Don't keep it in a warm place, either.

3. Nor up against the ice, nor cube compartment, in your refrigerator. It needs coolness, not such extreme cold as to cloud it.

4. If cloudy, remove from excessive chill which has caused this temporary condition. Served immediately, it would have a weak head.

5. No jiggling or jouncing before serving.

6. Pry off bottle caps briskly, and plunge can opener boldly, to avoid spray effects.

7. When pouring, tilt glass so that beer makes its entrée on the slant; then straighten for a collar.

8. Glasses should be washed in a solution of salt or soda. Never soap. And do not dry with a cloth.

9. Ale and pewter are particularly congenial.

10. Steins with hinged lids keep beer fresh for leisurely drinkers.

And here are three old-time combinations to vary your pursuit of hoppiness:

PORTER

(Named for porters who in the 16th to 18th century went after the stuff when the master was abed.)

1 part ale
1 part beer
1 part two-penny (a milder beer)

'ARF AND 'ARF

1 part ale
1 part beer

HUCKLE-MY-BUTT

1 quart beer
½ pint of brandy
2 eggs
Sugar to taste
Small amounts of cinnamon, cloves and nutmeg
Stir thoroughly until well mixed.

Punches
TO BOWL YOU OVER

PUNCHES — Cold

Bearing no resemblance to the sloppy "pink lemonade pond" that functions, amid dirty glasses and wet tablecloth, at nondescript dances where the budget for "refreshments" is modest to the point of prudery—these are punches with *punch*. An honest-injun bowl of cheer is a natural hub of a party, and though you'd best have a Scotch-and-soda bar for die-hards who regard a punch bowl as a quaint curio, you'll be surprised at the converts you win with some of these mixtures—particularly if you ladle them into stemmed Delmonico glasses or outright tumblers rather than those cute-handled cuppies known as knuckle-traps.

[165]

A punch recipe holds good only as regards proportions; quantity needed will have to be figured separately according to size and vim of party. With some groups the turnover may be leisurely—say, a bowl an hour. With others, it will take *two* bowls—one under attack in the living or dining-room, and the other in process of concoction in the pantry, with steady alternation. At any "event," give guests free ladle privileges and they're in business for themselves, quaffeteria style.

ARISTOCRAT SPARKLING PUNCH

1 bottle burgundy
4 ounces brandy
1 quart sparkling water
2 bottles champagne
1 cup cube sugar

Dissolve sugar in a cup of sparkling water and pour into punch bowl. Add burgundy and brandy, stirring well. Place block of ice in bowl, and add champagne and the balance of sparkling water. Garnish top of ice block with strawberries or raspberries, or other fruit in season, and float thin slices of two oranges on top of punch.

BRANDY PUNCH

Juice two oranges
Juice six lemons
1 cup powdered sugar
½ pint Curacao
1 quart brandy
Spoonful Grenadine

Pour into punch bowl over a large piece of ice. Add 1 bottle soda water.

BOSTON FISH HOUSE PUNCH
(Feeds fifty)

Into the bosom of a mammoth punch bowl put:

1 tumbler melted sugar or plain syrup
1 tumbler lime juice (or 1½ tumblers lemon juice)

Mix thoroughly, making sure that all sugar is dissolved.
Now add:

1½ bottles superior Jamaica rum
1 bottle de luxe American brandy
1 tumbler peach brandy
3 quarts champagne (cuvéed within our shores)
Hunks of ice

The impact of this punch is guaranteed to knock Santa Claus's beard right off its moorings, or break your lease if you so desire.

BOWLE

This light, refreshing summer drink served so often in Europe offers a good way to use plain white wine. You put fresh crushed fruit in wine and let it stand several hours before serving. The Continentals make bowle when strawberries arrive and go right through the season, using whatever fruit is in market. Here's a sample:

STRAWBERRY BOWLE

Place in a bowl one quart of washed and hulled strawberries. (Use wild strawberries, if possible.) Cover with 1 pound sugar and 1 wineglass of water. Shake bowl slightly to mix ingredients and put in icebox to stand about eight hours. When ready to serve, add three bottles of well-iced Moselle or Rhine wine. Do not add ice.

CHAMPAGNE PUNCH

. . . the official potion that directly follows the kissing of the bride (or the making of a million, or the Big Announcement) ranges all the way from pure champagne poured over ice and decorated with fruit to champagne stepped up with brandy, rum and liqueurs. Esky recommends:

IN THE GRAND MANNER

(Allow one fifth of champagne to each guest)

For every bottle of champagne add one pint of sparkling water, one wineglass of Maraschino, one wineglass of yellow Chartreuse and one full glass of the best cognac. Use one-half lemon and one orange, sliced, for each portion. Put a large chunk of ice in the bowl and serve cold.

CHAMPAGNE PUNCH

To each bottle of champagne add one bottle of club soda, one pony of brandy, one pony of Triple Sec liqueur; the rind of one orange, cut very thin. Little or no powdered sugar. And no lemon. Deposit berg of ice.

Decorate with sliced fresh pineapple and orange, and plenty of fresh mint. Crushed fresh strawberries add a gala touch to looks and flavor.

Variation: Cointreau instead of Triple Sec.

CHATHAM ARTILLERY PUNCH

1½ gal. Catawba wine
½ gal. St. Croix rum
1 quart London dry gin
1 quart ★ ★ ★ brandy
½ pint Benedictine
1½ quarts rye
1½ gal. strong tea
2½ lb. brown sugar
Juice of 18 oranges
Juice of 18 lemons
1 bottle Maraschino cherries

Mingle and let rest in a cold spot for 2 days. Then add 1 case champagne and serve.

It's a drink you'll remember, if you remember anything.

CHAMPAGNE CUP

Carve and shave a piece of ice 8 inches long so it will stand in a pitcher and leave 1½ inch space all around. In this space place 3 round slices of orange, 3 round slices of pineapple, and preserved cherries in between. 3 long slices of fresh cucumber rind are next put in place. Now add 1 bottle of champagne, and 2 ponies each of brandy and Benedictine, and stir. Fresh mint is used as top decoration.

CHAMPAGNE PUNCH

(Recommended for summer; serves about 10)

Slice four fresh pineapples, put them in your punch bowl and cover with sugar. Pour over this one pint of cognac and one pint of Jamaica rum, eight ounces of Curacao and the juice of six lemons. Put a cake of ice in the bowl and then slowly pour in four quarts of champagne. Decorate with slices of fruits.

CHRISTMAS RUM PUNCH

(Cold)

Juice of four oranges
Juice of two lemons
Diced pineapple
½ cup granulated sugar
1 pony Curacao
1 small bottle Maraschino cherries
1 bottle old Jamaica or New England rum
1 bottle club soda

Place in punch bowl fruit juices, cherries and liquid of cherries; add garnishment consisting of 1 orange thinly sliced and 2 lemons ditto, and the diced pineapple. Also the sugar, Curacao and rum. Let stand for 2 hours. When due to be served, add ice (chunk) and club soda.

CLARET OR BURGUNDY CUP

To each bottle of claret or burgundy add one bottle of club soda, one glass of sherry, one pony of Triple Sec, and one pony of brandy; also the rind of one lemon cut very thin; powdered sugar to taste.

Decorate with fresh pineapple, orange, and one slice of fresh cucumber rind. Let brew a short time before serving, then add a boulder of ice and, if available, a flock of fresh mint. Fresh (or frosted-packed) raspberries and peaches are appropriate dunnage.

COLD APPLE TODDY

Roast 1 doz. apples with their skins on. Mash while hot. Add 1 lb. sugar and 2 quarts of boiling water. Then 1 quart apple brandy and 1 pint peach brandy. Cover so as not to squander aroma. And don't go sniffing at it.

When cool, strain coarsely, permitting pulp to come through. Add 1 pint sherry. Bowl with ice.

CREAM IN YOUR COFFEE

3 quarts of hot coffee, turned loose upon:

    1 quart vanilla ice cream
    ½ bottle Jamaica rum
    Bowl with ice. No décor

DIXIE PUNCH

    ½ jigger gin
    1 jigger Southern Comfort
    ½ jigger lime juice
    2 dashes Grenadine
    ½ slice of pineapple

Mix drastically in an electric mixer, without ice.

Then pour onto shaved ice in a mint julep goblet or Collins glass, decorated with pineapple and slice of orange.

FESTOONERS' HIGH TEA

    Rind of one lemon, cut thin
    5 oz. lemon juice
    2 quarts green tea, cold
Mix these well, then add:
    1 bottle whiskey or brandy
    5 oz. bouquet rum
    4 oz. Curacao
    1 bottle Angelica wine
    1 bottle American champagne or carbonated Moselle
Stir lightly and place in bowl containing berg of ice. Fruitage ad lib.

Also conducive to clambering is

FISH HOUSE PUNCH

¼ cup sugar and splash of water to dissolve. When dissolved add:

    Juice of 1 dozen lemons
    1 bottle fine old Jamaica rum
    ½ bottle brandy
    1 jigger peach brandy
    1 quart water

Let stand 2 hours in bowl with berg of ice, stirring frequently. Hard part is keeping prowlers at bay.

FLORIDA PUNCH

    1 oz. grapefruit juice
    1 oz. orange juice
    1 oz. heavy rum
    ½ oz. brandy

Shake and strain into tall glass filled with cracked ice.

FRUIT CUP

Take whatever fruit you have on hand in season, such as peaches, strawberries, plums, raspberries. Wash the fruit, slice, put in a bowl with half a cup of sugar and one cup of brandy, rye or rum. Let it stand over night and when ready to use pour into a gallon of chilled Chablis, Pouilly Fuisse or the best dry domestic white wine available. Variations: Use 1 cup sugar . . . add a quart of sparkling water and a glass of gin. The top of the bowl may be dressed with the fruits of the season.

GIN BOWL

    1 gallon dry white wine (foreign or domestic)
    1 bottle of gin
    1 cup of green tea
    3 lemons sliced

This can be stepped up considerably by the addition of one cup of heavy rum or brandy.

JEFF. DAVIS PUNCH

    1½ pints lemon juice
    3¼ pounds sugar, dissolved in water
    12 bottles claret
    1½ bottles sherry
    ½ bottle brandy
    ½ pint Jamaica rum
    1 cup Maraschino liqueur
    3 bottles ginger ale
    6 bottles mineral water or soda

Garnish with 2 lemons sliced thin; half of a cucumber sliced with peel on; one orange sliced.

If too strong, water may be added till the quantity reaches 5 gallons. Best if made 24 hours before using, adding ice, the ginger ale and mineral water just before serving.

JUBAL EARLY PUNCH

1½ gallons of lemonade
3 pints brandy
1 pint Jamaica rum
3 quarts champagne

Dissolve 1½ pounds of sugar in the lemonade before adding other ingredients. Bowl well iced.

KEUKA CUP

1 cup diced or crushed pineapple
1 orange, sliced
Juice of half a lemon
1 tablespoon Grenadine
2 teaspoons sugar
1 bottle champagne

Commingle and chill, avoiding dilution by wilted ice. Serves 6-8 diffident people or 3 greedies.

MINT JULEP, Community Style
(A lifesaver for country hosts)

Take your punch bowl and place it on a table under a tree. Next fill it half full of chipped or shaved ice. Now in a separate crock place about fifty fresh mint sprigs. Pour over these a glass of water, a glass full of rum, one-fourth pound of powdered sugar and then macerate the leaves thoroughly. When infused, pour this through a cocktail strainer, over the chipped ice. Do not permit any of the stems or mash to seep through. Next pour on two bottles of best bourbon. Now place straws around the edge of the bowl, the sort that will last a few moments. Use as many straws as you have guests. At a given signal, tell them to heave to.

NOEL ON THE NOSE

Assemble and boil together for five minutes:

½ cup sugar
¾ cup water
6 strips lemon peel
12 cloves
3-inch stick of cinnamon

Let cool and strain. Now add:

1 cup orange juice
½ cup lemon juice
1 cup juice of canned pears
1 bottle American red wine
1½ cups sparkling water

Pour over ice hunk in the punch bowl. Garnish with orange and lemon slices and cut-up canned pears.

ORANGE CUP
(For 12 people)

Juice of six oranges
2 pints carbonated water
Sweeten with sugar and put in punch bowl with
16 ounces of rum
2 ounces of Curacao
Iceberg.

PICNIC PUNCH
(Ideal for washtub and cake of ice)

1 pineapple, cut up
12 lemons, cut up
1 gallon gin
2 gallons white wine
1 pint of rum

Makes 30 picknickers *very* happy.

RED WINE CUP

1 bottle of claret or burgundy
1 bottle of club soda
1 wine glass of sherry
1 pony Curacao
1 pony brandy
Rind of 1 lemon, cut very thin
Smidgen of powdered sugar

Adorn with fresh pineapple, orange, fresh mint and slice of fresh cucumber rind. Let stand an hour or so for interjubilation of ingredients. Add large berg of ice when ready to serve.

REGENT PUNCH
(One gallon)

1 pint black or green tea, brewed strong
Thin-cut rinds of 4 lemons
1½ lbs. granulated sugar
Juice of 6 lemons and 6 oranges
1 pint brandy
1 pint rum
1 magnum (or 2 bottles) champagne

Put the lemon rinds into the tea while the latter is still hot, allowing them to seep together. Add the sugar. Set aside to cool.

When cold, add the lemon and orange juices, the brandy and the rum. Place in punch bowl with one or two large chunks of ice, adding the champagne immediately before serving. Garnish with orange and pineapple slices.

RUM PUNCH

Into a bowl put ½ cup granulated sugar and juice of 4 large grapefruit. Stir to dissolve the sugar and add 1 bottle of rum, 4 oz. brandy and 4 oz. of Benedictine, 2 teaspoons of bitters, and the juice of 1 lime. Stir well and add ½ nutmeg grated and the peeling of 1 lime.

SAUTERNE PUNCH

Slice some peaches and apricots (twice as many of the former), add a little brandy, cover with sugar and let stand for a few hours. When ready to serve, put the mixture in a bowl or pitcher and pour over it chilled sauterne and charged water. Ice slightly so as not to weaken the drink.

SCOTCH PUNCH

This all-purpose drink should be in any country household. It can be put down in the spring, say a gallon every week, and set to rest in the cellar, properly labeled.

The recipe was given Esquire by Howard MacAdams, who got it from his grandpappy in Scotland. It goes like this:

2 quarts of Scotch whisky
1 pint of good brandy
1 cup of green tea
Rind of six lemons
1 teaspoon of cloves
1 tablespoon of allspice
30 lumps of sugar

Seal this in a glass jug and allow to stand at least six weeks before serving. Served with ice, either cracked in the glass, or a chunk in the punch bowl, the single potion is modified.

SINCLAIR LEWIS'S FAVORITE

⅓ pint lime or lemon juice
¾ lb. of sugar dissolved in water
½ pint cognac
¼ qt. peach brandy
¼ pt. Jamaica rum
2½ pts. carbonated water

Add large piece of ice and serve from punch bowl.

TEA PUNCH

Use a pint of strong tea, a pint of sherry and a half pint of Jamaica rum. Add the juice of Maraschino cherries (a small bottle). When cold, add bits of orange and lemon peel before serving.

WHITE WINE CUP

1 bottle of white burgundy or dryish Graves, 1 bottle of club soda, 1 wine glass of sherry, a pony apiece of anisette and brandy; rind of 1 lemon; powdered sugar in moderation; thin slices of fresh pineapple; mint; ice.

PUNCHES — Hot

In most cases these warmers of the inner man can be made by the mug in the same proportions as those given for group gurgling, but where such perennial favorites as hot buttered rum and hot milk punch are involved, we've given both "bowl" and individual recipes.

AL LONG'S SPECIAL HOT TODDY

Juice of one lime
Sweeten 2 parts Drambuie, 1 part raspberry
2 oz. Scotch whisky
3 oz. boiling water

Mix and bring to boil.

ALE FLIP

Beat separately 2 egg whites and 4 yolks. Combine them, adding 4 tablespoons of moistened sugar, and ½ nutmeg grated.

Put 1 quart ale in saucepan and bring to boil. Pour into it the egg-sugar mixture, gradually, stirring as you add.

Transfer the steaming result to robust pitcher and pour back and forth rapidly between this pitcher and its twin brother, each time holding the pourer high above the receiver, till a handsome froth is attained.

Serve in mugs or large goblets. One pillow to every customer.

APPLEJACK ALGONQUIN

1 teaspoonful baked apple
1 lump sugar
1 jigger applejack

Fill glass with hot water. Sprinkle with nutmeg.

ARCHBISHOP PUNCH

Stick cloves into a good-sized orange and roast it in a warm oven. When the skin is brown cut into quarters, seed, put into a saucepan and cover with a bottle of claret. Add sugar and let it simmer on fire until hot.

ARRACK PUNCH—HOT

Into a glass mug put:
1 oz. of orange juice
1 oz. of lemon juice
1 teaspoonful sugar
1 jigger Arrack

Fill up with hot water. Stir.

Give a ball of black tea a bath in it for two or three minutes, then remove. Add a slice of pineapple.

BISHOP

Stick an orange full of cloves and roast it in front of the Yule log (or in the oven) until soft and brownish; cut it in quarters, pour over it a quart of hot port wine, and let simmer for half an hour. Serve in punch glasses. The aroma is almost as good as the flavor.

BLACK STRIPE
(Served anywhere in the tropics)

1 tablespoon of honey dissolved in hot water
½ cocktail glass of old rum

Fill glass with hot water, grate nutmeg on top.

BLUE BLAZER

1 jigger Scotch or rye
1 lump sugar
Very hot water
Set liquid on fire and pour from one glass to another
Twist of lemon peel on top

BRANDY PUNCH

Take the peel of two lemons, a pinch of cinnamon and a bit of nutmeg, mace and cloves. Add this to three quarters pound of sugar and a half pint of boiling water. Let it simmer on the fire and then strain. Now add a bottle of brandy and the juice of two lemons. Added effect is gained by setting on fire before serving.

CAFE GROG

Mix a pony of Jamaica or Bacardi rum, two lumps of sugar, a slice of lemon, a spoonful of brandy and a demi-tasse of black coffee. Heat and serve hot.

CHRISTMAS RUM PUNCH
(hot)

6 oranges
½ gallon sweet cider
1 bottle Jamaica rum, bestest
Sugar to taste
Whole cloves
Ground cinnamon and nutmeg

Stick the oranges full of cloves and bake them in the oven until they soften. Place oranges in the punch bowl, pour over them the rum and granulated sugar to taste. Set fire to rum and in a few minutes add the cider slowly to extinguish the flame. Stir in cinnamon and nutmeg, and keep the mixture hot.

EGGNOG
(For Solo Drinking)

Open fresh egg into large glass. Add two teaspoonfuls powdered sugar. Add small amount of milk and fill glass with very hot rum. Mix well and add dash Angostura bitters.

ENGLISH CHRISTMAS PUNCH

Take two bottles of good red wine, add one quart of strong tea, and the juice of one lemon and one orange. Heat thoroughly and just before serving, supporting on irons across the bowl two pounds of sugar soaked in rum. Light the rum and as the flame dies add the rest of the bottle of rum.

FLAMES OVER JERSEY

1 qt. apple brandy
1 cup sugar
1 oz. to 1 jigger Angostura bitters
Lemon peels, to taste

Set afire and stir, with blue flames flickering (lights more easily if warmed first). Then douse flames with 1 quart boiling water, stir and serve pronto in glass or silver mugware.

GLOW WINE

2 bottles claret or other red wine
1 cup granulated sugar
6 cloves
Peel of ½ lemon
Piece of cinnamon

Bring to boiling point and serve at once with a slice of orange.

GLUEHWEIN

Boil in an earthen jug one glass of good claret or burgundy. (Never use a fortified wine.) In the pot put about 3 inches of a cinnamon stick, 1 clove, 3 lumps of sugar, 1 slice of orange peel and 1 slice of lemon peel. If a quantity is made it is better, allowing the earthen jug to stand on a slow fire and brought to near boiling point slowly.

GUARDSMAN'S PUNCH
(For Six or so)

1 ounce of port wine
1 pint of fresh green tea
4 ounces of sugar
Peel of one lemon
1 glass of brandy
1 bottle of Scotch whisky

Heat and serve piping hot.

HOT BRANDY

1 teaspoon sugar, dissolved in boiling water
1 wineglass brandy

Fill ⅔ with boiling water. Grate nutmeg on top.

HOT BUTTERED RUM
(Bowl)

1 qt. New England rum
3 qts. sweet cider
1 cup brown sugar
Enough butter to dapple the surface
1 cup boiling water

Dissolve sugar in 1 cup boiling water, add cider and heat to boil, then add rum. Butter. Serve piping in punch bowl, flurried with ground cinnamon.

"Is the groom ready?"

HOT BUTTERED RUM
(Individual)

Dissolve 1 or 2 lumps of sugar in a little hot water, add a wineglassful of rum, a piece of butter the size of a small walnut, and fill the mug or glass with hot water. Sprinkle nutmeg on top. (A teaspoon of spices such as cinnamon and cloves may be added to this mixture, or you might garnish with clove-studded lemon.)

HOT BUTTERED TODDY

Bestow in deserving mug:
- 1 hooker doggonedest best whisky
- 1 ounce orange juice
- 1 teaspoonful sugar

Fill up with hot water. Stir inhalingly. Add about a quarter of a pat of butter as a floater on top.

HOT LOCOMOTIVE
- 1 yolk egg
- ½ tablespoon sugar
- 1 pony honey

Stir these well with a spoon. Add:
- ½ pony Curacao
- 1½ wineglass burgundy or claret

Place over fire until boiling. Pour from cooking dish to mug several times. Add slice lemon and little cinnamon.

HOT MILK PUNCH — 1
- 1 tablespoon sugar
- ¼ wineglass rum
- ¾ wineglass brandy

Stir in large glass and fill with hot milk. Add nutmeg.

HOT MILK PUNCH — 2
- Half wineglass of rum
- Half wineglass brandy

Add spoonful powdered sugar. Mix well and pour into large glass. Fill glass with very hot milk. Add few grains nutmeg.

HOT MILK PUNCH — 3
- 1 teaspoon powdered sugar
- 1 pony Curacao
- Dash of orange juice
- Measure of rum

Mix in highball glass, fill with very hot milk and add a slice of orange and a few grains of nutmeg.

HOT MINT BURGUNDY DELIGHT
- 6 fresh crisp mint leaves
- 1 piece lemon peel
- 1 tablespoon sugar
- 3 oz. (or 3 tablespoons) burgundy

Muddle well together and add a few drops of Maraschino cherry juice syrup, one small stick of cinnamon and two whole cloves. Then add 3 oz. or 3 tablespoons of burgundy and an equal amount of hot water. Stir and serve.

HOT IRISH PUNCH
(Bowl)
- 12 lumps sugar
- 2 lemons
- 1 bottle Irish whisky
- Cinnamon
- Cloves
- Boiling water

Rub sugar lumps on lemon rinds. Then squeeze lemons and muddle sugar in lemon juice. Add whisky, cinnamon, cloves and boiling water to dilute as per own judgment.

HOT IRISH PUNCH
(Individual)

Dissolve 2 lumps of sugar in a little hot water in large glass. Add small amount of lemon juice, and one wine glass Irish whisky. Fill glass with hot water and stir well. Add nutmeg and slice of lemon.

HOT RUM
- Dissolve 2 lumps sugar in hot whisky glass with a small amount of hot water
- 1 wineglass dark rum
- ½ lemon (juice)

Fill glass with hot water and sprinkle cinnamon on top

HOT RUM PUNCH
- 1 pt. Puerto Rico rum
- ½ pt. cognac
- ½ wineglass Kümmel
- ½ wineglass Benedictine
- 1 lemon or lime peel
- 1 orange peel
- 1 sliced orange or grapefruit
- 1 sliced lemon or lime
- Sugar to taste

Put all in bowl, add 3 pts. boiling water. Stir well and serve.

HOT SCOTCH
- 1 or 2 lumps of sugar
- Dissolve in hot whisky glass with a little hot water
- 1 wineglass of Scotch whisky
- Lemon peel

Fill glass with hot water, stir and add nutmeg.

HOT TODDY
(Bowl)
- 1 quart rye, bourbon, Scotch, apple brandy or grape brandy
- 2 quarts boiling water
- Clove-studded lemon slices
- Bits of stick cinnamon
- Sugar to taste

Pour boiling water over spiced and sugared liquor, stir then serve steaming hot with one of the lemon slices in each drink.

HOT TODDY
(Individual)

Mix double-shot of favorite whisky or brandy with 1 teaspoon (or less) sugar. Fill glass with hot water and garnish with clove-studded lemon slice and bits of stick cinnamon.

HOT WINE PUNCH

Boil three spoonfuls of sugar in a half pint of water, add six cloves, three small pieces of stick cinnamon, rind of whole lemon cut very thin. When this comes to a boil, add one bottle of good claret or burgundy and serve piping hot.

HOT SPICED WINE

Put a bottle of good American burgundy or claret, without uncorking, into a deep pot of water atop a fire. Let it heat up, but don't let it actually boil, rescuing bottle when on the verge. Uncork and pour into preheated pitcher. Add hot syrup made with sugar and water, spiced as desired. Toss in sliced (or halved) lemons and oranges and any other flavorful cargo that occurs to you. Serve in glass mugs with a stick of cinnamon in each.

In instances where more intensive grape glow is required, a bottle of brandy is substituted for the wine, with 1½ quarts of water as dilutor. Where party opinion is stalemated on the question of Wine vs. Brandy, the solution is Hot Wine *with* Brandy — the brandy inserted to the extent of 3 ponies per bottle of wine; spices and décor same as in Hot Spiced Wine. The only hard and fast rule is: Never let the wine or spirits boil.

JAMAICAN HOT TEA PUNCH

1 pint voluptuous bodied bouquet rum
1 pint best brandy
2 oranges, sliced
1 lemon (or lime), sliced
3 pints hot tea, freshly brewed
Sugar to taste

Mix these in large metal pot on stove or in front of Yule fireplace. Mull by plunging in a red-hot poker as a stirrer. Makes six generous drinks, preferably served in jorums.

LAMB'S WOOL
(A corruption of "al maes abhal" ancient term for a harvest holiday, Nov. 1.)

Put six baked apples in a large dish. Cut or break apples so that their pulp is exposed. Pour over these one quart of hot ale. Sugar to taste and add ginger and nutmeg in small quantities.

MARCIA DELANO'S NORTHERN

1 tablespoon sugar
1 egg
Beat till stiff
½ glass Puerto Rico rum
¼ glass brandy

Fill glass with boiling water. Stir and serve with grated nutmeg on top.

MARTINIQUE MILK PUNCH

Bring a quart of grade A milk almost to the boiling point. Take from fire and add the yolks of three eggs. Beat well, then add four tablespoons of sugar, and one-quarter teaspoon of cinnamon, nutmeg and vanilla. Next add the peel of one lemon. Add one glass of rum and serve while still hot.

MULLED ALE

Heat an iron poker till red-hot; immerse it slowly in a mug (preferably pewter) of ale, taking care not to cause an overflow.

MULLED WINE

1 pint Burgundy or Claret, and extra glass of same
½ nutmeg
Sugar to taste
Yolks of 4 eggs

Grate nutmeg into pint of wine; sweeten to taste. Place on fire and bring to boil, then set aside for the moment.

Beat and strain the egg-yolks, adding to them the glass of *cold* wine; then mix the result gradually with the *hot* spiced wine and pour back and forth half a dozen times.

Put total mixture on the fire and heat slowly till piping and thick. Ladle it up and down.

Serve in mugs with laths of toast on the side.

MULLED WINE WITH EGGS

Beat separately the whites and yolks of a dozen eggs. Pour two bottles of red wine into a saucepan thinning with half amount of water. Just before it comes to a boil, mix the whites and yolks together and stir them slowly into the hot wine. Serve from a pitcher with nutmeg grated on top.

NEGRITA GROG

¼ brandy
¼ rum
¼ sugar
¼ strong tea

Add a small glass Curacao, mix well, then pour into a large glass until it is half full. Fill the glass with hot water, slice of lemon on top.

NEGUS — 1

Pour a pint of port wine into a bowl and add ten lumps of sugar that have been rubbed on a lemon rind. Add the juice of one lemon. A small pinch of nutmeg. Now add a quart of boiling water and serve while hot.

NEGUS — 2
(Stronger)

Pare off yellow rind of one lemon in thin strips. Put into double boiler with juice of same, two tablespoons of sugar, and one bottle of port wine. Heat, stirring until sugar is dissolved. When hot, add one cup boiling water and strain into preheated pitcher. Pour into glasses or cups with or without a flick of nutmeg.

Serves a dozen unless really thirsty.

NIGHT CAP

Beat up a yolk of a fresh egg, add pony of anisette, one pony orange Curacao, one pony of brandy. Add hot water and leave a call for 2 o'clock.

OLD CASTLE PUNCH

Take a granite saucepan and melt two pounds of loaf sugar in one quart of water, letting the mixture come to a boil. Now reduce the heat under the pan and add two bottles of Rhine wine, not permitting the mixture to boil. Soak a lump of sugar in a silver spoon and set it afire holding it over the pan. Pour gradually over the sugar a pint of good rum. Serve very hot as it comes off the fire.

REGENT'S PUNCH

Take two glasses of white wine and add one glass of Madeira and a half glass of rum. Mix this with one pint of very hot tea.

RUM FLIP
(For British Sailors)

1 egg
½ tablespoon powdered sugar
1 glass of rum, brandy, port wine, sherry or whisky

Heat well, stirring constantly.

SACK POSSET
(A Two-Pot Circus)

Introduce to each other in a saucepan:
½ pint sherry (not "cooking" sherry)
½ pint ale

Slowly bring to a boil.

Meanwhile, in another saucepan, similarly heat up a quart of milk.

Pour the boiling milk gradually into the sherry and ale. Sweeten to taste. Add grated nutmeg.

Transfer to preheated dish or jug, equipped with a cover, and stand near fire for two or three hours. Quaff in mugs, preferably of the Toby type.

SANO GROG

Into a highball glass put a teaspoonful of powdered sugar, a pony of whisky, a pony of Curacao, a pony of Jamaica or Bacardi rum. Add three times the quantity of boiling water. Serve with a slice of lemon on top.

SKI JUMPER'S THÉ DANSANT

1 pint strong hot green tea
Juice of 4 lemons and 6 oranges
½ pound granulated sugar, stirred till dissolved
1 wineglass Curacao or Triple Sec
1 bottle rum, heated

Serve hot and watch your slaloms.

SKIPPER'S PARTICULAR

1 pint Jamaica rum
½ pint cognac
2 ounces Kümmel
2 ounces Benedictine
Rind of 1 lemon
Ditto of 1 orange
3 pints of piping hot water
Sugar as you please

SOLDIERS' CAMPING PUNCH

1 large kettle boiled strong coffee
4 pounds lump sugar
4 bottles brandy
2 bottles Jamaica rum

Pour brandy and rum over sugar and place over fire until sugar is dissolved. Add to coffee mixture and stir well.

SUN VALLEY

Heat a quart of thick cream almost to the boiling point, add two tablespoons of powdered sugar. Beat the yolks of four fresh eggs with a little milk and add this to the cream. Now add a large glass of rum (Jamaica type) and stir thoroughly. Serve in cups.

TOM AND JERRY

Take as many eggs as persons served. Beat up the whites and yolks separately. Add one teaspoonful of granulated sugar for each egg and mix whites with yolks. When ready to serve, take two tablespoons of this batter and put in a large mug or tumbler. Now add one pony of brandy and one pony of Jamaica rum, stirring constantly to avoid curdling. Fill to the top with hot water or hot milk and stir until smooth. Usually a little grated nutmeg is sprinkled on top.

(NOTE: Some, finding water too thin and milk too rich and filling, use half hot milk, half boiling water. Vary the proportions of rum and brandy, emphasizing one or the other, or try it with bourbon and brandy, bourbon alone or bourbon and rum.)

WHISKY PUNCH

One pint of whisky and two glasses of brandy are mixed with the juice and peel of one lemon. Then add one wineglass of boiling ale. Stir in one-half pound of powdered sugar and a quart of boiling water.

ZERO NIGHT PUNCH
(6 to 8 Persons)

½ cup granulated sugar
1 quart milk
2 whole lemon peels, pared very thin

Place in double boiler, and let come to a boil. Infuse 5 or 6 tea bags for 1 or 1½ minutes. Remove bags and add 10 oz. apple brandy. Boil for 2 or 3 minutes, and serve very hot with a little nutmeg on the top.

THOMAS AND JEREMIAH

Into 1 big tall glass, pour 1½ jiggers of rum — white preferred. Add a touch of lime or lemon juice (preferably lime). Add brown sugar to taste. Fill with hot cider.

WASSAIL BOWL

Put one pound of sugar in a bowl and over this pour three quarts of beer and four glasses of sherry. Add small amount of nutmeg and ginger and float a sliced lemon on top.

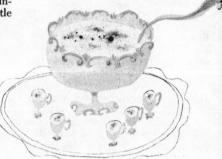

Egg=Nog
SEASONED TIPPLING

To tradition-steeped Christmas celebrants, the season would be bleak unless thickly upholstered with Eggnog. Basically eggs, sugar, liquors, milk and cream, served very cold in glass cups, the eggnog is sometimes underpinned with rye or bourbon, sometimes with brandy and rum. Try these, mixing up 2-egg batches until your experiments have convinced you of the best method:

VIRGINIA EGGNOG

One dozen eggs of the freshest. Separate. Put whites aside for the moment. Beat yolks strenuously. While still beating, slowly add 12 tablespoons of granulated sugar and continue *à tempo* till sugar is entirely dissolved. Slowly pour in 1 generous pint *cognac*, still stirring the while. Follow with ½ pint (on the slim side) *full-bodied rum*. (The completed concoction should not taste of rum-in-the-nude. In other words, the rum must not boss the mixture. If it is very pungent, pull down the rum content and increase the cognac. In any case, the quality of the cognac will determine the character of the brew. So have your cognac good!) Pouring the liquor into the yolks has the effect of cooking them more lovingly than any stove could. Now take 1 pint milk and ½ pint heavy cream. (Cream may be whipped, but this makes the result a bit rich, so to some tastes plain cream is preferable.) Stir in milk and cream. Clean off egg-beating equipment and go at the whites till they will stand without hitching. Fold the whites into the general mixture. Then stir in 1 grated nutmeg. If outcome is too sweet to suit taste, extra brandy may now be added till it fits. Will serve 10 to 12 people. For open-house purposes, you would need double, triple, or quadruple this amount. For convenience's sake, some people make this eggnog the day before the party and put it in the refrigerator till wanted. Parked there—or even on the pantry window sill—it will keep perfectly for several days if air-tight glass jars are used.

BALTIMORE EGGNOG

Take six eggs (fresh). Beat the yolks and whites separately. Beat until very light. Add ¼ pound of sugar to whites and ¼ pound of sugar to yolks. Beat again. Stir into the yolks one quart of rich milk and one quart of rich cream. Then stir in very slowly ¾ pint of *Old New England rum*, or *Jamaica rum* (a good heavy rum is best) and ¾ pint of good brandy. Whiskey may be used if desired, but real Maryland eggnog never has whiskey in it. Add ½ grated nutmeg and about two dozen whole cloves. Let stand in the refrigerator for about four hours before serving. When ready to serve, shake well to mix the milk and cream, which have a habit of separating.

ANOTHER BALTIMORE EGGNOG

One-fifth bottle *cognac,* one pint *Jamaica rum,* one-half pint *apple brandy,* one-half pint *peach brandy,* two dozen eggs, two pounds powdered sugar, three and a half quarts of milk (or three quarts milk, one quart cream), one pint of thick cream. Beat the yolks of eggs until light, add liquors, starting with cognac, until the eggs are cooked. Next add sugar, beating it in, then the milk. Let stand in refrigerator or on cake of ice for 6 hours—or, if you're in a hurry, until cold. When ready to serve fold in the whites stiffly beaten.

AND STILL ANOTHER

(This one with Bourbon)

1 doz. fresh eggs
1 doz. tablespoons granulated sugar
1 pint best bourbon whiskey
1 pint heavy-bodied bouquet rum
1 wineglass peach cordial
1 quart milk
1 quart cream
Grated nutmeg

Segregate egg yolks, beat them and add to them the sugar, working it in gradually; then half of the milk. Still stirring, insert the whiskey and the rum. Let stand 15 minutes or so to give these elements a chance to get well acquainted; then add the other half of the milk, and also the cream, likewise the peach cordial.
The whites of the eggs which have undergone a separate lashing till stiff, are now neatly folded into the mixture, which gets a light shower of nutmeg as a send-off.

CALIFORNIA EGGNOG

Take six fresh eggs and beat the yolks and the whites separately, particularly the yolks. Into the yolks, after having been beaten some time, beat six tablespoons of sugar till smooth, six tablespoons of whiskey and one-half teaspoon of grated nutmeg. Then add the beaten whites. After adding the whites, add the following: six tablespoons brandy, three tablespoons rum.
When this is all beaten together, add one-half pint cream whipped stiff. This makes twelve glasses.

HOLIDAY EGGNOG

Take six fresh eggs and beat the yolks and the whites separately. Add ½ cup of granulated sugar to the yolks, beating it in and add ¼ cup sugar to the whites after they have been beaten. Stir into the yolks one pint of rich cream and one pint of milk. Then stir in slowly one pint of good *rye, bourbon* or *brandy* and the one ounce of good heavy *rum.* Set aside for three or four hours so that the eggs will cook in the whiskey. When ready to serve, beat the whites in lightly and sprinkle nutmeg on top if desired. For serving, place in a container of ice.

OLD VIRGINIA EGGNOG

(Thick)

12 eggs, new born
2¼ cups granulated sugar
1 quart finest brandy
1 pint Jamaica rum, rich and ripe
1 gallon heavy cream

Beat the 12 yolks relentlessly, adding the granulated sugar, then alternate shots of the brandy and rum till full amounts are incorporated. Then three-fourths of the heavy cream and, foldingly, half of the egg whites, prebeaten in a side dish. Whereupon, beat up other half of egg whites stiffer than stiff, adding to them the cup of powdered sugar, plus (lightly stirred in) the other quart of cream, and fold this side show into the main show. Twelve hours' rest in a cool place of safety will be beneficial. Partakers will need spoons as this calls for spadework.

FROZEN EGGNOG

(As served in New York's Algonquin)

12 egg yolks
1 pound sugar
1 gallon cream, whipped
1 pint brandy
1 pint Jamaica rum

Beat the egg yolks very light and add the sugar, then the whipped cream. Freeze till firm. Then add the brandy and rum and turn freezer rapidly a few times to mix well. Eat with holiday cake. Serves 24.

RAPPAHANNOCK EGGNOG

1 doz. egg yolks (no whites used at all)
12 even. tablespoons pulverized sugar
3 pints bouquet bourbon whiskey
3 wineglasses peach brandy
2 wineglasses full-bodied rum with plenty of "nose" to it
3 pints milk
1 pint whipped cream

Beat yolks in a kitchen bowl for 30 minutes. (An electric mixer is a good reprieve.) Add the sugar gradually, with no letup; then, shot by shot, the 3 liquors, followed by the milk. Last of all, the whipped cream. If the latter isn't interpolated until the next day, so much the grander.

LEONINE EGGNOG

12 eggs, recently from Mrs. Cluck
12 level tablespoons granulated sugar
3 pints bouquet bourbon (rye if you prefer)
1 quart milk
1 pint heavy cream
Nutmeg

Crack eggs, separating yolks from whites. Setting latter aside for the nonce, go at yolks with an egg-beater, plying it furiously. Gradually add the sugar, beating it in till entirely dissolved. Now enters the whiskey, poured slowly and stirred, its action on yolks being equivalent to a gentle cooking. Then the milk, followed by the cream (whipped cream if you prefer extra richness), likewise stirred in.

Clean off egg-beater and tackle the whites till they stand without flinching. Fold them into the general mixture. Stir in one grated nutmeg. Will serve 10 to 12 people. If it's the whipped cream version, they'll need spoons.

The only thing more horrible than a really first-rate hangover—one with long, matted hair and a guttural voice—is the hangover remedy which well-meaning friends force down your gullet the morning after. Although the medical profession in general seems to take the attitude that you've made your own hangover so you're welcome to groan in it, one heroic group of physicians has come up with these pointers:

1. Much of your morning-after misery is due to the anesthetizing after-effects of ethyl alcohol; you and your organs are still partially paralyzed. Your sleeping stomach should be given TIME to get back in working condition before you throw ice-water, coffee, Hair of the Dog or *anything* into it. Thus, the best thing to "take" for a hangover is *NOTHING*.

2. Though your tongue is parched and your mouth tastes as if you have been sitting up all night licking Lithuanian postage stamps, don't drink ice-water. If your mouth is so dry it is un-

bearable, simply wash it out with water. Later, if you must go through the motions of sitting at the breakfast table, sip a half cup of *warm* water—*slowly.*

3. Upon arising, try to force yourself to do a little mild exercising—or, if that seems impossible, stand at the open window and breathe deeply as many times as you can stand it. An oxygen tent is the one real aid to a hangover, but since so few homes are equipped with oxygen tents these days deep breathing will serve as a substitute.

4. Only when you begin to feel actually hungry, meaning that your gastric juices are beginning to function again, it is safe to take an alkalizing salt or a laxative.

5. And *then* what you need is a pick-me-up composed of (1) something to give your stomach a kick in the pants and (2) something easily digestible for nourishment. No. 1 is the reason why so many "remedies" contain tabasco, bitters or absinthe. No. 2 explains raw eggs, the most digestible food on the market. Since The Hair of the Dog courts alcoholism, we recommend the non-alcoholic Prairie Oyster school, or the mild beer varieties of "cures." But inasmuch as all this requires a great deal of will-power and is largely a matter of conjecture anyway, the following list includes more potent pick-ups.

Incidentally, prevention is always more successful than cure. Short of sane drinking, here's the best preventive Esky knows: before falling into your spinning bed, dose yourself thoroughly with soda or any of the commercial alkalizing salts.

BARBATOGE
Fill a glass with champagne; add a teaspoonful of brandy and a dash of Curacao.

BLACK VELVET
Half champagne, half stout.

BUILDER-UPPER
In a tall glass filled with ice, insert a long lemon peel — as you would for a Horse's Neck — hooking one end over the edge of the glass. Then put in 2 parts brandy to 1 part Benedictine and fill the glass with ginger ale.

CRIMSON CRINGE
Plain gin with a dash of Grenadine!

FERNET BRANCA
This is a thick, black bitters with quinine in it. Sometimes it is added to rye, with a few dashes of Pernod and a lump of ice in an Old-fashioned glass.

FLIPPANT HEN
An egg in a short glass of beer.

PICK-ME-UP
½ Dubonnet
½ cognac
⅓ Anisette
Lemon peel
White of egg
Cracked ice
Shake well, strain and be picked up.

PICON BITTERS
Picon bitters dashed into lime juice.

PORTO FLIP
4 oz. port wine
1 raw egg
1 oz. thick cream
Dash of Benedictine
Shake with cracked ice; strain into wineglass. Sprinkle with nutmeg.

PRAIRIE OYSTER
1 teaspoon Worcestershire Sauce
Tiny drop Tabasco
1 raw egg
Sprinkling of salt and pepper
Down at a gulp.

SEA CAPTAIN'S SPECIAL
(Distilled dynamite which may beg the question by putting your hangover off — until tomorrow.)
In an Old-fashioned glass, place half a lump of sugar and douse it with Angostura. Add 1½ jiggers of rye and 1 lump of ice. Fill the glass with champagne. Top it off with 2 dashes absinthe.

SPIRIT OF '76
Absinthe (Pernod) and the white of bromo.

SUISETTE
Absinthe (Pernod) and the white of an egg.

Tipples for Teetotalers

SOFT . . . AND EASY

The secret of entertaining non-drinkers lies in attitude rather than latitude. The only drink-equipment you need is a fruit juice for cocktail-time, a soft drink for hard-drinking-time; but to be a perfect host you need some think-equipment which is sometimes as rare as the guest who doesn't drink.

Think how *you* would feel if, by a great surge of will power, you managed to go on the wagon—then were constantly ridiculed or urged to have "just one" by well-meaning hosts. Then, when *you're* doing the honors, make it a point never to make a point of abstinence.

Include "tomato juice" or the like just as you include sherry in that list you rattle off in your "What'll you have?" speech—so that non-drinkers will know at the outset that their "foibles" are not going to inconvenience you. Then restrain yourself from comment (including the I-wish-I-had-your-courage sort of false admiration) as you pass the puerile potion. There *are* teetotalers who are also crusaders, but you're not likely to entertain many of them; there *are* abstainers who smugly revel in praise of their will power, but they're just the ones who'll put a guilt-edge on other guests if you let them get started.

So, for the good of the party, make no ado about those who do not drink. Have "dry" drinks available, serve them in glasses like those that pack punch for the other guests, and change the subject.

For the special case, ulcers, for instance, milk is usually in order: and that means just plain milk, without a dash of sympathy. A glass of milk on a tray of Martinis can seldom enter the room without bringing forth the "little mother" type of so-called humorous remarks —but if you get into the act with a dead-pan, "Here's your milk punch," at least you leave it up to the ulcerous unfortunate as to whether or not he wants to give his case history. Even if he's hardened to the razzing, he'll appreciate your considerate try to spare him his 10,000th discussion on Ulcers and How I Got One.

Aside from fruit juices, ginger ale, cola and other soda pops, about the only classic teetotaler's tipple you're likely to need is the . . .

HORSE'S NECK

Peel the whole rind of a lemon, in one spiraling piece. Place it in a tumbler, with one end hanging over the top. Add 2 cubes of ice, a dash of bitters, then fill the tumbler with ginger ale.

MOM COLLINS

When your other guests are drinking Toms, make the same for your dry friend — leaving out only the gin!

...and Be Merry

**HOW TO BE HAPPY
THOUGH HOST**

To good food and good drink add one more element, and your reputation as a host is assured. The element: effortless hospitality. Its ingredients: on the following pages.

"Who wants to play 'spin the bottle'?"

THE SOBER DUTY OF A HOST

The mark of a perfect host is that he has a good time at his own party — but not *too* good. For though he seems to be just another guest, he is really very busy staying sober enough to continue his subtle hosting.

Every man should determine early in life how much liquor he can carry without losing his poise, equilibrium, reputation and civil liberties — but knowledge of his capacity-quotient is particularly important to a host. The amount, of course, is quite variable — depending on the type of liquor, the hour of your last meal, your metabolism and even your mood. Some men can handle with poise and even distinction a half-dozen whiskey-and-sodas, while three martinis impel them to pinch the hostess. Others can drink over a half-dozen martinis, but are liable to be left for dead after three whiskey-and-sodas. The only way to determine how much *you* can drink of what, under any given conditions, is by experimentation. But experiment at other people's parties! When you're a host, watch for your own danger-signals with double care.

You've had a few if . . .

You find yourself thinking up forceful rebuttals for an argument you lost the other day, an argument which, at the time, didn't seem particularly important.

You hold eight diamonds to the ten, jack, a singleton spade and four small clubs and bid one heart, figuring that, although you are vulnerable, a psychic bid, in an effort to save rubber, is a fine strategic move.

There is a fly in your drink, but instead of taking the trouble to remove it, you quaff down your drink, merely taking the precaution to avoid consuming the fly in the process.

The first thing you get when you switch on the radio is a jazz orchestra. You remark that they are playing a swell tune. It happens to be one which you have heard five or six times previously without being impressed.

[185]

You start arguing politics, and make dogmatic statements about economics and sociology although you are by nature a cautious person who customarily qualifies all statements in such a fashion that you always have an out.

You tell that story in mixed company — the one which, when you first heard it, seemed slightly dubious for such an occasion.

It is just before dinner, and your passing dividends have just emptied the shaker. You fail to catch a question from the lady on the sofa next to you because you are wondering if you can get out to the kitchen to mix another batch before dinner.

You hold forth at some length on various celebrities you have encountered lately although you are chronically a person who is impressed by few of them and who actively dislikes the majority.

Dancing with a girl twenty years your junior you try that step which you have seen her Yale escort execute with such precision — and you aren't displeased with the result.

You think it might be fun to send a telegram to somebody.

You sit down at the piano, reel off a couple of tunes, and feel that you are going pretty well. You are delighted when somebody makes a request.

You are in the process of mixing another Tom Collins for yourself. It seems like too much trouble to bother with the lemon squeezer, so you seize half a lemon between your fingers, and squeeze a few drops of juice into your glass. The result tastes all right, although, when starting fresh, you customarily use all the juice you can get out of a whole lemon.

IS THERE A DRUNK IN THE HOUSE?

Since your guests may not be as careful as you to stay on the sober side, you'd best bone up on How to Handle a Drunk on the Premises. Your object, whenever a drunken guest begins to annoy the rest of the party, is to lure the lush into a bedroom and get him to take a nap. "Let's have a drink in here" or "I must speak to you alone" are the approaches most likely to succeed. Thereafter, the use of Mickey Finns is not particularly recommended; you can often achieve the same effect with bed or chair combined with just one more very strong slug.

"All right, everybody now—sing!"

S'PRISE!

Liquor is quicker, but plain old-fashioned hospitality also sets your guests at ease and assures their enjoyment of an evening in your home. Hospitality seems to be composed of two parts sincerity and one part preparedness. In the home of the congenitally good host, no one is ever unexpected. An Emergency Shelf in your pantry should be always equipped to provide a little something for drop-in callers to munch on. The bar is always ready with something to sip. But, most important of all, the host is always ready to pretend he is delighted to have the company of his guests.

Of course, it ain't necessarily so. And sometimes enough is enough. It may not be Emily Post-ish, but in this busy day it's good sense to know how and when a good host is a poor host. Since the beauty of hospitality is its sincerity, the minute you start wishing people would go home it's time they did. So here are a few ways to . . .

SPEED THE PARTING GUEST

(If you have home movies, you need read no further; just threaten to show them and you'll show even the genus spongae the way to go home.)

1. Turn to your wife or straight-man and say, "C'mon, c'mon, let's be getting on home so these people can get some sleep." Then look honestly embarrassed when said wife reminds you, "Why, we are at home, silly."

2. When you've planned an evening of quiet or letter-writing and the doorbell rings, put on your hat and coat before you answer the door. "Why hello, hello! Gee, I wish you had let me know you were coming over; I'm already late for such and such. I was just leaving; can't I drop you somewhere?"

3. After an uninvited house guest has taken complete charge of your household, rearranged your furniture, run up a cross-country phone bill, charged all his laundry and cleaning to you, killed your dog with cakes and candy . . . there's only one way to get rid of him.

Tell him you're moving, have all the furniture loaded on a big red van and tell the driver to keep driving the furniture around the block until your guest has left. This may cost you $275.67, but it will save you a nervous breakdown.

4. When your cocktail guests have stayed long past the dinner hour, when you're sick of cigarette smoke and gags that don't sound so side-splitting any more, make sure that there's an adequate liquid supply on hand, announce that you're late for your dinner date, and just go out into the night. Not very cordial, but often the only tactics to adopt unless you're willing to have your cocktail party turned into a supper party and perhaps even a breakfast.

5. Even before the over-staying guest finishes his statement, *agree* — instantly, uncharacteristically and with only a slightly impatient tone in your "yes, yes."

6. Fix the radio: "You don't mind? I've been meaning to do this for weeks." Or, better still, fix the clock and keep asking what time it is. Even if the ruse fails, the evening will not have been wasted — provided, of course, that clock or radio *needs* fixing.

7. Arrange with your dog to demand to be taken out, so you can explain, smiling weakly, "We always walk the dog just before bed-time; guess he thinks I've forgotten him." With appropriate "There-there-Duke—we'll go out soon's" in the dog's direction, of course.

BE PREPARED

When your guests *are* expected, and of course welcome, you'll enjoy the gathering more yourself if you make sure that everything is in readiness before your guests arrive. Cooking underway, table set, ice and liquor ready, ash trays out, canapes ready to serve, etc. It's usually safest to dress first, finish your last-minute chores later, in case anyone arrives early; then you'll at least *appear* to be ready.

Once the party has officially begun, your major job is to keep it from breaking up into cliques or settling down into polite boredom. For a good start, provide your guests with a conversational opening the very moment you introduce them; don't settle for "Miss Jones, this is Mr. Collins," but add something like "Tom has just come back from Washington, Jane. He can probably bring you up to date on your old hangouts." From there, of course, Mr. Collins has to find out why Miss Jones should be so familiar with Washington night-life, and Miss Jones must ask about his trip. Before they finish playing "do-you-know," they'll be old friends.

If one of your guests is shy or a stranger or both, draft him or her as your assistant. When she has something to pass or to do, the shy girl will be forced out of her corner and made to feel a part of the group in spite of herself. The same technique sometimes works in breaking up cliques: you can call one or two people away from a closed group, put them to doing some small thing like picking out the next records to be played, and then introduce new people to the old group.

Incidentally, as host you yourself should avoid being caught in a long discussion or an entrenched circle. But unlike the guests, whom you must sometimes rescue from monologuists or drunks, you can always break away if necessary with a simple "Excuse me. Be back as soon as I can." Be as much of a free agent as you can, rushing in where a host's soothing words or a change of subject seems indicated.

And then there's the classic trick for causing guests to circulate: put the food at one end of the room and the drink at the other.

GOOD TALK

Whatever the sort of gathering in your home, the major entertainment will very likely be conversation. As a mere human being, of course, you should know the ins and outs of good conversation. As a host, such knowledge is essential, for one of your jobs is to steer the talk. You will, of course, make sure that the conversation at no time excludes any one of your guests — the comparative stranger who doesn't know the people under discussion, say, or the athlete who is quite naturally fidgeting after prolonged conversation about art. You will create openings for the shy, switch subjects where necessary to bring the talk into line with one quiet guest's background, squelch shoptalk when it ceases to furnish interesting tidbits for the uninitiated and becomes instead a lecture or a technical discussion. You won't let the conversation embarrass any guest; you'll soothe tempers and act as arbiter if arguments get out of hand.

For this job of steering conversation, perhaps the prime qualification is to be a good conversationalist yourself. And who is a good conversationalist?

His talk is casual, easy, varied. He rarely talks for more than three minutes at a time unless others ask questions to keep him going.

He suits his topics to his audiences. He does not drag out his personal affairs or his innermost convictions for casual acquaintances. With them he can keep up a perfect, enjoyable chatter about the weather, the caprices of Rhode Island Reds or yesterday's front-page murder. He'll talk about bridge only to those who play bridge, about a new play only to those who have seen the play. He reserves intimate conversation for intimate friends. When he tells you something, you have a feeling he thought it would interest *you*, not that he wanted to tell it to *somebody*.

His phrases are crisp, his remarks have a beginning and an end. And no rambling bypaths.

It's not easy to put a finger on his success. But this you know: when you have said good-bye you realize you have had a good time. You never emerge from his house with a worse opinion of yourself than when you entered. From him you get no insight into your faults, your ignorance. You could almost believe that he hadn't noticed the idiotic remarks you made during the talk on Italian submarines.

In retrospect you remember two things:

That he listened with brilliant intensity. It was flattering to talk in the face of such attention.

Those few wisecracks or jokes cling to your memory. You laughed when he said to the too-fertile lady novelist: "Good God, my dear woman, are you with book again?" And his answer when someone slyly accused him of being involved in a scandal: "It's very flattering but untrue. We're strictly perpendicular friends." You smiled frequently but the remarks always fitted specific cases. There was little that could be lifted from its context and repeated in another conversation.

Working toward that general goal, it would be well to remember these Eight Cardinal Sins of Conversation:

SINS, VENIAL AND MORTAL

1. "He was an old varlet."

Anyone who tosses rare, obsolete words into his conversation makes his listeners pay less attention to what he says than how he says it. But pedantry isn't the only form of conversational snobbery. Sometimes a man who did brilliantly in Professor Snitchkins' English IV chooses to say, "I ain't," "I knowed him," "I went for to see him," because these expressions sounded amusing when spoken by a rustic. Some forms of speech like some vintages of wine don't travel well.

2. "So I had a *Wiener Kaffee.*"

How many English-speaking people know what this means? How many know *corrida, Weltanschauung, oi sunetoi, dolce far niente, béguin, en papillotes, quid pro quo, Wanderjahr, flâneur?*

Foreign words unless anglicized or clearly known to the majority of educated people should be shunned. Unless the speaker wants to be considered a snob.

3. "So he said, 'Come along.' "
"And I said, 'I simply can't.' "
"And he said, 'Why not?' "
" 'Why?' I said. 'Because I made a date with Eddie.' "

Edith Wharton made the observation that good novelists use dialogue sparingly — only when it is desirable to tell the exact words spoken by a character. The same holds for conversation. Yards of dialogue can sometimes be summed up in a foot of narrative. The above phrases could better be said, "He urged me to come but I explained I had an engagement." Half the words and clearer expression.

4. "I got into New York at seven and then this man took me to dinner at the Waldorf."

Well, *what* man? It is sometimes perfect technique to keep the characters in one's conversation anonymous but references to "these people," "this friend," "somebody I know" give the conversation a curious blurred quality and make the speaker sound like a sneak.

There are two ways to introduce characters into conversation. One is to be crisply anonymous: "A friend of mine told me that . . ." (not "this friend"), a cousin of mine wanted to play tennis," "a red-headed harridan who sat next to me on the bus."

But occasionally a story should be better documented. The method, then, is to start off at the beginning:

"I had a letter to a man named George Redwood in Cleveland. The day I got there I sent the letter and the next morning he phoned, asking me to lunch with him. He's about thirty-five, unmarried. He's a lawyer, writes articles for law journals. He's a golf champ, too, so when he suggested we play at his club. . . ."

Or:

"You've heard me speak of Ted Gorham, my roommate in college. He's just busted into the movies so when I was in Hollywood I phoned him. He was having a party and invited me over. That's how I met. . . ."

It ought to be easy to decide when to introduce characters by name with a brief account of their works and achievements. In general, characters who enter a conversation briefly and casually should be left nameless. If the speaker intends to refer to them constantly they should be identified at the outset.

5. "That reminds me."

People are reminded of altogether too many things in conversation. If the talk is about the Spanish Revolution and someone is reminded that Aunt Esther's janitor is a Spaniard, the conversation is done for. Every time "that reminds me" flashes through the cerebrum, it should be followed by an examination of conscience: "I'm reminded of some-thing, yes, but has it anything to do with the subject in hand?" If the answer is no, self-control is required. If that looks dubious, the re-minded one should step up to the cocktail bar and silently repeat "that reminds me" with each sip until the attack has passed off.

6. "William Powell was in it. It started off in Singapore where he was a beachcomber. Then there was an explosion. . . ."

There must be a special compartment in hell for people who relate the plots of movies, books and plays. And in this compartment there must be a special chamber with a thermostat apparatus keeping the temperature at 3,000° Fahrenheit for those who are too sophisticated to reel off plots from beginning to end but who don't hesitate to prattle about special scenes: "There's something remarkable about the novel — *in spots*. For instance the scene where the uncle confronts his nephew with the evidences of the theft. A terrific mistral was blowing. It was laid in Nice, you see."

7. "Do you get the point?"

There's only one proper reply to people who say, "Do you get the point?" "Do you follow?" "Sure you understand what I mean?" It is "I doubt if there is any point but in any case I'm not following and of course I don't understand what you mean."

8. "I'm not boring you, am I?"

What does the speaker expect? What would he do if he got a truthful answer? The very suspicion that one is boring another ought to freeze up the tongue.

But sometimes a speaker will say, "I'm not boring you, am I?" when he knows very well he's interesting everyone in sight. The motive is sometimes nervousness, sometimes a mistaken idea of making a dramatic pause. It provides a second good reason for not asking people if you are boring them. In every company there are some individuals who don't know whether they are bored or spellbound. Suggest boredom and they'll yawn. They are the kind who would be bored by the spectacle of George Bernard Shaw eating a cannibal.

These general precepts hold good whatever the subject of conver-sation — but when you get into serious discussion you need additional rules. If you and your friends are content with cocktail-party chit-chat and aimless talk about personalities and personal experiences, skip this next section. But if you would like either to improve your own batting average in serious discussion or to use your home as a gather-ing place for friends who like large talk, the following suggestions of Mortimer Adler may prove invaluable.

"My—but these winter evenings are long!"

HOW TO TALK SENSE IN COMPANY

from an Esquire article by Mortimer J. Adler, professor at the University of Chicago and author of *How to Read a Book*.

A distinguished educator recently pointed out a paradox about our country. We have achieved wonders in mechanical communication, but human communication has been breaking down. People still gather socially, but more and more they turn to the radio or bridge; and if they talk, they tend either to talk about trivial things or, if they begin talking about serious matters, they tend to get into bitter and fruitless disputes. Yet there are rules for good conversation — rules which make discussion both pleasurable and profitable. To be able to persuade someone to see a point your way — to win his agreement by moving his mind, not by bludgeoning or intimidating him — is certainly as pleasant as winning at bridge or golf through an exercise of skill. To learn something as a result of being genuinely open to persuasion is a profitable use of conversational time.

Now the rules, even though they are "ideals," are neither hard to understand nor impossible to follow. The next time you meet with your friends and begin discussing, say, politics, why not place a copy of these rules in the hands of the coolest-headed member of the group? Appoint him chief umpire and bouncer. See if it doesn't make a difference.

An orderly conversation has a beginning, a middle and an end. The rules fall into three groups, corresponding to the three phases of discussion. First, there are the preconditions for serious conversation, without which it cannot be undertaken at all. Second, there are the rules to be followed during the course of the discussion. Third, there are the precepts that deal with its conclusion.

I. Beginning a Discussion

Pick the right occasion. There are times for small talk and times, so to speak, for big talk. A dinner party is a bad place for big talk. Whenever conversation must be larded in between other activities, such as going to the theatre and going to bed, it might just as well be trivial. You must always have plenty of time. Good talk is usually slow in getting started and long in winding up. A gathering in which many of those present are strangers is usually a small-talk group. An evening of relaxation, when most of those present are tired, is no occasion to solve the problems of the world. But when friends are gathered and they share an impulse to talk about their common problems, then serious discussion can take place.

Pick the right people. Don't try to discuss everything with everybody. Even some of your best friends may lack competence on certain subjects. Some people aren't interested in some subjects. Sometimes it isn't competence which is lacking, but the affinity of temperaments. Some people "just don't get along together." If you happen to know that Green and Robinson hate each other, keep the conversation on the weather. And be sure that everyone present is going to participate. People who whisper on the sidelines disrupt discussion as fatally as kibitzers spoil bridge.

Don't argue to win. Of course, you want to persuade, but you should also be open to persuasion. Good discussion is an *exchange*, not a blitzkrieg. You know the difference between brawling and fencing. There is the same difference between wrangling and arguing.

Don't argue for argument's sake. Don't pick an argument on every point regardless of what you really think. Don't disagree just to keep the argument going. There is no point in going on and on. Better taper off into small talk before everyone is antagonized and discussion becomes a feud.

Don't be polite. Discussions are often nipped in the bud because people don't want to quarrel. They suppose you can't argue without losing your temper. They don't want to quarrel with their friends and, if they suspect they disagree on fundamental issues, they definitely avoid serious conversation. This is an unfortunate mistake. The minor agony of examining a difference of opinion is one of the best expressions of friendship. Those who are willing to take pains in honest and forthright discussion are helping, not offending, each other. (When I say "Don't be polite," I don't mean that you should be rude. The boor who interrupts all the time ruins any conversation.)

Don't listen only to yourself. Don't sit around thinking of a bright remark with which to break in and win applause. It is not your private train of thought which matters most. If you lapse into soliloquy, you will lose track of the argument; and then, no matter how good your next idea, it is likely to be irrelevant. Of course, you may get a good idea at a moment when someone else is making a long speech. It is hard to be patient — but it is the only way to talk sense.

These rules state the preconditions of conversation. Though some of them may actually operate during its course, they really govern the mood and attitude with which you enter discussion.

II. Carrying on a Discussion

Find out what the issue is. Until the issue is clear, it is impossible to tell what points are relevant and what are not. The best way to make the issue explicit is to state it.

Take one thing at a time. This is a good rule in talking, as it is in living. Every serious problem has many angles. Our first obligation is to separate a jumble of related questions into a number of distinct issues. Deal with one at a time. Let's say you are discussing religion. That's a complicated subject, involving many questions, each with an order of points. They can't be discussed all at once. If you try, you bog down in confusion. Cover, say, the historical question about church origins before you take up the theological question about church doctrine, and that before you consider the political question about church practices.

Stick to the issue. Irrelevance is the rock on which most conversations are wrecked, and the worst of it is that, unless everyone is on the lookout for it, the victims don't realize before it's too late that they got off the course. A familiar enemy (though often an innocent one) of intelligent conversation is the man who is "reminded of a story" by something someone said. If the story is relevant — fine. But nine times out of ten it isn't.

Keep moving. After a point has been settled push on to the next one. This doesn't mean you shouldn't come back to a point if it needs reopening. But it does mean a conversation should be a progress. The man who hasn't listened attentively usually raises from the dead some point that was settled. Backing and filling is one of the mortal diseases of conversation.

Don't take things for granted. Since few conversations begin at the beginning, and something is usually taken for granted, the rules might be better stated as follows: ask your companions to grant the assumptions you are making. We frequently suspect that the other fellow is making assumptions, though precisely what they are we seldom know. We too infrequently recognize that we ourselves are also making assumptions. The best cure is for everyone to try making his own assumptions explicit and beg the others to accept them *pro tem*. Sometimes the assumption can itself be argued, but when that is not possible, because it would take you too far back, it has to be granted for the sake of argument. Otherwise, sooner or later, somebody says, "But wait a minute, Joe. What makes you think we all agree that men are equal?" And the preceding conversation is a total loss. If you see the point of this rule, you also see that all argument is either about the assumptions themselves or their consequences. I can grant your premises, and still think you have reached a wrong conclusion.

[197]

Don't disagree until you understand. Unless you can state the other fellow's position just as well as he can, you have no right to oppose him. The man who says, "Now look here, you're saying . . ." usually misstates the other fellow's position. Begin, "Let me see if I can state your position," and unless he agrees that you've done it, you can't tell him he's wrong.

Don't agree until you understand. To agree with something you don't understand is inane. We all have the tendency, at times, to say, "Uh huh," when we should be saying, "Wait a minute — I'm not sure I get you straight," or "What's your proof of that?" Most of us are too prone to suppose we understand. Moving on to the next point is important, but we oughtn't to agree just for the sake of motion, or because we are too lazy to pursue the matter.

Use arguments, not authorities. If George Washington was against entangling alliances or third terms, it may be worth mentioning. Great men have a right to our consideration. But great minds have made mistakes, and those that were right on a certain point a century ago may be wrong today. Authorities may support your position; but reason alone can make it tenable.

Don't take a vote. Just as authorities may be wrong, so a majority of your friends may, at any given moment, be wrong. Everyone in the party may disagree with you, and you may still be right. And you can be wrong even if the majority agree with you. Counting noses settles nothing except the numbers of Ayes and Nays. Voting may follow arguing, but it should never take the place of argument.

Beware of examples. "Why, I know a fellow who . . ." Everyone knows a fellow who. Examples may be helpful, but they may just as often be harmful. And the discussion starts going in circles when, after you've cited an example, everybody else cites one to prove something else. An example is like an assumption. You ought to ask permission to use it. Unless everyone sees its direct relevance, it can do no good.

Never argue about facts. You cannot settle by argument the precise size of the national debt, or how far it is by air time from New York to the Azores. If you have doubts about a fact someone has cited, express them, but don't argue. Perhaps you can stop talking long enough to find the answer in the *Britannica* or the almanac. If that cannot be done, accept the dubious fact for the purpose of discussion, or put it on ice until you can ascertain the truth about it.

Explain your disagreement. If, after you understand the other fellow's position, you still disagree, you do so for one or more of the following reasons: you think that he simply lacks knowledge of some relevant point; or that he mistakenly supposes he has knowledge when he doesn't; or that he drew the wrong conclusions from things you were willing to admit were so; or that he drew the right conclusions but didn't push them far enough. You ought to be able to tell your opponent precisely what you don't see eye to eye about. Disagreement never gives way to agreement unless the difference is located. Trying to define it helps you find out when the disagreement is only apparent, due to your divergent use of words. This happens frequently. People who are of one mind are often separated by the babel of tongues.

[198]

III. Ending the Discussion

Don't expect too much from discussion. If you engage in argument with no hope of reaching agreement, you expect too little. If you suppose agreement can always be reached, you expect too much. At one extreme, the hopeless folk suppose that everything is a matter of opinion and that one opinion is just as good as another. If everyone is entitled to his own, there's no profit in discussion, and ping-pong seems more enjoyable than conversation. At the other extreme, the overhopeful fail to distinguish between the realms of knowledge and opinion. Reasonable men can agree wherever knowledge is possible, but there are many matters about which even reasonable men can only entertain opinions.

Distinguish between theoretical and practical questions. This helps you follow the preceding rule. Whether 2 plus 2 equals 4 is what is known as a theoretical question. When you discuss problems of this sort, you should expect agreement on the truth. But when you discuss practical problems, problems which concern *what should be done in this case*, you are in the realm of opinion. Here honest, intelligent men, trying to be reasonable, may disagree.

Distinguish between principles and cases. Not all practical discussions are about what should be done *in this case*. Many times we discuss the general principles which underlie our moral, economic or political conduct. The general principles we must appeal to in arguing questions of policy are always true everywhere and for all men. Reasonable men can agree about the nature of justice; they can disagree indefinitely about whether a certain business deal was just or unjust. Arguments about *practical* principles are like theoretical disputes. We can hope to reach agreement. But in the application of those principles to particular cases, reasonable men may disagree because of different estimates of the probabilities and different judgments about the circumstances.

Don't stop with agreement. Argument is not the only form of profitable conversation. Men who agree can often help each other clarify a point by discussing it. Conversation is a useful device for exploring a theme about which there is general agreement. You may all agree that Fascism is a bad form of government and yet spend many evenings (many years, for that matter) helping each other discover the reasons why. People who stop talking when they agree seldom probe their beliefs very deeply.

Don't go on forever. Even in matters where agreement is possible, discussion sometimes reaches an impasse. After all, man is an animal, even though rational, and there always is, as William James pointed out, a certain blindness in human beings. When you see it is fruitless to go on, change the subject. If the conversation is paralyzed by the obstinacy of the opponents, let it die naturally. And don't whip a dead horse.

These three sets of rules are what might be called the technical precepts for talking sense. They direct you in the use of your mind. But these technical rules will be useless unless you can also follow the "emotional rules." Many of the technical rules, especially those which concern the preconditions of discussion, have emotional aspects. But throughout its course *reasonable* discussion is impossible if emotions run away with it.

Of course, our emotions play an important role in everything we do and say. *But they don't help us talk sense.* When you find yourself getting excited or angry during a conversation, take a trip to the water cooler. If that does not help, stand up and say, "Friends, I'm sore as a boil. I'm hitting below the belt, but I can't help it. I'm mad." It will do you good, and the rest will admire you for admitting it.

If another member of the group gets fighting mad, you have only two alternatives. Soothe him in a friendly way. If that does not work, change the subject. He's probably just as nice a fellow as you are, but someone happened to hit him in a tender spot. Get off the spot. The barkeeper's advice, "If you want to fight, you've got to fight outside," is indispensable to good conversation.

And how do you know when your emotions are getting the better of you?

First, you find yourself shouting the other fellow down. Or you stop thinking and merely repeat your claim over and over, each time with greater heat and less light.

Second, you find yourself making irrelevant references to his grandmother, his nationality, his occupation or his personal habits. All such tactics go by the name of *ad hominem* argument. It is an argument against the man, rather than against his ideas. The most exasperating form of *ad hominem* is the bedfellow argument. You say, "So you agree with Hitler," as if that necessarily made the other fellow wrong. All bad thinking and arguing is some kind of irrelevance, but the emotionally motivated type always gets personal in one way or another.

Third, you find yourself being sarcastic, or trying to get the laugh on your opponent, or baiting him by harping on unimportant mistakes he has made. All these devices are calculated to goad your opponent into losing his temper also. If he resists all your efforts, and keeps cool, he will probably enrage you further. When a discussion reaches this stage, it becomes a battle of wits in the worst sense of those words.

Fourth, you will find yourself suppressing points which you see, but which weaken your case.

Finally, you find yourself stubbornly refusing to admit what you see, namely, that you are in the wrong. By this time you have so completely lost your head you cannot remember the wise counsel that there is no point in winning an argument, or even in standing pat, when you know you're wrong. Unfortunately, you will remember it after the evening is over, when passions have cooled. If you let yourself get out of hand this way very often, you will eventually ruin your disposition.

By following these rules, and controlling your emotions in order to do so, you will find pleasure and profit in serious conversation. The better you follow them, the more pleasure and profit.

Games

THE LIFE-SAVERS

OF THE PARTY

But there comes a time in every host's life when conversation is better replaced by GAMES. When your guests know each other so well that they've nothing new to say to each other . . . when your guests are such complete strangers that they seem in dire need of an organized ice breaker . . . when your guests, friends or strangers, are of such divergent views and interests that a normal conversation may result in hopeless argument or boredom, propose a game. Here are a few suggestions, most of which can be adapted to the evening-for-two (either as a prop for the benefit of unexpected callers or as a genuine device for passing the early evening) as well as to the gang gathering.

[201]

BELOTE: THE OLD FRENCH GAME

Here's the Gin Rummy sequel for which it was necessary to go back to the days of Madame Pompadour. It moves faster than bridge and has an essence of poker. Here is a complete set of rules for Belote as presented in an ESQUIRE *article by P. C. Elston:*

Belote is played with thirty-two cards and a box of chips. You diminish the fifty-two card deck for Belote by throwing out the twos, threes, fours, fives, and sixes. Belote can be played by two, three, four, or five persons, and there is no dummy except when five play. The object is to make your contract, or to prevent your opponents from making theirs. If, after naming the trump, that side fails to fulfill its contract (to make more points than the other side), then all of the points of the one who has named the trump are scored by the other side.

POINTS: 1. All tens rank above all kings, coming just below aces. 2. In the trump suit, and in the trump suit only, jack is the high card and nine is the next. The others follow in regular order: ace, ten, king, etc. Points are scored as follows: each ace, 11; each ten, 10; each king, 4; each queen, 3; each of three jacks, 2; jack of trumps, 20; nine of trumps, 14; bonus for taking last trick, 10. Total, 162.

In addition to the 162 regular points there are "announcement" points which add excitement to the game in having luck a priority over skill. These announcement points are:

Belote – king and queen of trumps held in same hand	20
Tierce – any straight flush of three held in same hand	20
Cinquante – any straight flush of four held in same hand	50
Cent – any straight flush of five held in same hand	100
Four aces, tens, kings or queens held in same hand	100
Four nines – held in same hand	150
Four jacks – held in same hand	200

Fours of a kind outrank straight flushes.

When Played by Four Players

DEAL AND BID: The dealer gives two cards together to each player, and then three. He turns the twenty-first card face up and bidding then starts. By bidding we mean simply the accepting of the card turned up as the trump, or passing. All suits have the same value. The bidding is started, not by the dealer, but by the player on his right. The successful bidder takes the exposed card into his hand. That gives him six cards and he has two more to be dealt to him before the bidding is over. Each of the other players has three more to be dealt to him. This bidding on a partial hand, with two cards yet to come, gives a poker flavor to the game.

THE BIDDING: Since the regular points are 162, and you have a partner to help you, it is reasonable to name a trump if you see as many as forty probable points in the first six cards. In making this estimate, possession of three out of eight trumps may be given a value of ten, in addition to the points that may be scored by the individual cards. With less than forty in sight, it is more prudent to pass.

The first round of bidding is on the suit of exposed card only. If all four players decline to accept that suit as trump, each one passes; then, on the second round, any other suit may be named. If all pass for the second time, then it is a new deal. If a bid has been made, then the remaining cards are dealt out, two only to the bidder (who has picked up the exposed card), and three to the other players.

PLAY: No matter who has made the trump, play is started by the player on the right (or left) of the dealer. It is while the first trick is being played that announcements are made. Any player who has one to make should make it as he plays his first card on the first trick. After his first card has fallen on the table it is too late. This is a feature that calls for strict attention. The only exception to this rule is in the case of the "belote" announcement; that is, king and queen of trumps held in the same hand. This announcement should be made by saying "belote," and later "rebelote" as the trump king and queen are played out. The reason for this will appear later.

ANNOUNCEMENTS: Announcements are valid in accordance with their rank. Thus, if the player who plays first announces a tierce, and the opponents make a higher announcement, then the first announcement does not count. In the case of two or more tierces it is the highest one that counts, the ranking of the cards in this matter being precisely as in poker, the ten taking its normal position between jack and nine. If announcements are of equal rank, the one announced first prevails unless the one announced later is in the trump suit. Partners' announcements score concurrently; that is, if you hold the highest one you thereby validate any lower one that may be held by your partner, even if his is lower than one held by your opponents. There may be, of course, two tierces in the same hand. Both count in case the higher one is the highest one announced. Immediately

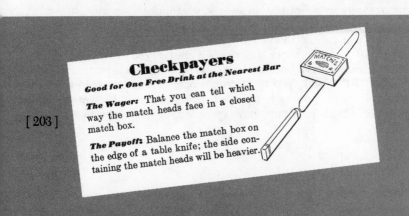

after the first trick is played, all valid announcements must be laid face up on the table. When all have seen them, they are taken back into the player's hand and play proceeds. The exposed trump card should also be left on the table until after the first trick is completed.

Announcements, since they add to the total score, increase the liability of the bidding side. Thus an announcement of 100 lifts the total score to 262 and makes it necessary for the bidders to make 132 points in order to fulfill their contract.

NO-TRUMP: This is a spicy feature. It cannot be an original bid. It can be bid only after another suit has been named for trump. When any player names a suit for trump, he thereby opens the door for a no-trump bid, which is the only overbid. If the exposed card is an ace, it is obviously dangerous to name that suit for trumps unless you are protected by another ace already in your hand, for the probability is that your opponents will pick up the free ace on the board and declare no-trump. The possession of two aces is a minimum warrant for a no-trump bid.

After a suit has been named for trumps, the other players in proper turn should say "pass" or "no-trump" before play starts. If any player says "no-trump" out of turn, that should annul the hand because too much information has been given thereby.

You can go no-trump over your partner's bid as well as over your opponents'. It is conventional to do so if you have a minimum of two aces, or one ace with an announcement of fifty or better. Usually a better score will be made this way than if you leave your partner in with his original bid.

The attraction and the risk in a no-trump bid lie in the fact that its *score is doubled.* Since the trump value of jack and nine are out, all four aces being high cards with tens next, the total score without announcements is 130 instead of 162, but the doubling brings this up to 260. The score of all announcements is also doubled. Last trick, being doubled, counts 20, and is usually more important in no-trump hands than in trump hands. In fact the winning or losing of a no-trump bid is very likely to depend upon which side takes the last trick, and careful attention needs to be given to the cards that are out.

One convention in connection with no-trump bidding is worth bearing in mind. It occurs when the exposed card is an ace and, on the first round, all players have declined to name that suit trumps. If, on the second round of bidding, your partner names some other suit trump, that is a command for you to take up the ace on the table and declare no-trump. The presumption is that your partner has at least one strong suit to the ace. Of course, the player between your partner and yourself may go no-trump, and thus relieve you of further responsibility as to the bidding.

BYLAWS: It is obligatory, in case you cannot follow suit, to trump, unless you have no trumps. The only exception to this is that, even though you cannot follow suit, you are not obliged to trump when your partner is master of the trick. Of course, you must play a trump card if trumps have been led; and, even though your partner may be master of the trick, you *must trump over him* if you hold a *higher trump* than the one he has played. It is obligatory to over-trump if possible whenever trumps have been led, or whenever an opponent has become master of a trick in which you cannot follow in the suit that has been led. If you cannot follow in a suit that has been led, and an opponent has trumped it, *you also must trump* even though compelled to play a *trump lower* than his.

A tie score is called at *litige*. In this case, the non-bidders score their points, but the points of the bidders are held in suspense until the next hand has been played, and then awarded to the winners of that hand.

When one side takes all the tricks it is called a *capote*. In that case a bonus of one hundred points is awarded to the winning side, but the ten bonus for the last trick is not counted. A capote in no-trump scores two hundred points. This capote feature affects the play of the hand. When you see that there is a chance to make a capote, you should play to make it, rather than prudently salvaging cards that risk being trumped. Usually one saves tens, but sometimes one misses a capote by doing so.

In case of capote, the side that has taken no tricks has no claim on the score of the other side even though by virtue of *announcements* it may have a larger score. Nor can a side that has taken no tricks win a game on that hand even though its announcement points carry its total score beyond the goal that has been agreed upon; in such a case, all points count, but an additional hand must be played to determine the winner. In other words, you cannot go out when you are capoted. BELOTE AND REBELOTE: As stated before, the announcement of "belote" is made as the king and queen that compose it are played, belote being called for the first one played, and rebelote for the second. Since belote is not scored unless it is properly announced, if the bidding side sees that it is going to be set, and if one of that side holds the belote, that player may prefer not to say "rebelote," thus avoiding the risk of giving twenty additional points to the opponents. On the other hand, announcement of "rebelote" may just save being set. In such an event one needs to know how the points are running. In case of a decision not to announce "rebelote" it is better, in order to avoid possible misunderstanding, to make the statement: "I am not announcing rebelote" as the second card (king or queen) is played.

The "arrete" is a feature that often has dramatic value at the end of a close game. Suppose the play is for 1,200 points. One side has 1,160, the other 1,170. Play starts. As soon as either side has taken in enough game points (not announcement points) to make a total of 1,200, a player of that side may say "j'arrete." That ends the game, even in the middle of the play of a hand, unless the side that says "j'arrete" is the side that has bid, in which case the hand must be played out to make sure whether the contract is fulfilled or not. This

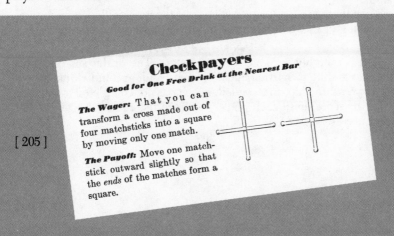

Checkpayers

Good for One Free Drink at the Nearest Bar

The Wager: That you can transform a cross made out of four matchsticks into a square by moving only one match.

The Payoff: Move one matchstick outward slightly so that the *ends* of the matches form a square.

"arrete" feature may enable the side that has the weaker cards on the last hand to nose out a victory by reaching the goal before their opponents pass it. On such a hand it is, of course, a great advantage to have the first play and to make all possible scores as quickly as can be done.

SCORING: The game is usually for twelve hundred points. The score may be written down, but it is more convenient to score with counters having values of 10, 50, and 100. Score is to the nearest ten, and five gets the benefit. Thus 64 would score 60, but 65 would score 70. Count only the lower scoring one, and, to find the other, subtract that score from the known total of game points plus announcement points.

When Played by Three

In the three-handed game each player is for himself. The contract is to make more points than either, but not both, of the other players. In case of failure to do so, the contractor's points go to that player who has the highest score. In case of capote, the player who takes no tricks scores no game points and each of the other players scores an additional fifty points; but the player who is capoted is entitled to his announcement points unless he is the one who has made the contract. In the event that two players are capote, the player who has taken all the tricks scores one hundred extra points.

Six cards are dealt, three at a time, to each player before the bidding starts, and three afterwards. Thus the play is with nine cards in each hand instead of eight.

The exposed card does not go automatically into the hand of the bidder, as in the four-handed game, but even in case the suit of that card has been named as trump, the exposed card can be "bought" by any player who has the seven of that suit, the seven being laid down when the exposed card is taken up. This may be done either before or after the last cards are dealt, but it must be done before play starts. After the last cards are dealt, the bottom card is also exposed. This is merely to reduce the number of unknown and undealt cards to three.

After each hand has been played, each player's score must be counted separately on account of the cards that are not in play.

When Played by Two

The two-handed game observes the same rules as the three-handed game except that there are twelve unknown and undealt cards. In case of capote, one hundred additional points are taken by the winner. To deal is a slight disadvantage since the non-dealer has first bid. For that reason it is a rule that the deal goes to or remains with the winner of the preceding hand. In case of no bidding, the deal changes hands.

Since there are twelve undealt cards, the two-handed game invites the taking of greater risks than the three- or four-handed game.

When Played by Five

This is a highly sociable form of Belote. The dealer sits out. This involves a shift in partnerships on each hand, and individual scores are kept. More chips are needed. A game is not completed, no matter what the score, until each player has been the dealer as often as any other player.

GIN RUMMY

Here's Gin Rummy, the card craze that crashed the gates of Holly-wood, and traveled east like a prairie fire. Perhaps you "thumbs down" these ESQUIRE rules, but after consulting a crop of crack players, we decided there must be a different variation for every player. So instead of using Betty Grable's method, here is a set of rules compiled by ESQUIRE, which we hope will end all conflicts and shilly-shally at the Gin Rummy table:

RULES FOR PLAYING GIN RUMMY FOR TWO, THREE OR FOUR PLAYERS

THE PACK — Full pack of fifty-two cards, which rank in sequence from king (high) down to the ace. In scoring, kings, queens, jacks and tens count 10 points each, all other cards their face value; aces are 1. Suits have no rank.

NUMBER OF PLAYERS—Two, except as described below under "Gin Rummy for Three Players" and "Gin Rummy for Four Players."

DEAL—Ten cards, one at a time. After the deal, next card is turned face up on the table to begin the discard pile (the talon) and the remainder of the deck is placed beside it, face down, to form the stock.

OBJECT OF GAME — To form sequences of three or more cards in the same suit (as four, five and six of hearts) and combinations of three or four cards of a kind (as three or four kings).

PLAY—Beginning with dealer's opponent (pone), each player in turn draws one card from the talon or stock; after the draw, he dis-cards a card from his hand face up on the talon to maintain his hand at ten cards. At the beginning of the deal, if pone refuses the turned-up card, dealer may take it; if both refuse, pone draws from the stock.

Play continues in this way, with each player attempting to improve his hand, until the end of the deal; in the meantime, neither player may meld (place on the table) any sequences or combinations, but must keep them in his hand. The deal ends when one of the players scores a down as described below, or until all except two cards in the stock have been exhausted (in the latter case, game is a draw and no one scores).

THE DOWN — When a player can meld enough cards so that his remaining, unmatched cards add up to 10 or less (as four, three and ace), he may declare a down by exposing his cards and announcing the points he has remaining, doing this after making his draw and at the same time he makes his discard. Opponent then melds all his sequences and combinations and in addition may also "lay off" by playing cards on the other player's melds. Opponent then announces his remaining points; score for the deal is the difference between these points and those of the player who declared the down.

SCORING—Player who declares the down wins the hand and receives credit for the score, if his point value is less than his opponent's. If not, or if the values are equal, opponent wins and receives a 10-point bonus in addition to the point score.

CONTRACT GIN RUMMY

Contract Gin Rummy is an entirely new game, combining some of the principles of contract bridge with the pace and gambling element of ordinary gin rummy.

In the interests of avoiding serious mayhem, it is suggested that all hands study the rules below, before dealing:

Step I — Seating

As in bridge, partners sit opposite each other. In the ensuing explanation use this chart as your guide and consider yourself as "A" — your partner thus being "C."

(A)

(D)   (B)

(C)

Step II — Dealing

The dealer is determined by high cut. Let us assume that "A" has won the deal:

(a) He deals ten cards to each player including himself.

(b) He places the remaining cards, of which there are twelve, face down in center of table.

Step III — Evaluating Your Hand

Each player arranges his ten cards, as in ordinary gin rummy, by placing the sequences, the threes of a kind, and the "possibilities" together. Everyone is now in position to evaluate his hand for purposes of bidding.

Step IV — Bidding

Bidding is based on the player's forecast of how many cards he thinks he will have to draw from the center of the table in order to "knock" with ten or less. The maximum bid is ten, and the minimum bid is obviously one. If a player thinks his hand is so poor it will take more than ten draws for him to "knock" he may pass. Bidding procedure follows:

(a) The dealer is first to bid.

(b) Each player is only allowed two bids before the bidding closes.

(c) A double or a redouble is counted as a free bid.

(d) Bids from 10 through 6 receive smaller bonuses and smaller penalties than bids of 5 through 1 (consult the score chart on page 210 for the actual count).

(e) In the first round of bidding it usually is best to make as high a bid as possible. A high bid means a bid which allows the bidder the maximum draws up to 10. There may be instances, however, where a player's hand may be so good that he may immediately want to shut out all other bidding with, say, a 5 bid. This would be considered a low opening bid and only an exceptional hand would justify such an opening.

(f) After the first bid is in, each succeeding bid must be lower than the last previous one.

(g) Bidding proceeds to the left as in bridge.

(h) The bidder making the lowest bid wins the bid and his partner becomes the dummy.

Step V — The Dummy

(a) After his partner has won the bid, the dummy must shuffle his cards so that he disarranges their order. He then places them face down on the table.

(b) Assuming, as an example, that "A" has won the bid, "C" consequently being the dummy, follows step (a) as above. Player "A" then proceeds to discard any number of cards in his hand which he thinks weakens it.

(c) He places his discards in the center of the table on the top of the twelve cards left over from the deal.

(d) He now proceeds to pick blindly from the dummy's hand the same number of cards he has discarded. In this way he may either strengthen or further weaken his hand by adding other unwanted cards. That is his gamble.

(e) After he has done this, he places the balance of the dummy's hand in the center of the table and mixes it in with the twelve original cards and bidder's discards.

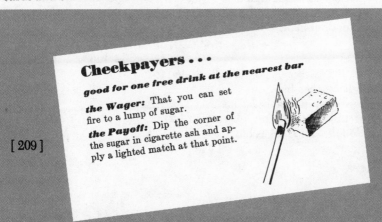

(f) The dummy may at this point sit beside his partner and inform him of the remaining cards that were in his hand. He may also assist in playing the game.

Step VI — The Play

(a) The bidder, player "A," turns over the top card in the center of the table as in gin rummy.

(b) That is all "A" does. It is now "B's" turn. If he cannot use this face-up card, "B" must give his partner "D" a chance either to accept or reject it before he may draw a down card from the pack. If "D" accepts the card, "B" automatically loses his turn. On the other hand, if "D" also refuses the card, then "B" draws a card and makes his regular discard. Since "D" and "B" are partners, it would be to "B's" interest to discard what he thinks would be helpful to "D."

(c) It is now "D's" turn (remember that "C" is the dummy and no longer in the playing of the game) either to accept or refuse the face-up discard.

(d) If he refuses it, he must ask "A" if "A" wishes it before he can draw another card. If "A" should accept it "D" loses his turn.

Step VII — Forcing a Lose

It will readily be seen from the above that it is possible to cause a player to lose a turn by accepting a discard which he has refused. It is naturally to the interest of the two players who are playing against the bidder to force him to lose his turn at drawing. Since he has contracted to draw a minimum number of cards in order to make his bid, he will obviously have great difficulty in making his contract if he is forced to lose many successive turns. Thus it would be to "D's" advantage to make a discard which he is quite certain "A" cannot use. And in most cases it would be advisable for "B" to take his partner's discards even though they may not fit into his hand at all, in order for "A" to lose his turn. Forcing a lose is the most important maneuver in Contract Gin Rummy.

Step VIII — Scoring

(a) If player "A" "knocks" and melds his hand, his opponents may discard on his hand as in regular gin. If he gins they may not.

(b) Assuming that "A" "knocks," his partial score, as in gin rummy, is the total of all the unmatched points held by both opponents, less of course, his own unmatched points.

(c) To this partial score he adds the bonus earned. (See below.)

(d) A game consists of 200 points — in other words, exactly double ordinary gin.

(e) Twenty points is counted for each box.

(f) A bonus of 100 points is given the winning couple.

(g) A "schneider" or "blitz" (a game which is won by a shut-out) counts for double the total.

Contract Gin Score Chart

	1-5 bid	6-10 bid
Bonus points to be added to gin score		
1. Bidder makes bid	20	10
2. Every play under bid	3	1
3. If doubled, then every play under bid	6	3
4. If doubled and makes bid	40	20

Penalty points to be added to opponent's gin score

1.	Bidder fails to make bid	0	0
2.	Every play over bid	3	1
3.	If doubled, then every play over bid	6	3
4.	If doubled, and bidder fails to make bid	20	10
5.	Bidder loses hand	20	10
6.	If doubled, and bidder loses hand	40	20

Demonstration Game

(In following the steps of this demonstration game, refer to seating chart at the beginning.)

(1) Assume "A" is the dealer.

(2) "A" opens the bidding with a bid of ten.

(3) "B" has a very weak hand and passes.

(4) "C" has a good hand and bids nine, thus underbidding his partner's hand to show strength and perhaps wishing to play the hand himself.

(5) "D" bids eight.

(6) "A" realizes that this is his last chance to bid. He therefore bids his minimum — six.

(7) "B" passes.

(8) "C" passes.

(9) "D" passes.

(10) "C" becomes the dummy and "A" plays the hand.

(11) "A" now discards three weak cards from his hand and picks, blindly, three cards from his partner's hand.

(12) The playing of the hand now begins with the bidder, "A," who turns up the first card from the stock in the middle.

(13) "A" improved his hand with the three cards he drew from the dummy and, after the fourth draw, he "knocks" with four unmatched points in his hand. He catches "B" with nineteen points and "D" with fifteen points.

(14) Subtracting four points (his unmatched cards) from both "B" and "D's" score, he receives a total of twenty-six points.

(15) To this he adds ten points, the bonus for making the bid, and two additional points — one point each for every play under his bid of six.

(16) Thus, the total score for partners "A" and "C" is thirty-eight.

If bidder "A" had been doubled, the scoring would have been as follows: "A" would have received the regular twenty-six points as in the previous example from the unmatched cards in his opponent's hand. In addition to this, he would receive twenty points for being doubled and making his bid, and three points each for every play under his bid, which would make six additional points. His and his partner's total score, therefore, would be fifty-two points.

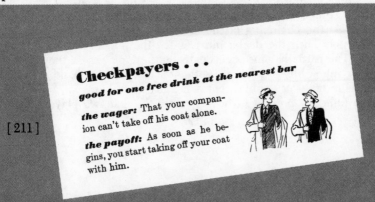

Pif-Paf is a fast, exciting gambling game, yet so easy that a rummy player could learn it after just a few moments.

Pif-Paf (pronounced Peef-Paff) is a simple combination of rummy (not gin rummy) with some of the exciting features of poker. Perhaps that's why it is an equal favorite of both men and women.

Pif-Paf is best with *four to eight players*. It is played with *two decks* of cards combined. Nine cards are dealt to each player; the remainder of the pack is placed face down in a center pile.

The object of the game is to match up the entire hand as in rummy — in sequences of three or more cards of the same suit (seven, eight, nine of hearts; nine, ten, jack, queen of clubs, etc.), or in sets of three or more of the same denomination (three sevens, four queens, etc.).

Sets of three or more of a kind, however, must always be of three different suits; two sevens of hearts and a seven of spades will not do. Four of a kind must have one pair of the same suit; five of a kind, two pairs. Six of a kind offers no difficulty; it can always be made into two sets of three.

The first card of the center pile is not turned up as in rummy. It is drawn by the player at dealer's left, but he may reject it. If he discards it, it may be claimed only by a player who needs it to complete his entire hand; otherwise, the first man picks again, then discards any card. The next player may either take up the last discard or draw from the center pile. Each discard may be taken only by the player next in turn, but one which will complete another player's hand may be claimed no matter who throws it. If the same discard puts more than one player out, it goes to the player nearest in turn.

Before the play begins, however, there is a little matter of betting to be done — and that's where poker comes in.

Let's assume five players in the game — A (the dealer), B, C, D and E. At the beginning of the deal each player puts one counter in the pot. Then the dealer must match the pot, so A puts in five more. The cards having been dealt, the next player, B, may, if he wishes, raise "blind" (that is, without looking at his hand). If so, he puts in ten — or double what A has to put in. C may also double in the blind by putting in twenty. Only the first two players have this right, but either or both of them may decide to look before anteing. If he looks, however, he may not raise; he may only match the last player's ante or drop out.

In this hand both B and C decide to raise. D and E, of course, have looked at their hands. D has a poor hand and drops; E puts in the necessary twenty counters and plays along. As dealer, A has already put in five so he needs to put up only fifteen more; B adds another ten and stays in; and now comes the big thrill. C, the last blind raiser, has the option of re-raising. (Only the last blind raiser has this right. B would have it if C had not raised in the blind; A would have it if neither B nor C had raised.)

If C decides *not* to re-raise –· the betting is over and the play begins. But if C likes his hand and puts in forty — the betting is wide open; thereafter any of the players may raise in turn, each raise doubling the last ante. Obviously, you need plenty of counters when the game gets hot.

Once the betting is over the play is rapid. Each player tries to match up his entire hand; nothing else counts but "going out." The first player to go out takes the pot and deals the next hand. That's all there is to it.

So much for the rules; now for the matter of skillful play.

Skillful play at Pif-Paf is a matter of knowing a few simple principles, and then of figuring out the right thing to do at the right time. There are two distinct phases of Pif-Paf science, the betting and the play. The betting comes first.

The first thing to realize is the tremendous advantage to betting blind. Don't refrain from using this privilege on the argument that it makes the game too steep. Reduce the stakes if necessary, but bet blind whenever you have the opportunity.

If you are the dealer, you have no choice; you must make your blind bet.

When you are third man, and second man has doubled dealer's blind bet, you have an enormous advantage if you double again in the blind. At worst you have an even bet, because at the start your chance to win is as good as anyone else's. If you should happen to have a good hand, which gives you a better-than-even chance, you alone have the privilege of raising and increasing the stakes. If you have a poor hand, no one has the right to raise you and you may play along, occasionally lucking out a victory on a hand you would have thrown away in any other circumstances.

There is an equally valid reason why you should invariably make your blind raise when you are second man (that is, when you are at the dealer's left).

Suppose you do not raise. This makes the dealer the only blind bettor; he alone will have the right to raise. You look at your hand and find that it is just fair. So you stay. Then it comes back to the dealer and he raises. Again your hand is just good enough for a call. And now other players start raising, and by the time it comes around to you again the bet is over 100, whereas you originally thought your hand was worth betting about 15 on. Not being one to throw good money after bad, you drop out and have lost what you put up before.

If you make your maximum blind bet early, when your chance is as good as anyone else's, you save yourself all sorts of problems later.

If the man at your left does not make his blind raise in turn, you become the last blind bettor and have all the advantages of that position. If he does make his blind raise, you may look at your hand before deciding to play along. And if he then raises, everyone else will have acted before it comes around to you again and if there is any sky-high raising you can drop out if you wish.

What sort of hand warrants staying in? What sort of hand justifies a raise?

Any experienced rummy player can look at a hand and tell you whether it is a good one or a bad one. It isn't entirely a matter of the ready-made matched sets that are dealt to you. The following hand is only fair:

This hand has a ready-made combination in clubs, but only the spade possibility on the side; no other card is of value. But here is a hand which the rummy player would call good, though it includes no matched set:

♠ Q 10   ♣ 10 9   ♥ 9 7 6   ♠ 3 A

Any one of ten cards — ♠ J, ♦ 10, ♥ 10, ♣ J, ♣ 8, ♠ 9, ♦ 9, ♥ 8, ♥ 5 or ♠ 2 — will give you a matched set and leave you still with a handful of combinations which can be turned into matched sets on the draw of the right card.

The decision to stay in or to raise is partly a social one. If you are playing in a wide-open game, in which everyone likes to see action even if the odds are against him, you will make yourself highly unpopular if you insist on playing them close to the chest. If you are playing in a hardboiled game, with everyone out to win, you will be a sucker if you buck the odds. From the standpoint of the hardboiled game, here is how you should play:

If drawing a single specific card will put you within one card of going out, you should raise. Here is an example:

♠ K Q J   ♥ 10 9   ♦ 9 7   ♥ 6   ♣ 3

The jack or eight of hearts, or the eight of diamonds, will leave you in a position to go out if you draw one card. Raise.

If you have no more than two worthless cards in your hand, stay in, but do not meet a raise. If you have no more than one worthless card in your hand, stay in and meet a raise. Here is another example:

♣ Q J   ♥ 10 9   ♦ 9 7 6   ♠ A 5

Every card in this hand except the ace and five of spades may help toward making a matched set; stay in. If the pot is raised, drop. Change the ace of spades to the seven of hearts, giving you this hand:

♣ Q J   ♥ 10 9 7   ♦ 9 7 6   ♠ 5

and you should meet a raise, because you have only one card which is complete deadwood.

Players of other rummy games have learned to watch their points: they would rather be stuck with a deuce, which counts only 2 against them, than with a face card, which counts 10 against them. In Pif-Paf the cards you have left are immaterial. The sole objective is to go out.

Kings and aces are the least valuable cards to the other players; these cards fill sequences only at one end (K-Q-J or A-2-3) while any other card may fill a sequence at either end. When choosing among worthless cards to throw away, kings and aces should be saved to last. Dangerous discards — cards which some player across the table probably needs — should be made early. In the later rounds a player may need just one card to go out, and may claim your discard whether you are next to him or not.

"Duplicates" — two identical cards — look good but are worth little. In this hand:

♦ K J 8   ♣ 5 4 3   ♥ 7 7   ♣ 8

if the six of diamonds is picked up, it should be saved and one of the sevens of hearts should be thrown away. With wild luck, a six-card sequence may be made in clubs or diamonds; there is less chance of making up four or more sevens.

In Pif-Paf you should concentrate on getting three of a kind. Four of a kind are not worth much, except in unusual circumstances. It is usually better to throw away the fourth card of a set, as in ♠ Q-J-10-9, than to give up a chance for a three-card set outside, as when you hold ♠ 9-8 and ♥ 8.

When you get within one card of going out you are entitled to pick up the vital card no matter who discards it, and your chance of getting it is multiplied many times. The first player to get within one card of going out almost invariably wins.

So, when you have two matched sets, it is worth while to pick up a good possibility, rather than draw blindly from the unknown cards. For instance, if you have:

♠ 9 8 7   ♥ Q ♠ Q ♦ Q   ♣ 5
            ♥ 3   ♠ A

and the player before you discards the ♥ 5, pick it up fast and throw the ♠ A. You will now have 5-5-3, and can go out if you can get the ♠ 5, ♦ 5 or ♥ 4. Nothing you could have drawn from the stock could possibly have put you in better position.

As in all rummy games, it is necessary in Pif-Paf to watch the cards that are discarded, and to remember the cards the other players pick up and so figure out what they are saving and what they want. The information gained from the most careful observation may cause you to break almost any "rule" that might be laid down.

Furthermore, any rule may fail to work out to your advantage every now and then. If the thought of that is liable to cause you any disappointment, console yourself with the thought that the uncertainty of Pif-Paf is what makes it so much fun.

[215]

DEALER'S CHOICE
by Winston Hibler

The great American game of Poker is played by everyone from old-maid aunts in the front parlor to the boys in the back room. Several million players prefer the game "Dealer's Choice" to straight Stud, so for those dealers who like to name their own poison, here are 20 games of "Dealer's Choice" as compiled for an Esquire *article by Winston Hibler:*

Five-card Stud with the Hole Card Wild—Deal it and bet it like straight Stud. Here's the twist—your hole card is wild and all like it in your hand. If you have a five in the hole and a five and an ace up, you have Three Aces and they *should* win, but Doc may have made his Straight, so take it easy.

Roll 'em—Another five-card Stud game. Two cards are dealt, face down, to each player who turns up whichever one he chooses and the high hand bets. Each card, thereafter, is dealt face down, and each is bet before the next card is dealt. The player may turn up his hole card or the one he has just received, but he must, of course, always have one card in the hole. What usually wins it? Well, what wins at Stud? It's the same thing.

Roll 'em, Hole Card Wild—This one is a beaut, and you had better call in a C.P.A. to figure out your hand for you when the last card is dealt. Deal it the same as Roll 'em, but remember that the card you choose to keep in the hole is wild and all like it; so if you have two aces, turn one up and keep the other down in order that you may have two wild cards with which to work. If you catch another pair you will have Four of a Kind, or your wild cards will fit into a Straight or a Flush. If, however, you don't improve when your last card is dealt, turn up your other ace to make you Three Aces. A Flush or a Straight usually wins it, but the Three Aces will stand up once in a while.

Bet or Get Out—Five cards in all. One card is dealt each player, face down. The player to the left of the dealer starts the betting each time a card is dealt. All five cards are dealt face down, and no player may check, he must either bet or get out. You may play this game with the deuces wild, or the treys, or the tens, or whatever your favorite wild card happens to be, but it is really a better game just as it is.

No Peek—Five cards are dealt, face down, to each player and no bet is made until each has his five cards. No player is allowed to look at his hand, and if he does so, his hand is dead and he forfeits any right to the pot. The player to the left of the dealer turns one card and bets or checks. If he bets, all players wishing to remain in the pot must call. The NEXT player to the left then turns his cards until he has topped the hand to his right, but if he turns an additional card when he has already beaten the hand ahead of him, then his hand is dead. As soon as a player beats the hand to his right he bets and all must call if they wish to see their hands. As soon as any hand is raised out or drops out, the high hand may bet again. The betting and turning goes on until all the hands are turned or the players forced out. Same hands win as in Stud.

Here are some of the twists that can be given to Draw Poker:

Aces or Better—This is simply Draw Poker with the exception that it takes Aces or better to open. It is designed primarily to build up bigger and better pots. If no one has Openers on the first round, the same dealer deals again and everyone antes. The next round it takes Kings or better, and so on down to Jacks and then up again until some player has the required Openers. It has never been explained why all the players do not ante more in the first place, open on Jacks and have it over with; but there it is, take it or leave it.

Legs — Again this is straight draw with nothing wild, but this time the pot stays on the table until any one player has won it TWICE, then it is won for "keeps." And here's a warning: Don't play this one near quitting time, for it may be well into the wee hours before one player *does* win twice.

Pig — A combination of Stud and Draw. Three cards are dealt to each player and the player to the left of the dealer bets on his three cards; after the betting is complete, another card is dealt and that is bet; then another. You have five cards now, haven't you? All right, play it out as you would in Draw by discarding and drawing to your hand. Any pair opens, or you can open on "your hat." The game is a bit more interesting, incidentally, when played with wild cards.

Spit in the Ocean — Even Hoyle has this one, so we'll skip it.

Here's what can be done with that game the Old Timers used to call "Whiskey Poker."

Dizzy Liz — Five cards are dealt to each player and four to the center of the table. It takes Jacks or better to open. When the pot has been opened and the betting complete, one of the center cards is turned and the betting starts again; and so on until all of the four cards in the center are face up. The player who makes the best hand with his five cards and the four in the center is the winner. The cards in the center are NOT wild; they simply play as part of each player's hand.

California — The same as Dizzy Liz except that *five* cards are dealt to the center and one turned up as a starter before the betting begins. No Openers are required, and the player to the left of the dealer starts it off by betting or checking. In these last two games a Full House is usually the hand that wins it; so if you are sitting there with two pairs, stop yelling for your wife to go out and mix a round of drinks — do it yourself and save money.

Omaha — Still another version of the above; but just to make it wilder than it is, the dealer puts a chip on one of the cards that is face down in the center, which when it is turned up is wild and all like it. Some fun, but you better have Four Aces or a Straight Flush when that last card is turned.

There are perhaps half-a-dozen other versions of Dizzy Liz, but your imagination is as good as anyone else's, so see what you can do, using the above games as a foundation.

Now to the pot-builders. The various forms of the famous old Seven-Toed Pete are becoming more and more popular. More cards on which to bet, and so more money in the pot.

Baseball — Deal it like Seven-card Stud with the first two and the last card dealt face down. The nines are wild; the four spot dealt face up to a player gives him an extra card; a three spot strikes him out, and out he goes — no matter how much he has invested in the pot.

The player who has a four spot up receives his extra card usually after all of the other players have been dealt their card for that round. A three or a four spot in the hole plays as any other card in the hand. The betting is the same as in any Stud game; the first three cards are bet and every round thereafter. It usually takes a Full House to win this one, but a Flush will stand up now and then.

One-eyed Jacks — Seven-card Stud with the two one-eyed Jacks wild.

Seven Cards, Deuces — You know this one.

5 and 10 — Seven-card Stud with the fives and tens wild. But you must have at least one of each. In other words, if your first three cards are fives, you have three fives and nothing more; but if you should happen to catch a ten on one of the next four cards it will give you four wild cards. Deuces and treys are sometimes substituted for the fives and tens. With less than Four of a Kind in this, you're not interested.

Low Hole — Seven-card Stud with the lowest card in the hole wild and all like it. The last card which is dealt to the player face down usually makes or breaks the hand.

Look . . . if you have two fours in the hole and two Jacks face up, you have Four Jacks; but if you should be so unfortunate as to catch a trey on that last down card, then your lowest card in the hole is a trey and you have a Full House and no more. Anything can happen in this game, so look for Royal Flushes and Fives of a Kind.

444 — Four down, four up, and the fours are wild. Bet on the first four cards and on each card thereafter. Fold up with less than a high Full House.

333 — Three down, three up and the threes are wild. Bet on the first three cards and on each card thereafter. A Straight or better should take the money.

High-Low — This variety is applied to the straight versions of Stud and Draw; it is just another form of the time-honored Low Ball. The player plays his hand for either high or low, but does not have to announce which way he is playing it until the last card is dealt. The highest and the lowest hands split the pot. Ace is always high and cannot be used as a low card except as part of a Straight in the high hand.

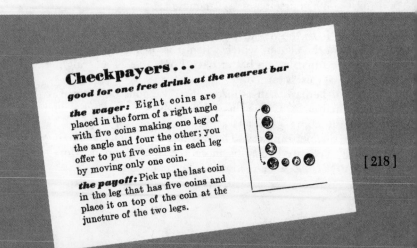

Checkpayers . . .
good for one free drink at the nearest bar

the wager: Eight coins are placed in the form of a right angle with five coins making one leg of the angle and four the other; you offer to put five coins in each leg by moving only one coin.

the payoff: Pick up the last coin in the leg that has five coins and place it on top of the coin at the juncture of the two legs.

PLAYING POKER TO WIN
by George F. Browne

The most difficult point to master in the art of poker is the fine science of quitting. Especially when the cards are running right for it takes a foxlike cunning to sense precisely when they'll peter out.

This lack of perception accounts in a large measure for the high mortality among "luck" players. Scudding along under a stiff breeze they blandly ignore squalls ahead. So reach for your hat and hit the deck if the high tide you've been riding slowly begins to ebb. The crest of your wave has been reached and the breakers, if disregarded, will shower you with regrets. On second thought, since bidding the shorn lambs a cheerful adieu hardly seems cricket, it might be best to master a subtler technique for clinging to the booty.

The bright thing to do, then, is to drop out of active competition until the cards again start rolling your way for the long shots, till now completed with ease, will soon bog down like an Italian blitzkrieg. Consummate artistry should be used so the hedge is not apparent and chips previously flung about with plutocratic abandon should be doled out with artistic finesse. Lay back and ride along, for a tight play now will show a profit when taps are sounded.

"But if you want a really unbeatable combination," argue the experts, "this style of play will have to be combined with a mastery of mathematical probabilities."

And at that there must be something to this mathematical angle, for Johnny MacGregor, as canny a Scot as ever mickeyfinned a jack-

[219]

pot, is one of its most rabid enthusiasts. And although the game's a hobby with him it's a pasteboard gold mine, simply because he's a specialist at mathematically booting a minor hand into a major victory.

"Among the uninitiated," says Mac, "the fall of cards is supposed to be controlled by the fickle goddess 'Chance.' What they don't know is that a good many years ago skeptical mathematicians embalmed this erratic jade and dug up the laws of probabilities; laws which discount chance entirely. Mathematical patterns must exist in all things, poker included, and cards honestly shuffled must fall with a relative frequency. Their progression is as unchanging as the days of the week, the fall of the tides or the path of the sun."

And therein, wrapped up and ready for delivery, lies the meat of the MacGregor Equation. Not a parcel of thinly sliced baloney but porterhouse steaks of wisdom from a master strategist whose successful maneuvers will put chips in your corner and logic in your play.

For his is no theoretical musing. Experiments show, and you don't have to take his word for it (try it yourself), that in each thousand deals the following hands will appear.

No rank	503	times
One pair	422	"
Two pairs	47	"
Triplets	21	"
Straights	3	"
Flushes	2	"
	998	

The other two hands will contain either full houses, fours or straight flushes.

But of that, more later. The first thing to bear in mind at the next weekly session is that the deck contains 2,598,960 poker hands. Only one of these can be dealt to you. So finding a gold mine in Central Park will be a lot easier than annexing that Royal Flush you've been yearning for. Hope, however, springs eternal but since dreams must be shattered let's start the blasting by figuring your exact chance of getting an unbeatable combination on the deal.

The only unbeatable hand in straight poker is, of course, the straight flush. Using a full deck (52 cards), there are ten possible straight flushes in each suit; in the four suits, forty. These highly profitable nuggets nestle snugly somewhere in the 2,598,960 hands the deck provides. Since only forty straight flushes are available, and since any of the other combinations may turn up, your chance of jarring a straight flush loose is confined to one-fortieth of the total combinations. You have therefore 64,974 possibilities. However, receiving only one hand, you have only one chance of success, while stacked against you are 64,973 chances of failure. The odds against snaring a straight flush on the deal, therefore, are 64,973 to 1. This includes the four Royal Flushes.

The odds against getting any other combination on the deal can be arrived at by the same process. Unless you have a flair for figures you won't care to figure them out. Anyway the table following will save you the trouble. The first column shows the number of combinations of each type in the deck.

ODDS AGAINST HOLDING VARIOUS HANDS ON THE DEAL

QUANTITY	HAND	ODDS AGAINST
40	Straight flush	64,973 to 1
624	Four of a kind	4,164 to 1
3,744	Full house	693 to 1
5,108	Flush	508 to 1
10,200	Straight	254 to 1
54,912	Triplets	46 to 1
123,552	Two pairs	20 to 1
1,098,240	One pair	1¼ to 1
1,302,540	No pair	EVEN
2,598,960		

If you have looked at the table you will note an almost even chance of getting a pair on the deal. But even a pair has its advantages when its mathematical possibilities of improvement are known. It shouldn't be sneered at for it improves, if high enough, to a 3 to 2 winner over a two-pair entry.

This is not guesswork. It's the mathematical certainty of the unchangeable laws of probabilities. As MacGregor says, "The improvement of any hand depends entirely on the undeviating pattern in which cards fall." This pattern can be dissected, translated into figures and the odds against improvement of any hand calculated. However the process is tedious and involved so a ready reference table showing the odds against improvement has been set up below.

A daily workout with this table should sharpen your playing, put a razor edge on your technique and account for many scalps heretofore immune.

ORIGINAL HAND	CARDS DRAWN	IMPROVED HAND	ODDS AGAINST
One pair	3	Two Pairs	5.25 to 1
	3	Triplets	8 to 1
	3	Full house	97 to 1
	3	Fours	359 to 1
	3	Any improvement	2.5 to 1
Two pairs	1	Full house	11 to 1
Triplets	2	Full house	15.5 to 1
	2	Fours	22.5 to 1
Four-straight (open ends)	1	Straight	5 to 1
Four-straight (interior)	1	Straight	11 to 1
Four-flush	1	Flush	4.5 to 1
Three-flush	2	Flush	23 to 1
Two-flush	3	Flush	96 to 1
Pair with odd Ace	2	Two pair Ace high	8 to 1
	2	Triplets	12 to 1
Ace	4	One pair	4 to 1
	4	Two more Aces	63 to 1
Ace and King	3	Either paired	3 to 1

Now to get back to MacGregor's strategy. When holding two pairs, if you are sure you are fighting triplets, your best line of defense is to throw away the smaller pair, when lower than tens, and buy three cards.

The advantage of holding an ace kicker with a pair is a perennial argument. But not from the standpoint of its mathematical probabilities of improvement. Some players are for it, some agin' it. Confidentially, it smells. It is true that when holding the kicker the probability of ending up with two pairs is slightly better than when holding the pair alone. This advantage is more than offset, however, by the probability of the pair to improve to triplets, a full house or fours. The odds are as follows:

ORIGINAL HAND	CARDS DRAWN	IMPROVED HAND	ODDS AGAINST
One pair	3	Two pairs	5.25 to 1
"	3	Triplets	8 to 1
"	3	Full house	97 to 1
"	3	Fours	359 to 1
" plus kicker	2	Two pairs	5 to 1
" "	2	Triplets	12 to 1
" "	2	Full house	119 to 1
" "	2	Fours	1,080 to 1

After taking a look at that table you won't need the MacGregor equation to tell you to heave that kicker you've been holding into the ashcan.

And believe you me, there's dynamite in pairs. Especially when a high pair or a small two-pair hand gets caught in a crowd of them.

To convince yourself of this, deal out four hands containing respectively a pair of aces, a pair of sevens, and a pair of jacks. The remaining hand can hold a pair of sixes and tens. Or, if you prefer, use pairs of your own choice. The object, for purposes of comparison of the effective value of a crowd of pairs, is to have one fairly low pair, one intermediate pair and one high pair; plus one low two-pair hand.

When this has been done, have each of the pairs discard and draw three cards while the two-pair hand discards and draws one. In the majority of the cases you will find that the low or the intermediate hand has improved over the high pair, or the two-pair hand. The reason for this becomes clear when consideration is given to the fact that the low and intermediate pair hands have two opportunities for improvement as against the high pair's one. Also there are three opportunities for improvement of all the pairs against the two-pair's one.

As a matter of fact, the small two-pair hand misses the bus, seven out of ten times. In a battle against three one-pair hands, one of the singles after the draw will hold two pairs half of the time and one of them will hold threes, one-third of the time. The small two-pair hand catches the bus in less than one out of three tries.

When holding threes, it is well to inveigle small pairs in, so do not frighten them off with a raise before the draw. On the other hand, when holding a pair of aces, shake off the small fry by a raise. Before doing so, however, be careful to see that no two-pair hand is around, otherwise you'll do his dirty work and in addition may have to battle him alone and unaided.

In considering a raise be governed by the strategy to be employed. To frighten out weak hands that lose often and require a large profit for the risk they are taking, raise to the limit. To keep hands in, take it easy, for you want to see lots of weak hands around. In this event a moderate raise will do. After the draw, you can let loose. The pot is then bigger, weak hands that have improved will mistakenly attempt to protect their investment, and your chances of being seen are proportionately greater.

While you may not be out for a killing, you certainly want to draw blood, so extreme care should be used in opening. Your chances of being squelched in a seven-handed game are lessened if you open only with a pair of kings or better; a six-handed game, queens; a five-handed game, jacks. If one of seven players before you passes, try considering it a six-handed game and open with queens; a five-handed game if two pass and open with jacks. Quite a few of your entries may be lost in this manner, but that will be overcome later, for players who have won several pots on your entries are inclined to come in readily when you open.

Bluffing is an art in which, unless you are a master strategist, you should rarely indulge. The bluff of threes is the most successful. In this, imitate a normal two-pair hand. Raise to the limit before the draw and buy only one card. See a raise after buying, or better it, and you will probably corral the pot. This trick also confuses your opponents who, when sizing you up for two pairs, can never be sure they are right. A good rule is to play a third of your threes that way.

Play a pair of aces, once in a while, as you would threes. Raise moderately and buy two cards. Also play two pairs occasionally as you would a pat hand. While the latter dodge will not always deceive the wiseacres it will chase some of the dangerous one-pair hands to cover. This is the easiest bluff to carry, as the only stratagem required is to raise to the limit before the draw, nonchalantly waive aside the proffered cards and wait for the fadeout. For this bluff the choice position is next to the dealer. Be careful not to overdo this, for a pat hand should show up no more than seven times in a thousand deals, and a pat hand oftener than that may justly be suspected of bluffing. Reducing the margin, a pat hand shows up in a seven-handed game once in twenty rounds, and in a five-handed game once in twenty-eight rounds. The odds are about five to two in a pat hand that a straight or a flush has been dealt.

The equation says that a good time to pull up stakes or lay low is during a steady losing streak. Believe it, please. While you may not want to leave the game, don't become discouraged and desperate. Forcing brings nothing except additional losses. Play carefully and coolly. Wait till you get decent cards before going to town and, by all that's holy, lay off the long shots. Take a walk out to the washroom, it kills sluggishness and revives wilted energy.

A certain rhythm in which he repeats himself is subconsciously employed by each player. The pattern of this melody in your opponents should be carefully studied, and, with experience, you will almost always be able to tell what will be done in any situation. And now, if you can't win with all this information, I'd suggest you stop playing cards. I have.

BLUFFING AT BRIDGE

by Hart Stilwell

The time comes in the life of every bridge player when he gets sick and tired of following suit to the opponents' high cards, and finds that he has, without any visible explanation in logic, indulged in a remarkable bid.

Perhaps he feels that it will change his luck. I knew a player who held stubbornly to this theory. When I was his partner I was always on the lookout for an earth-shaking bid, based on a few tens and eights, after a protracted session of worthless hands. I was seldom disappointed.

"I got sick of following suit," he would explain after we had gone down a few thousand points. "Thought maybe I would change our luck."

Of course when the opponents got through with his bid it was usually too late for a change of luck to do him, or me either, much good. But at any rate, he had broken the monotony of following suit, for it seems that when a man starts getting a run of worthless hands, the distribution is usually 4-3-3-3.

Sometimes I believe his idea is not so bad. I know that every man who plays bridge is likewise tempted on occasions, but few yield to the temptation. There is a modest tingling of pleasure from suddenly calling out "four spades" when you have nothing higher than a jack or queen. You are flinging a challenge into the teeth of fate.

Some of these bids have met disaster. Most of them have. Those I manage to forget in a hurry. No man enjoys remembering the time he went down six, doubled and redoubled, and I say redoubled for a man's partner usually has a nasty habit of redoubling on such occasions.

But when the screwball bids pay off, then I love to linger over them on some quiet afternoon months or even years later, playing the hand over once more, watching the look of astonishment on the faces of the enemy as their aces and kings are ruffed away, and gloating once more over that overtrick which was the crowning insult of all.

I am gloating right now over just such a hand. I had been meekly following suit until it began to lose interest. Any hand I picked up with a king in it began to look big, and I felt a strong desire to bid welling up within me. My partner must have realized this, for he sat there in stony silence when I was doubled, when he had sound reason to redouble if my bid had been based on anything near the values that it indicated. In fact, his thinking was even worse than that, for later he confessed to me that he was contemplating going to a small slam. I still shudder when I think of it.

I sat South, then, and drew this mess of pottage:

	North	
	S — Axx	
	H — KQJxx	
West	D — xx	East
S — Qx	C — Kxx	S — K
H — xxx		H — Axxxx
D — QJxxx	South	D — AKxx
C — xxx	S — Jxxxxxx	C — Axx
	H — none	
	D — xx	
	C — QJxx	

The gentleman on my right, East, dealt and opened one heart. He had been doing it all evening. The only time there was any variation was when he opened one spade instead of one heart. I don't think I had played a hand in fourteen hours. When I did get some face cards they were clubs, and I was always outbid. When I finally work out my own system of bridge, there are going to be no clubs in the deck — just a few extra spades and hearts. They are the cards to hold.

So I figured it was time I played a hand. Holding this pile of junk I bid four spades at once, before I had time to reflect on the complete lack of logic in the bid. I realized that even a modest amount of thought on the matter would have resulted in a pass, so I was careful not to indulge in this thought.

This four-spade bid rode all the way back to East, and after a casual glance at his ace and kings, and knowing full well that I was in a humor to make a bid regardless of what I held, he doubled.

When it arrived back at my partner he started studying his hand, and no matter how hard I looked at him he kept right on studying it and wouldn't pass. Finally, when I was on the verge of shouting at him to go ahead and pass, he did pass. I eased back in my chair, figuring I would lose no more than nine hundred or eleven hundred points, since we weren't vulnerable. I figured it was a cinch to take at least four of my spades, and I might even take a club — who knows.

Well, the opening heart lead brought down the dummy and a shower of delight with it. The spectacle of that dummy, with a heart lead through it, was worth all the bad sets I had suffered in three or four months.

And what followed was worth twice as much.

I put up the king which brought out the ace which was ruffed. I played over to the ace of spades, got rid of my two diamonds on the queen and jack of hearts, which was perfectly safe since the queen was the only outstanding trump and it was high. Then I made the enemy a present of the ace of clubs and the high trump, thus making the doggone bid with an overtrick.

East got up and put on his hat and walked away. I haven't seen him since then, and sometimes I worry about him, for as he went out the door he was muttering. "No man objects to losing at bridge, but to sit at the same table with anybody fool enough to bid four spades on that hand and lucky enough to make five. . . ."

That was a noble incident in my bridge career.

I recall another flurry into the realm of the fantastic that has given me much to gloat over. We were so far behind that anything might happen. It did.

I dealt and again sat South, since nobody objected. I picked up the stack of junk shown in the South hand below:

```
                         North
                       S — Kxxx
                       H — AKxxxx
                       D — Ax
        West           C — x              East
     S — QJxx                          S — Axxxx
     H — none                          H — xxx
     D — Jxxxxx                        D — KQxx
     C — AJx            South          C — K
                       S — none
                       H — QJ10x
                       D — x
                       C — Qxxxxxxx
```

After a casual glance at my hand I opened with three clubs, in spite of the then current rule that to open with three in a minor suit you must have the top honors. West passed and my partner bid three hearts. East passed and I bid six hearts, on the theory that if my partner couldn't make it, he had no business bidding at all.

East opened the ace of spades and began abusing me for foolish bidding as I put down the hearts and clubs and the diamond. It always seems odd to me that people will berate you for making a bid which they expect to set. But when East started looking for Spades and couldn't find any, he stopped talking. My partner ruffed the spade ace and led a club. The rest of the tricks were in the bag — at least, we put them in the bag. If there was any way to defeat the contract, East and West never discovered it.

There are plenty of bridge players who might have opened three clubs on the hand. I am not proud of that bid at all. It's the six-heart bid that strikes my fancy. A man might even go back over the hand carefully and justify the six-heart bid. But I hope nobody does it. I love to feel that it was a pure venture into the unknown — and one that paid off nicely.

The interesting part of the hand to me is that six spades could have been made by the opponents.

I even derive a certain fiendish satisfaction from some screwball bids that have been set and set badly. For many is the time when a careful check afterward will reveal that I saved a thousand or so points by such a bid. I never fail to remind the opponents of this, which is another reason why I am extremely popular as a bridge player.

One such hand sticks in my crop, quite pleasantly, at the moment, and I reproduce it here in order to gloat over it a bit more. On this hand I sat North, my partner being a gentleman from South Carolina who flatly refused to occupy that position.

The hand follows:

```
                        North
                        S — xx
                        H — xxxxxxx
       West             D — xxx              East
       S — AJx          C — x                S — Kxxxx
       H — Q                                 H — AK
       D — AKQxx                             D — Jxxx
       C — xxxx         South                C — AK
                        S — Qxx
                        H — Jxx
                        D — x
                        C — QJxxxx
```

You will note upon careful examination that I held what is known in the profession as a yarborough.

The gentleman on my right, West, dealt and bid one diamond.

Well, I didn't pass. I knew East for a malicious sort of fellow who could think of nothing more satisfying than setting somebody. What particularly delighted him was to hold the high cards in your trump suit and then double. Evidently he held them. At least I didn't.

So I decided to bid just enough to get doubled. I bid three hearts and East doubled. Thus the bidding ended.

Well, I went down, of course. I lost every trick it was possible to lose, I guess, going down for a penalty of five hundred. But the hand, and particularly my bidding, was an outstanding success. The vulnerable opponents had an iron clad cinch for six spades or seven diamonds, and could have made seven spades by finessing for the queen.

Certainly a small slam would have been bid, except for East's malicious yearning to see me squirm while he took the high trumps.

What irritated the enemy on this hand wasn't so much the points

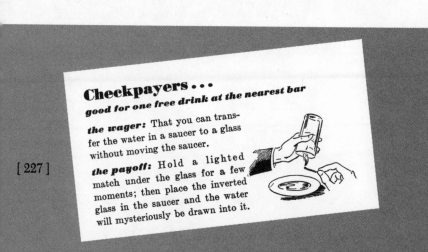

they lost. It was my bidding. They claimed that it was even dishonest and against the rules to bid three hearts holding no honor cards. Perhaps it is. I wouldn't know. But I do know that if that is dishonesty, there are times when it will give a person a certain degree of mild satisfaction.

Incidentally we won the rubber, which didn't make East and West feel any better.

Now I am not advising you to set out on a course of wild bidding on hands that are doomed, on the face of things, to meet a sudden and disastrous fate. Such bidding would soon take the interest out of bridge, at least for your partner.

I am merely pointing out that there are times when a thing can go just so far and then it not only ceases to be entertaining but it becomes a downright nuisance.

In times like that almost any kind of a diversion is likely to enliven the proceedings. When the diversion, in the form of a fantastic bid, pays off — then, brother, you've been through a real experience in bridge. You've got something sweet you can look back on.

Here's a streamlined version of Contract Bridge dreamed up by Squire Albert A. Ostrow for the Knights of the Square Table. This three-handed game of Contract with oomph, flashed into the mind of Mr. Ostrow one evening on the boring 5:38 local, and from that Bridge for Three reached its final shape . . . the perfect game for three marooned bridge hounds with no fourth in sight.

Deal four hands, one to each player, the left-over hand remaining face down. The dealer then opens with his bidding just as though he had a partner. The second hand may support this bid, overcall, or make an opening bid over a pass. The same goes for the third hand. If the third hand bids a suit already bid in partnership, *he* becomes the declarer. (That means that if the first bidder bids spades, either or both of the other two hands can raise in spades. If both so raise, however, the third hand becomes declarer.)

When the final contract is reached, declarer may choose *any* of the three hands for his dummy, regardless of previous bidding, raises, etc.; if he picks a partner hand, bonuses and overtricks are split. However, if he chooses the blind hand, he's rewarded with full bonuses.

In the event declarer elects to choose one of the two other players' hands as dummy, the remaining player plays with the blind hand, and the game resolves itself into the familiar pattern of Double-Dummy.

If, on the other hand, he chooses the blind hand, the other two players become defending partners and play proceeds exactly as in four-handed bridge.

There is a 300-point bonus for the game, with all overtricks as in the standard score, nonvulnerable Partials get a flat 50 points per man, regardless of the level of the bid. Penalties are the same as the regulation game, always nonvulnerable. When there are two defenders against a contract, penalties are split. If there is only one defender, he collects full penalties.

There are few rules, so as to keep the game as streamlined as possible, but these few additional are essential:

1. Declarer is barred from taking a doubling hand for his dummy.

2. An opening lead is barred from the blind hand. (This shuts out the possibility of a player seeing two hands before making his opening lead.)

3. If a third hand bids a suit already bid in partnership, he becomes the declarer.

SEVEN GAMES OF SOLITAIRE

Designed for desert island and B.O. sufferers, these seven intriguing solitaires are also useful when your guest is either inept at or bored by the better known card games. Make it double or quadruple solitaire and the good card-player's evening will not be ruined, as it would be if he were forced into bridge, poker or another game where his own fun depended on his opponent's or partner's skill.

LEONI

For two decks. Build up on the Aces in suit to Kings. Build down on the Kings in suit to Aces. Only the exposed card of each Auxiliary pile is available but any card in the Reserve pile is playable.

Leoni combines several types of routine with an interesting result.

Withdraw from the pack one Ace and one King of each suit and lay them in rows as shown. The balance of the double-deck is then dealt into thirteen piles in the form illustrated but in this manner:

As you deal (from left to right) you count, and every time a card dealt corresponds to the number called, that card is placed aside in an Exile Pack and its place refilled from the hand. Starting with "One," you lay down six cards in a row as you count, the seventh starting a new row. Every thirteenth card goes into a pile of its own, fanned out as shown. And if as you count "four" a Four turns up, you put that aside, face down, and deal another card in its stead. (J counts 11; Q, 12; K, 13.)

The pack exhausted in this manner, examine the available cards and make all possible plays. Then pick up the top card of the Exiles and, if not suitable for play on one of the Foundations, slip it under that pack whose numerical order (from left to right) corresponds to its pip value. Referring to the diagram: if the first Exile turned up should be a 3, it would go underneath the pile topped by the 7 of Clubs in the illustration. Then remove the top card from that pile and slip it under its correct numerical pile (as indicated by the denomination), continuing this routine until you find a card that can be played on a Foundation.

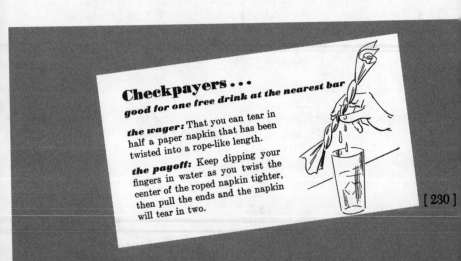

After playing it, and any others which may be suitable, the next card in the Exile pile may be drawn: played if possible; or placed under its numerical pile as before. This same procedure prevails throughout.

If it happens that all the cards of a packet are of the same denomination but of different suits, you may transfer the top card to the bottom of that same pile, continuing until a suitable card for play is uncovered. After the Exile pile has been exhausted you may pick up the remaining Auxiliary packets from right to left in order and, without shuffling, re-deal once.

SHAH OF PERSIA

For two decks. Build up on the Aces in suit to Queens. Marriages (building down in sequence but in suit of alternate color) may be made on the outer or Auxiliary circle only. A Reserve card cannot be played until the removal of the Auxiliary in that column releases the former.

Here is a tough one! Discard seven Kings from a double deck, placing the eighth in the center as Shah, then place the eight Aces in a circle around the Shah to form the Foundations. Now deal another circle outside of the Aces of eight more cards from the pack, examining the board for possible plays and refilling resulting vacancies from the hand.

Another circle of eight cards is then dealt, completing the Reserves; possible plays made and vacancies refilled as before. Then a third circle (not illustrated for lack of space) is dealt, completing the Layout: this final circle comprises the Auxiliaries. The remaining cards are held in the hand, face down, and dealt as needed.

Plays are now made according to the rules: Remember that you may make marriages on the outer circle only — that is, Reserve cards cannot be married among themselves but can only be used to build up on the Aces or down on the Auxiliaries. And you cannot do that, even, until the removal of an Auxiliary releases the next card in that column or spoke.

When the three cards in any column are played off, leaving a vacant lane to the Foundation, you can start a new spoke with any two cards from the Auxiliary circle. Then you must deal the next two cards from the pack to those newly vacated spaces.

OVER AND UNDER

For two decks played separately. Build on the Left Foundation in suit and ascending sequence. Build on the Right Foundation in suit and descending sequence. Place discards in rotation in four piles.

Here, for a change, is a double-deck game in which you don't shuffle both decks together but play them separately. And it's tough.

The first card dealt is the Key Card, placed on the table to start a row of four piles of two cards each. As they appear, the other cards of this same denomination will go in this row unless the Foundations have been built up to receive them.

The Key Card also determines the Foundations, so we'd better look at the illustration for further light. The first card dealt in the diagram was an 8: therefore, the four cards one point higher will constitute the Left Foundation Square as they appear. Although they would never come out all at once, we've put the 9's here for the sake of clarity. In the opposite or Right Foundation Square will go the four cards one point lower than the Key — in this case, the 7's as they appear. And upon both Squares you build according to the rules.

Unsuitable cards as dealt are placed below the Layout in four separate Talons or Stock Piles, always in rotation from left to right. Builds are made as you go, and when the first deck is exhausted, the

[232]

second is dealt. Eights (or whatever the Key Card was) still go up above unless they can be properly played below on a Foundation, and the routine is the same throughout for the second deck. If you manage to play off all the Key Cards to their respective Foundations, you win.

QUEEN OF ITALY

For two decks. Build up on the Foundations in alternate colors. Build down (marry) on the Auxiliaries in alternate colors.

This is a good game calling for close concentration. First, deal eleven cards from the pack in a horizontal row constituting the Reserves. Only the extreme right-hand card (8 Spades in illustration) of this row is playable, each move releasing the next card to the left. Now deal three cards below this row as shown — examine the three and determine which of them will soonest release the end Reserve. Select this for the first Foundation and move it over to the left (directly under the 9 Diamonds in the picture).

The two remaining cards are now transferred to a third row as indicated by the blanks in the illustration, and seven more cards dealt to this row, making nine Auxiliaries. Following the diagram, it is apparent that the 6 Hearts would soonest release the available Reserve (built in alternate colors, remember!) so this 6 is moved down under the 9 Diamonds. As they appear, the seven other 6's (or whatever the Foundation proves to be in your game) will go in this row to be built upon in accordance with the rule. The other two center cards (10 and J in the picture) now come down to the blank spaces in the third row and the remaining Auxiliaries are dealt.

Possible plays are now made, vacancies in the Auxiliary row being refilled from the hand — Reserve vacancies, of course, being left open. Auxiliaries cannot be married among each other, all plays to this row coming from the hand; neither can Reserves be played to Auxiliaries

— they go on Foundations only. The object is to build each Foundation card on up through its family of thirteen, and every effort must be made to clear away the Reserves. One re-deal permitted.

FLOWER GARDEN

For one deck. Build up on the Aces in sequence and suit. Build down on the exposed cards of the Beds in sequence but regardless of suit. This is probably the best single-deck game in captivity and a good example of the pure-skill type.

Deal six packs of six cards each, arranged as illustrated to form the Garden Beds. You now have sixteen cards left (the Bouquet) which you can lay out on the table, face up, or hold in your hand as you prefer. In any event, you can study them to your heart's content, thus cutting yourself off from the luck alibi. All you do now is follow the rules. Bouquet cards can be played on the Foundations or on the top card of any Garden Bed. But the unwritten law is that once you've removed a card from the Bouquet, you cannot play it back there

again. However, exposed Garden cards may be moved from one Bed to another or played on the foundation Aces which are placed, as they turn up, as indicated by the blank cards in the illustration. A King in the Beds, incidentally, can be moved only to a vacancy caused by clearing off some other Bed or, eventually, to its proper Foundation pile. The system is to move your cards back and forth so as to clear off cards needed for the Foundations, continuing this jockeying until you've built the Aces to Kings.

LA NIVERNAISE

For two decks. Build up on the Aces and down on the Kings in sequence and in suit. As many cards in each of the Line piles may be studied as there are vacancies in the Flanks.

Deal two vertical columns of four cards each (called the Flanks) with space enough between for two Foundation columns as indicated by the blanks. As they appear in dealing, one Ace and one King of each suit go in these columns.

Then deal a horizontal row of six piles of four cards each: the Line. Only the top or exposed card of these piles is available for play, each move releasing the card beneath.

At this point make any plays to the Foundations which show, always giving preference to a Flank card rather than a Line card. You will soon learn that Flank vacancies are precious, so cultivate them early. Indeed, if you can't play a Flank card from the original layout (after a Foundation appears), shuffle the deck and deal again, for you haven't a chance!

The play proceeds from this point by dealing four cards at a time to each of the Line piles. Make your plays at the completion of each deal (full round) but do not replace cards played from the Line until an entire pile has been exhausted. Then refill with four cards from hand. After the hand has been dealt you may pick up the Line packets in rotation from left to right and, without shuffling, resume dealing as before. This can be done twice. In planning your plays you are entitled to examine the Line piles in accordance with the rule above — which doesn't make the game any easier.

JAVANESE RUG

For two decks (shuffled into one). Build up on the Aces and down on the Kings in sequence and in suit. A card is available (playable) only when it has at least one narrow end exposed.

This is no game for a small apartment. But if you have the necessary space, it is an interesting specimen of the skill-judgment type.

First withdraw from the pack one Ace and one King of each suit, laying them in a horizontal row at the bottom of the board as shown. Then, following the illustration, deal eight rows of eight cards each, every other card placed horizontally.

The only available cards are those with at least one narrow end exposed: for example, playable cards in the illustration would be the 10, 6, 9, 2 Hearts and 3 Diamonds in the top row, and all others in the layout similarly "exposed."

All available cards in the original set-up are played on their proper Foundations according to the rules, and when no further plays are possible, cards in hand are dealt singly. Suitable ones are played where they belong; unsuitable ones are set aside in a Stock Pile, the top card of which is always playable. You may also build up or down (in suit) on this top card — a very valuable crutch which you'd better not overlook.

FOOTBALL FOR FEEBLE FULLBACKS

by Ernest Lehman

Fundamentals

1. Card-table football follows all the rules of college football.

2. The game is played by two people. They need have no more than a rudimentary knowledge of football.

3. The game is easiest to play, and most enjoyable, when the players visualize themselves as being teams on an actual field.

4. It's not really necessary, but some players find it helpful to keep a pad and pencil handy to jot down the location of the ball.

5. The player in possession of the ball holds the deck in his hand. Before each play from scrimmage, he states whether he intends to run, pass, punt or try a field goal.

6. After the player has stated what type of play he is about to make, he executes the play by laying up the card that is on top of the deck. The nature of the card then determines the result of the play.

7. As in real football, the player keeps possession of the ball (the deck) until he kicks, or has a pass intercepted or loses the ball on downs. When the ball goes into possession of the other player, the deck (the unused portion) is handed over to him.

8. When all fifty-two cards have been used up, the whistle blows and the quarter ends. The deck is then shuffled and another quarter is begun. In other words, four complete runs through the deck constitute a game.

9. At the end of the first half, there is a short intermission to enable kibitzers to get a hot dog and a bottle of beer, and to enable the coach (played by Pat O'Brien) to give the cards a pep talk.

10. Betting in the stands is positively prohibited.

The Plays

(Note: the kickoff, naturally, is the first play of the game. But, for reasons of clarity, we shall explain the various plays in what may seem to be no logical sequence.)

1. *Running Play* — An Ace represents a 4-yard loss; a King, a 3-yard loss; a Queen, a 2-yard loss; and a Jack, a 1-yard loss. All other cards represent yardage *gains* equal to the value of the card.

Example: You've received the kickoff and have run it back to your 30-yard line, first down and 10 to go. You say "I'm running," and you lay up a three. That indicates you have made a 3-yard gain, making it second and 7 on your 33. Again you say "I'm running," and you lay up a five. That's a 5-yard gain, making it third and 2 on your 38. Again you choose to run, and you lay up a Queen. A Queen is a 2-yard loss. That throws you back to your 36 — fourth down and 4 to go. Here's where you have to be a good quarterback. Is it worth the risk to run on fourth down in your own territory and perhaps lose the ball on downs? Or is it wiser to kick? We'll say you decide to kick. (And it's lucky you decided that way. The next card is a Jack. If you had run, you'd have suffered a 1-yard loss and lost the ball on downs on your 35-yard line!)

2. *The Punt* — is always made from a stripe. If you are not on one, you drop back to the nearest marker. If you are on your 36-yard line when you decide to kick, you make the boot from the 35. If you are on your 44-yard line, you kick from the 40. *Comprenez?*

After announcing your intention to kick, you lay up a card and multiply it by 5 to determine the length of the kick. In kicking, Jack counts 11; Queen, 12; King, 13; and Ace, 14.

A seven would give you a 35-yard kick. A Queen would give you a 60-yard boot. An Ace indicates a 70-yard kick. A four means a 20-yard punt, etc.

However, there is no 10-yard punt. If you lay up a two, it's a blocked kick!

Example: You decide to kick from your own 36. You drop back to the 35 and lay up a card. It's a Jack (11), giving you a 55-yard kick down to your opponent's 10-yard line, from which point he will make a runback. (If the kick had been a King — 65 yards — or an Ace — 70 yards — long enough to go to the goal line or over, the ball would then, of course, be put in play by the receiver on his 20-yard stripe. If you had laid up a two on your punt, giving your opponent a blocked kick, he would then have started his runback from the point where the kick was made, in this case the 35-yard line.)

3. *Runback of Kick* — Your opponent has just caught your kick on his 10-yard line. The ball is now in his possession, so you hand the unused portion of the deck to him and he lays up his runback card. If it is a picture (Aces are always pictures in this game), that means he is tackled immediately and downed at the point of reception, the 10-yard line. (In the case of the runback of the blocked kick, he'd have been stopped at the 35.) A picture on a runback indicates a zero runback. Any runback card other than a picture indicates a return of the kick equal to the value of the card.

However, there is one magnificent exception. If his runback card is the Ace of Spades, he goes all the way for a touchdown!

The Ace of Spades on the runback of a kickoff, punt, blocked kick or intercepted forward pass is always a touchdown.

Example: He catches your punt on his 10-yard line and lays up a Queen. The picture indicates he has been stopped dead on the runback, so it becomes first and 10 for him on his 10-yard line. If he had laid up a nine, he would have run the ball back to his 19, first and 10 on the 19. If he had laid up the Ace of Spades . . . STUDENTS??? (Slight pause for the roar of the crowds.) If he had blocked your kick on your 35-yard line and laid up a seven, that would have indicated that he had run the blocked kick seven yards to your 28, first and 10. A picture would have stopped him on the 35.

4. *Safety* — as in gridiron football, when you are thrown behind your own goal line, your opponent gets two points, and you take the ball out on your 20-yard line. In this game, on the goal line is as bad as over the goal line.

Example: You have the ball on your 2-yard line, you try a running play and lay up a King. The King throws you for a 3-yard loss into the end zone, and two points for the other guy. A 2-yard loss with a Queen would have had the same result. (Moral: Stay away from your 2-yard line if you can help it.)

5. *Touchdown* — when you carry the ball to the goal line or over — six points! (Don't gloat. He's liable to run back your kickoff for one of his own. How? With the Ace of Spades!)

6. *Point After Touchdown* — Immediately after scoring a touchdown, you lay up the conversion attempt. If the card is a two, three, four or five, you fail. Any card over five is good.

7. *Field Goal* — You may attempt a field goal at any time when you are within your opponent's 40-yard line (on his 40-yard stripe, or closer). When you state your intention to try a field goal, you must then lay up a picture to succeed. If you lay up a card that is not a picture, you not only fail to score the three points but you also lose the ball, and your opponent puts it in play on his 20-yard line. If you lay up a two, that, of course, is a blocked kick, and he takes over the cards for a runback from the line of scrimmage.

Example: You've worked the ball down to his 28-yard line but it's fourth and 9 to go, so you elect to try for a field goal. You drop back to his 30 and lay up a four. It's not a picture, so the kick is no good. He takes over on his 20. If you had laid up a Jack, Queen, King or Ace, the kick would have been worth three points and you would have then kicked off to him. However, if you had laid up a two, your opponent would have blocked your field goal attempt and run the ball back from the 30.

8. *The Kickoff* — when the game begins, high card has choice of kicking off or receiving. The ball is kicked from the 40-yard line.

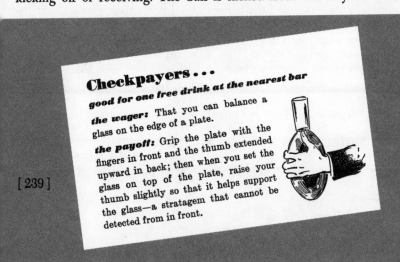

Checkpayers . . .
good for one free drink at the nearest bar

the wager: That you can balance a glass on the edge of a plate.

the payoff: Grip the plate with the fingers in front and the thumb extended upward in back; then when you set the glass on top of the plate, raise your thumb slightly so that it helps support the glass—a stratagem that cannot be detected from in front.

As with the punt, 5 is the multiplier, pictures count 11, 12, 13 and 14, and when the kickoff reaches the goal line or goes over, the receiver takes over on his own 20-yard stripe.

However, there is no blocked kick on a kickoff. A deuce constitutes a 10-yard kickoff (and a deucedly bad one, too). The kickoff is run back in exactly the same manner as the punt.

9. *Forward pass* — Don't worry. This only *sounds* complicated: It takes two cards (a passer and a receiver) to execute a forward pass, though the use of two cards constitutes only one down.

A. Completed Pass — When both cards are of the same suit, and the second card is not a picture, the pass is successful. To determine the net gain, you multiply the value of both cards. Here again, pictures represent 11, 12, 13 and 14.

Example: You announce a forward pass attempt and lay up the six of Spades and the nine of Spades. Since they are both of the same suit, you multiply 9 x 6 for a completed pass of 54 yards.

On another pass, you lay up the Jack of Hearts and the four of Hearts. Result: a nifty 44-yard completed pass. (The picture is all right, in this case, because it is the first card, not the second. If order had been reversed, the pass would have been no good.)

B. Incompleted Pass — When the two cards are of different suits, or the second card is a picture, the pass is unsuccessful.

Example: On an attempted pass, you lay up the six of Diamonds and the eight of Clubs. The cards are of different suits, so the pass is no good and the ball is returned to line of scrimmage.

On another pass attempt, you lay up the five of Hearts and the King of Hearts. Though the two cards are of the same suit, the pass is still no good — because the second card was a picture. If the order had been reversed, the pass would have been completed for 65 yards.

An incompleted pass, of course, uses up a down.

C. Intercepted Pass — When the second card is a black picture, the pass is intercepted. It makes no difference what the first card is. If that second card is a Club or Spade picture, you're in trouble. To determine how far your pass carried before it was intercepted, you lay up a third card and add value to the first card.

Example: You try a pass from the 50-yard line and lay up the seven of Diamonds and the King of Spades. The second card being a black picture, your pass has been intercepted, so you lay up a third card: the nine of Hearts. Adding the seven and the nine gives you a pass of 16 yards down to the 34, where the pass was intercepted. When you hand the cards to the intercepting player, he will start his runback from 34.

Another example: On an attempted pass from your own 30-yard line, you lay up the King of Diamonds and the Jack of Clubs. Moaning at the sight of the second card's black suit, you then lay up a third card: the four of Spades. Adding the King (13) to the four indicates that your pass carried 17 yards to the 47-yard line, into the waiting arms of your opponent, who will now run it back from the 47.

10. *Runback of Intercepted Pass* — This is identical with the runback of a kick. If you lay up any picture except the Ace of Spades you are tackled immediately at the point of interception. If you lay up any non-picture card, run the ball back for yardage equal to the card's value. If you lay up the Ace of Spades, you run interception back for a touchdown.

Strategy

1. If it's unwise on the gridiron, it's unwise on the card table. If you throw passes deep in your own territory, or run on fourth down, you are playing daring football. Sometimes you're lucky at it, and the kibitzers think you're a brilliant quarterback. More often you pay the consequences.

2. When you are within the enemy's 40-yard line on fourth down, it is usually wiser to attempt a field goal than to punt, unless you are so far behind that three points can't help much. Then a forward pass might be better.

3. When you near the end of the first half or the end of the game, don't attempt to go for a touchdown with a running attack unless you are sure there are enough cards left to carry you to the goal. If you are on your own 10-yard line, six points behind, and only five cards are left in the game, you know you can't possibly score a touchdown by running, even if you come up with four straight tens and a nine (49 yards). But you do have two chances for a last-ditch touchdown. In other words, instead of watching the clock, watch the deck.

4. If you can manage to remember which cards have already been played in the quarter, you will have a decided advantage in quarter-backing your game. For example, if you think that most of the pictures have already been turned up, you'll know there won't be much percentage in attempting a field goal in that quarter. With most of the pictures used up, you can try a ground attack unworried by possible losses from Aces, Kings, Queens and Jacks. On the other hand, if you haven't noticed any black pictures turning up, you'll think twice before throwing a forward. It could turn out to be a backward!

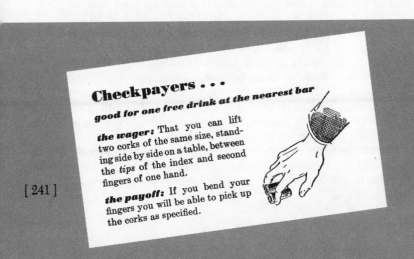

Checkpayers . . .
good for one free drink at the nearest bar

the wager: That you can lift two corks of the same size, standing side by side on a table, between the *tips* of the index and second fingers of one hand.

the payoff: If you bend your fingers you will be able to pick up the corks as specified.

SIX-PACK BEZIQUE
(Two-Handed Card Game)

Americans who know Pinochle won't find it difficult to get on to Six-pack Bezique. Non-Pinochle players may find the rules strange at first, but the game is essentially simple in its mechanics.

Let's play a sample game and find out. Take six packs of cards and remove all cards below the seven, leaving thirty-two cards in each pack — A, 10, K, Q, J, 9, 8, 7 of each suit. The cards rank in that order, with a ten winning from anything in the deck but an ace.

You'll also need poker chips, if you don't have a special Bezique scoring device. Scoring is too rapid and too high for pencil and paper. Put all the poker chips in a pile at the side of the table, a blue chip counting 1,000 points, a red chip 100 and a white chip 10. As you score, you will take the proper number of chips from the pile.

You and your opponent both shuffle the cards, trading portions back and forth so that the entire pack — there are 192 cards altogether — will be thoroughly mixed.

Now you each cut a card. Low deals first, and your opponent is the first dealer. He deals, one card at a time face down until you each have twelve cards. The undealt cards are toppled over at the side of the table to be the "stock." You pick up your hand:

♥ A   ♠ J   ♦ A 10 Q Q J 7   ♣ 10 J 9 7

You can't appraise your hand, of course, without knowing the principal object of play, which is to score for *declarations* (Pinochle players call them "melds"). Here are the combinations that count:

Table of Declarations

SEQUENCE (A-K-Q-J-10): In trumps, 250; in any other suit, 150.

MARRIAGE: K-Q of trumps, 40; K-Q of any other suit, 20.

FOUR OF A KIND IN TRUMPS: Four aces, 1,000; four tens, 900; four kings, 800; four queens, 600; four jacks, 400.

FOUR OF A KIND IN ANY SUIT (they do not have to include one of each suit): Four aces, 100; four kings, 80; four queens, 60; four jacks, 40. Four tens do not count.

BEZIQUE. This is by far the most important declaration. A bezique is always the queen of the trump suit and a specified jack of opposite color:

If spades are trumps, ♠Q and ♦ J.

If diamonds are trumps, ♦ Q and ♠ J.

If hearts are trumps, ♥ Q and ♣ J.

If clubs are trumps, ♣ Q and ♥ J.

Bezique counts only 40; but double bezique (two each of the proper queens and jacks) counts 500; triple bezique, 1,500; quadruple bezique, 4,000.

You must know the declarations to play; until you have learned them by heart, write them on a card and keep it beside you.

At the start there is no trump suit. The first marriage (or sequence) to be declared will establish the trump.

Now take another look at your hand:

♥ A   ♠ J   ♦ A 10 Q Q J 7   ♣ 10 J 9 7

Your opponent dealt; that makes it your first lead. You may lead any card; but what? Until you know what suit will be trump, you should hold on to all cards which might figure in the higher-scoring declarations. Especially you must keep all *queens and jacks*. You have no marriage with which to make the trump, and must be prepared for any. So you lead a worthless card — the seven of diamonds.

Your opponent plays the seven of spades. *It is not necessary to follow suit.* You win the trick because he did not play a higher card of the suit you led. Once there is a trump suit, a trump will also win from any lead of another suit.

The cards of the first trick remain face up on the table; the cards in the tricks do not count for anyone, so throughout the game they remain in a loose pile in the center of the table. Although tricks count nothing per se, there is one advantage to winning them: only after you take a trick may you declare and score one of the counting combinations. Usually, when you have nothing to declare you do not particularly care who wins the trick.

Now, having won the trick, and having no declaration, you draw the top card off the stock to restore your hand to twelve cards. Your opponent draws the next card. You drew the ♣ jack and your hand is:

♥ A   ♠ J   ♦ A 10 Q Q J   ♣ 10 J J 9 7

Having won the previous trick, you lead again. Still protecting your possible scoring cards, you lead the ♣ 9. This is a better lead than the seven, because to win it your opponent must play some possible scoring card. If the nine wins, you can declare your four jacks and score 40.

The ♣ 9 does win, and before drawing you put the four jacks face up on the table in front of you and take four white chips from the

pile. You draw — the ♥ K. Your opponent draws. Now you have:

♥ J   ♦ J   ♣ J J on the table

♠ A K   ♦ A 10 Q Q   ♣ 10 7 in your hand

The cards declared remain on the table, but you may play them as though they were in your hand. However, you want to keep the jacks for possible future beziques. You lead the ♣ 7.

Your opponent wins this trick with the ♣ 10 and declares the K-Q of hearts, scoring 40. Now hearts are trumps and the ♥ Q and ♣ J become the two most important cards in the pack. Other queens and jacks become of minor importance.

Your opponent, having won the trick, draws; you draw and get the ♦ K. Now you have:

♥ J   ♦ J   ♣ J J on the table

♥ A K   ♦ A 10 K Q Q   ♣ 10 in your hand

The lead is the ♣ 8; you put on your ten and win the trick. The ten is no longer likely to figure in a declaration, and you want this trick because you proceed to score 150 by adding the A, 10, K, Q of diamonds to the jack on the table. This gives you a non-trump sequence, known in the slang of the game as a "back door." Of course, you could have put down the ♦ K-Q first, scoring 20, and later added the ♦ A-10 for the 150 points; and now that you have declared the entire sequence, you may no longer declare the marriage. But in a high-scoring game like Six-pack Bezique, 20 points are not worth wasting time on. You draw another ace of hearts; your opponent draws. Your hand now is:

♦ A 10 K Q J   ♥ J   ♣ J J on the table

♥ A A K   ♦ Q in your hand.

You promptly lead the queen of diamonds from the table. This is an important feature of the game: Getting rid of that queen will permit you, the next time you win a trick, to put down the other queen of diamonds from your hand and score 150 all over again. You may not do this while the full scoring combination is on the table, so you break it up.

Your opponent wins your queen of diamonds and adds a jack of clubs to the queen of hearts he declared before; he scores 40 for bezique. He will not break up this combination; bezique is the one declaration that you do not break up, for to add a second bezique will score 500 more, provided the first bezique is still on the table; adding a third will score 1,500 more, provided the first two are still on the table, and so on. If a player is fortunate enough to get quadruple bezique, for a 4,000-point score, then he will break it up, for restoring it with one of the bezique cards will count an extra 4,000 each time.

You are permitted to "declare" two or more combinations at once, but only one may be scored at a time. Thus, if you have ♥K (trumps) and ♣J already on the table, after winning a trick you may put down the ♥Q and announce, "Forty for bezique and forty to score," the extra 40 being for the marriage in trumps. The next time you win a trick, you score the other 40. You may have any number of pending declarations at the same time, and after winning a trick you may choose which one to score.

Now your game is well under way, and in this manner play proceeds. When only ten or twelve cards remain in the stock, there is a mad scramble to win tricks and declare all available combinations, and to keep the opponent from making any declarations, for after the last two cards of the stock have been drawn there is no more declaring.

However, you try not to weaken your hand too much in this closing period, for there is a play-off which is important. Having drawn the last cards of the stock, you and your opponent pick up any cards you have exposed on the table, so that you each have twelve cards. The player who won the previous trick leads. The only object is to win the last trick, which counts 250 points.

In this play-off, the rules change radically. You must follow suit to the lead if you can. *You must win the trick if you can* by trumping if you cannot follow suit.

Having finished this play, you compare the total scores. The player with the higher score is the winner and adds 1,000 to his score, after which he gets the difference between his score and his opponent's.

Thus, if you have scored 4,320 points and your opponent has 3,690, you win 4,300–1,000, less 3,600, a difference of 1,700 points in your favor. (Anything less than 100 is disregarded, unless the winning of a close game depends on it.)

There is also the feature of the *rubicon*. If the loser has scored less than 3,000 points, the winner gets *all* the points that were scored: his own, plus the loser's, plus the 1,000 for game. The rubicon has a profound effect on the strategy of play. In the late stages of the game, when a player sees that he is virtually sure to be rubiconed, he refrains from scoring his declarations so as not to add to the winner's score.

The winner gets the rubicon privileges even if his own score is less than 3,000; if he wins 2,960 to 2,930, his total winnings will be 2,900+2,900+1,000, a total of 6,800.

Each deal represents a game, but there is one holdover rule from one deal to the next: the same suit cannot be trumps in two successive games. So, when you finish this game and start another, hearts cannot be trumps. If the first declaration happens to be the K-Q of hearts, it will count only 20 as a non-trump marriage, and the trump suit will still be unsettled.

Thus goes the play of Six-pack Bezique; and if you have trouble scaring up the six packs to start a session, you may console yourself with this thought: the sportier element often plays *Eight*-pack Bezique, just to make the scores still higher.

One other tip: don't play Six-pack Bezique in too solemn and serious an atmosphere; it simply isn't in the spirit of the game. The cognoscenti talk and kid each other as they go their merry way.

Checkpayers . . .

good for one free drink at the nearest bar

the wager: That you can stay under water for any specified length of time.

the payoff: Hold a glass of water over your head for the period agreed upon . . . then run, don't walk, to the closest exit.

1. Bookworm

Two books, Volumes 1 and 2, stand side by side in order from left to right on a bookshelf. Not including bindings, each book is one inch thick; the bindings are each an eighth of an inch thick. Starting from page one, Volume 1, a hungry bookworm eats its way to the last page of Volume 2. How many inches did he consume?

2. Doubling Lily

A circular pool, twenty-five feet in diameter, has a remarkable lily in its center. This lily grows by doubling its area each day. At the end of thirty days, the lily exactly covers the pool. In how many days does this lily cover half the pool's area?

3. Rope Ladder

An observant person noted a rope ladder dangling from a ship in a harbor, with its bottom six rungs underwater. Also, he saw that each rung was four inches wide and that the rungs were ten inches apart. If the tide rose at the rate of five inches per hour, how many rungs would be submerged in three hours?

4. Lieutenant

Richard Roe met a friend wearing a lieutenant's uniform. They shook hands and greeted each other warmly as they had not seen one another in ten years. With his friend was a little girl: "I've been married since you saw me the last time to someone you don't know," said the lieutenant. "This girl is my daughter." Richard asked the child's name, and she replied that it was the same as her mother's. "So your name is Margaret!" How did he know?

5. Weights

What four weights would you use for a scale to weigh any number of pounds from one to forty inclusive?

6. Smith, Robinson and Jones

Three railway men named Smith, Robinson, and Jones, and three businessmen similarly named, live in the State of New York. The businessman Robinson and the brakeman live in Albany, the businessman Jones and the fireman live in Rochester, while the businessman Smith and the engineer live halfway between these two cities. The brakeman's namesake earns $3,500 a year; the engineer earns one-third of the businessman nearest him. The railway man Smith beats the fireman at billiards. Name the engineer.

7. Truth and Lies

A strange island is inhabited by pure-blooded and half-breed natives who look alike, but the half-breeds always lie, whereas the pure-blooded always tell the truth. A visitor on the island meets three natives. He asks them whether they are half-breeds or pure-blooded. The first native mutters something inaudible. The second, pointing to the first, says, "He says that he is pure-blooded." The third, pointing to the second, says, "He lies." Knowing beforehand that only one of the natives is a half-breed, the visitor concludes what each of the three is. Can you?

8. Forehead Marks

Three men, A, B, and C, are tested for quick thinking. On the forehead of each a cross is marked which, they are told, may be either blue or white. They are then taken to an empty room. None of the three knows the color of his own cross or is allowed to speak to the others, but each one is told he may leave the room if he either sees two white crosses or determines the color of his own cross. A is a sharp fellow. He notes that both B and C have blue crosses, and after a few seconds of quick thinking, he leaves the room, having determined the color of his own cross. What was the process by which he determined the answer, and what was the color of his cross?

9. Fox, Goose and Corn

A man has a fox, a goose and some corn. He must cross a river; however, he can take only one at a time. If he leaves the goose with the corn to take the fox over, the goose will devour the corn. If he leaves the fox alone with the goose, Reynard will devour the gander. How shall he get them all across?

10. Hocus-pocus

Here's a cryptarithm, which poses a problem in addition, subtraction, division or multiplication with letters instead of numbers. The object is to find the numbers. One problem I concocted was in addition, thus:

$$
\begin{array}{r}
H O C U S \\
P O C U S \\
\hline
P R E S T O
\end{array}
$$

11. Cigarettes

A cigarette fiend in Zion City was out of cigarettes—and you can't buy cigarettes in Zion City. Desperately he hunted through his hotelroom, where he had been illegally smoking, and collected a total of thirty-six dead butts, too short to be smokeable. By experiment, however, he found that, with newspaper and ingenuity, he could make a more or less satisfactory cigarette out of every six butts. So he made and smoked as many cigarettes as he possibly could, at the rate of six butts per. How many did he smoke?

12. Trees

Perhaps only a rabid mathematician would feel thoroughly at home with the difficulties of the man who had ten young trees to plant and an *idée fixe* as to how they ought to be planted. He wanted them arranged in five rows, with four trees in each row, and he could afford only ten trees. Work that one out. It can be done.

13. Fly and Bicycles

Two cyclists start at the same instant from opposite ends of a twenty-mile road, and ride toward each other at a constant speed of ten miles per hour until their front wheels meet. At the instant they start, a fly leaves the front wheel of one of them and flies straight toward the other at a constant speed of fifteen miles per hour till he touches the other wheel; he at once flies back till he touches the first wheel, and so on, his journeys naturally getting shorter and shorter as the cyclists approach each other, till he is crushed between the wheels. How far did the fly fly?

14. The Classic: How Old Is Ann?

"*The combined ages of Mary and Ann equal 44 years. Mary is twice as old as Ann was when Mary was half as old as Ann will be when Ann is three times as old as Mary was when Mary was three times as old as Ann. How old is Ann?*"

15. Planes to S.F. and N.Y.

"Two planes leave San Francisco and New York at the same time, one bound on a non-stop flight for New York, the other on a non-stop flight to San Francisco. The distance each must travel is 2,500 miles. Each can fly ten miles to a gallon of gasoline, and each carries 250 gallons. Which plane crashed, and why?"

ANSWERS ON PAGE 279

KINSHIP PUZZLES

Just in case anyone drags up the old "I'm My Own Grandpa" song —which, by the way, was evidently swiped from Mark Twain's "Note Left by a Suicide":

"I married a widow with a grown daughter. My father fell in love with my step-daughter and married her—thus becoming my son-in-law, and my step-daughter became my mother because she was my father's wife.

"My wife gave birth to a son, who was, of course, my father's brother-in-law, and also my uncle, because he was the brother of my step-mother.

"My father's wife also became the mother of a son, who was, equally of course, my brother, and also my grandchild, for he was the son of my step-daughter.

"Accordingly, my wife was my grandmother because she was my father's wife's mother—I was my wife's husband and grandchild at the same time—and as the husband of a person's grandmother is his grandfather—I AM MY OWN GRANDFATHER!"

Certainly no one ever got into such a tangle before or since, and his seeking of the quiet of the tomb was entirely justified.

1. "Can a man marry his widow's sister?" is answered, of course, as above; but the statement "A man married his widow's sister" is perfectly correct and entirely explainable. Perhaps you would like to try unraveling it.

[248]

2. In-laws are the cause of trouble not only from a domestic standpoint. Here is a snatch of conversation overheard on a bus, which goes to prove the above statement: "That man's mother was my mother's mother-in-law; but he had a terrible fight with my father, and they still don't speak." The question is, what was the relation of the gentleman in question to the speaker?

3. Another combination of in-law-ship is involved in the following horrible-sounding bit (one man is speaking to another): "It's really quite simple, my dear chap. You happen to be my father's brother-in-law, my brother's father-in-law, and my father-in-law's brother." We are asked to provide marriages (within the legal limitations, of course) that would have brought about this astounding triple relationship.

The legal limitations, by the way, might be summarized to read: a man may not marry his aunt or his niece or the daughter of his deceased wife's sister (though he may, as stated above, marry said sister). Nor may he marry his mother, his grandmother, or his great-grand-mother. This last may sound preposterous, but solvers of puzzles partake of the quality which the Scotch impute to kings—they are "kittle cattle to shoe behind." If such limitations were not stated I greatly fear that some desperate toiler would tootle *Lohengrin* over a man and his grandmother, thereby making him his own grandfather and working up all sorts of startling relationships with the other members of his family.

4. A man had two friends, a brother and a sister. Their names were Augustus Smith and Sophronisba Smith. One day an attractive-looking young man appeared whom Augustus introduced as his nephew. The man naturally spoke of Sophronisba as his aunt, but the youth corrected him at once, saying that though he was the nephew of Augustus Smith he was not the nephew of Sophronisba Smith, Augustus' sister. As Bildad the Tishbite might have said, How come?

5. At a certain family party there were present one grandfather, one grandmother, two fathers, two mothers, four children, three grandchildren, one brother, two sisters, two sons, two daughters, one father-in-law, one mother-in-law, and one daughter-in-law. The party was held in a small apartment, with room for only seven people around the table. And yet all were served at once, without the slightest inconvenience. Perhaps you can explain this without recourse to relativity or the fourth dimension.

6. One favorite kinship puzzle is usually set out in the form of a story. This involves getting two people into a situation where there is no possible room for another party—say in a two-seater plane—

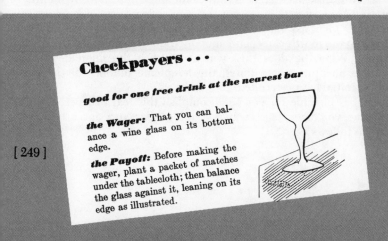

and then proceeding something like this: "Well, this plane would only hold two people, get me? And this pilot took my uncle up for a ride. After awhile this pilot started to stunt, and my nephew, who is a nervous sort of chap—" At this point someone usually interrupts with "You said it was your uncle in the plane, not your nephew." To which the narrator replies, "Oh, yes, my uncle and my nephew were in the plane. So this pilot didn't pay any attention to my uncle; in fact, he called to my nephew, 'You ain't seen nothin' yet!' and stunted worse than ever. So then my nephew reached for his parachute, but my uncle couldn't find the ring—" Just now some bright individual will say, "You mean the pilot was your nephew." To which the narrator replies with deliberation, "He is no relation to me at all." Then one of those last-analysis boys says, "You say the pilot is no relation to you?"

"Correct."

"And both your uncle and your nephew were in the plane?"

"Correcter than ever."

"And the plane would hold only two people?"

"Colossally correct."

"Two people, that is, counting the pilot as one?"

"I'm out of adverbs to express how correct that is."

"*Well!*"

"Oh, yes. The man who went up with that reckless pilot is my uncle —and he is also my nephew. Consequently I am his nephew, and at the same time his uncle."

The narrator can then explain, unless his listeners would prefer to work it out for themselves.

ANSWERS TO KINSHIP PUZZLES ON PAGE 280

TRICKS
1. NUMBER PLEASE?

1. This stunt will guarantee the success of your social life wherever a telephone directory is handy. Making a great point of the fact that you are neither peeping nor eavesdropping, have the victim write any three digits—let's say, for example, 632. Invert the sequence— here obtaining 236. Subtract the lesser from the greater, arriving at 396.

(What the victim does not know is that no matter what three numbers he chooses, upon inverting and subtracting, his final answer must be one of the following nine numbers: 99, 198, 297, 396, 495, 594, 693, 792, 891. For the present, merely remember this fact. You may check it later if you wish.)

2. Next, ask the victim to turn to the page indicated by the freely arrived-at answer, pointing out that you have no way of knowing this answer. Then ask him to glance over at the second column, count down to the fourth name, and announce aloud the initial letter of that name. When he does this, you accomplish the miracle—you announce, in appropriate tones, the telephone number of the party whose initial has been called.

3. It is possible for you to accomplish this feat because, one day at home, you have gone through your local directory and made a key-card as follows:

[250]

You have turned to pages 99, 198, 297, etc., and noted the telephone numbers appearing after the fourth name down in the second column on these pages.

Since each of these pages is almost a hundred apart, the initial letter of the party's name will be different in every case. Hence, all that is required, is that you jot down the initial and follow it with the accompanying phone number.

In performing this stunt, turn your back with the reasonable excuse that you do not wish to see the numbers that your victim is inscribing. This gives you a chance to remove your key-card from a handy vest pocket, and keep it concealed in the palm so that, when the initial letter is called, you can read off the corresponding phone number. (As a matter of fact, it is much more effective to memorize the key numbers, eliminating the use of the card.)

2. COIN TRICKS

1. One amusing little stunt with coins is to start with four—pennies or twenty-dollar gold pieces, as long as they are all alike—arranged like this:

—and by sliding them about, without lifting any of them from the table or employing any extra coins, get them into this position:

That is, arrange them so that if there were a fifth coin in the position shown by the dotted circle, all the original coins would touch it. It won't do to slide the lower right-hand coin over until it is as nearly in correct position as you can judge by eyesight; the position must be exact, not approximate.

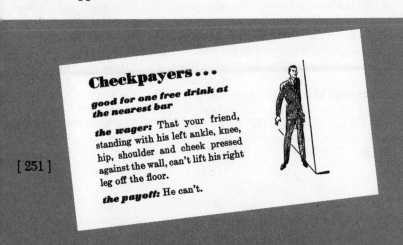

2. Nothing much to that one. Ah, but wait! Your friends are by this time interested; take five coins and arrange them like this:

—and then challenge anyone to arrange them so that they would exactly touch a sixth coin, like this:

—keeping to the conditions already laid down and accomplishing their object in only *four moves*.

It's not too difficult to perform this stunt in an unlimited number of moves; seven is what the novice usually requires. Others, a little more observant, will do it in six moves, and there is the standard solution in five. But for the four-move triumph, see page 280.

3. Another really topnotch coin problem is to take five pennies and five nickels and lay them in a straight line, alternating pennies and nickels, like this:

The two blank spaces indicated at the right of the row are to be used, as necessary, in solving the puzzle, which is this: to get all the nickels together and all the pennies together by moving *two contiguous coins at a time* to the vacant spaces. You might, for instance, slide the two left-hand coins around into the spaces at the right; then any other two contiguous coins could be moved into the vacant spaces left by the first pair, and another contiguous two into the spaces left by the second pair, and so on. The blank spaces must be left at one end of the row when you have finished; and only contiguous coins may be moved—that is, coins immediately beside each other. Coins between which the vacant spaces happen to fall are not contiguous. Five moves are enough to do the trick.

The specially good feature about this one is that the opening moves are disguised—no benefit is apparently gained by moving any one pair, though if you don't start with the right one you're sunk, as far as five moves go. Like all such puzzles, if given an unlimited number of moves it can be solved eventually; but the person who is betting with you is not allowed an unlimited number of moves—not if you're on the job.

4. A good deal of money has been won—and lost—on this simple proposition: take six coins, three of one kind and three of another—let's stick to pennies and nickels—and lay them out like so, with a blank space between each group, said blank space to contain only one coin:

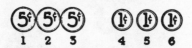

The trick is to get the coins to change places by moving one at a time either to a blank space directly or by a jump over a single coin, with this important condition: *no coin can ever move backward.* Obviously, in the case shown, the nickels can move only to the right, and the pennies only to the left. You can start by moving either coin No. 3 or coin No. 4 to the vacant space; or you can jump coin No. 2 over No. 3, or No. 5 over No. 4. You will find that you—and your betting companion—can get hopelessly locked up in this one if you aren't careful. It takes fifteen moves, by the way, and once you learn the trick of it it is a simplicity and a joy forever; you can do it so swiftly that even a watcher won't get on to the system.

5. Here is a little stunt which sounds a lot simpler than it is; Take six coins—they needn't be alike, though it makes the general layout neater if all six are the same—and lay them out in a row, three with heads up and the other three with tails on top. The puzzle is to get them arranged with heads and tails alternating—in three moves each move consisting of turning over a pair of adjacent coins. That is, at each move you turn over two coins, and the coins turned over must be next to each other. Of course, if you could turn over coins that were not adjacent the puzzle would be solved in one move by turning over the second and fifth coins; but adjacency is of the essence, as the barristers say.

SOLUTIONS TO COIN TRICKS ON PAGE 280

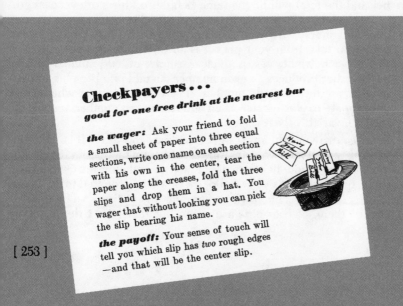

Checkpayers...
good for one free drink at the nearest bar

the wager: Ask your friend to fold a small sheet of paper into three equal sections, write one name on each section with his own in the center, tear the paper along the creases, fold the three slips and drop them in a hat. You wager that without looking you can pick the slip bearing his name.

the payoff: Your sense of touch will tell you which slip has *two* rough edges —and that will be the center slip.

1. One device to trap the unwary is so simple as to seem positively childish, and so obvious that one would think nobody could possibly fail to see it; and yet people consistently fall for it and are mightily mystified by it. Take a handful of coins from your pocket and keep your fist closed on it (you might jingle it a bit to show your opponent that you are holding more than one coin) and then tell the victim that he may take any number he likes from *his* pocket, odd or even as he chooses, and that you will bet that the total will be different from the number he chose—that is, if he selected an odd number, the total will be even, and vice versa. His bet, of course, is that his number and the total will be the same as far as oddness or evenness go.

On the face of it, it looks like a good fifty-fifty bet; but—it's a fraud, pure and simple. All you have to do is be sure that the number of coins you take from your pocket is an odd number; your opponent will *never* be right. It's quite clear, surely: an odd number plus an odd number produces an even number; an odd number plus an even number produces an odd number. Therefore no matter whether the unfortunate easy mark selects an odd or an even number of coins the total is invariably the reverse.

2. Of course you can always get somebody to fall for this: "I'll give you thirty cents in two coins, one of which isn't a quarter. Sold? The money's up? Good; here you are; a quarter and a nickel. One of them isn't a quarter. That's what I said; that's what I promised to do. I have given you thirty cents in two coins, and one of them isn't a quarter. One of them, of course, *is* a quarter, but that wasn't the idea. Pay me."

AFTER-DINNER WITCHCRAFT

If you would make a hit with the beautiful young ladies, don't step up to the piano, prattle on about Picasso or memorize the *New York Times* book reviews (let alone read a book itself). Turn on the mumbo-jumbo! Claim that you're a psychic and you're in — with fortune-telling, for instance.

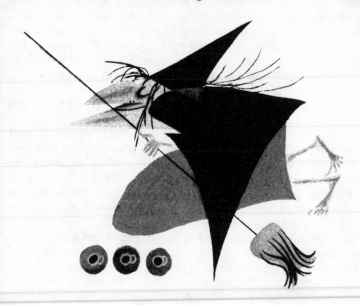

FORTUNE-TELLING

Fortune-telling, especially by cards, consists mainly of unabashed, facile, and highly greased fibbing. Pre-information helps, too. If you are not a good liar, practice lying in secret; go up to your mirror and let forth such a flow of lies that even your reflection blanches and turns away its head in shameful meditation that it is your exact counterpart. Moreover you must learn to so go on that the fib-flow is never stopped. When you can do this well, you are prepared to take your first lessons in card-laying.

Presupposing that you have learned to lie well, you must now exert what is loosely known as "hypnotic influence"; this is very easy as it consists mainly in astounding the "subject" through telling him or her that which is most apparently obvious concerning himself.

People having their fortunes told are under a kind of hypnosis anyway and will believe almost anything you tell them. And it needs only a glance to see whether your stab into the psychic has reached home and if you have struck, then you are indeed in luck. One little strike and you may go ahead and foretell her practically anything.

It is always well to foretell that she is going to fall in love with a young man. If she presses you to add his description and you can think of no one else, describe yourself.

There are a number of manholes in fortune-telling, which it would be well to avoid. Remembering Rule No. 1, of pre-information, and Rule No. 2, of superlative lying, keep well in mind Rule No. 3, which is, *use no known system*. If you lay down your cards in a known sys-

[255]

tem this very system may be very well known to your frail victim, and should this be the very unfortunate case you will probably soon find a Ming vase wrapped around your broken neck. On the contrary, you must lay your cards down in a most complicated arrangement—any arrangement will do provided it is not an arrangement you have ever seen before. After you lay the cards down you will now spend a long time studying them—the longer the better—and as you *crouch* over each card, you will mumble "Up-hump!" This signifies that you are getting a load of something pretty terrific and that you are endeavoring to piece this mess together although, apparently, you hate to do so. She will already be shaking in a quiver of apprehension.

And now, Mr. Psychologist, tell her a nice, good, pleasant fortune. She will be so relieved that she will be very predisposed to believe anything you say, if you say it firmly.

To tell the actual fortune, first draw a long breath (this will send blood to your brain and oil up the muscles in your tongue) and then spiel. Pointing from one card to the other you will now proceed to deliver as brilliantly as you can, and Heaven help you if you stop. If you find that you can think at all, try to draw upon every piece of eavesdropping or pre-information that you can. Don't look closely at the cards; the less you know about them, the better. Guide yourself firmly but delicately by her ejaculations; you must constantly know whether you are upon the right trail and consequently be prepared in an instant to swerve if disaster appears imminent. When a trail is hot she will brighten with confidence. When it is cold she will look at you clammily through half-closed eyes.

Let us suppose that early in the card-laying you have had the good fortune to stumble across a personage or situation which is obviously kosher and of the most tremendous interest to her. This incidentally is the most tremendous luck that can happen to any fortune teller. Not only can you now efficiently cook "his" goose, but you can also safely begin to coax and prod the "subject" with card after card—"by the way this card *would seem to mean* . . . that is true, isn't it?" etc., etc. And you need not worry. By this time she will be so completely under the card-laying hypnosis, so utterly astonished that you should have turned up something of secret but sizzling importance to her, that she will now scarcely permit you to tell her fortune, but *she will now proceed to tell it for you!* In the remote future she will always believe quite absolutely that you have told her the very things she actually told you, and loudly indeed will she sing your praises! And now, if you are only the least tiny bit unscrupulous she will gladly come up to hear you play Hindemith or to look at your priceless Picassos; why not cook her a Crêpe Suzette while you are about it?

But if you blush easily and are not a good liar, why not try table-tipping and have a table do your talking for you?

TABLE-TIPPING

Table-tipping also has the advantage of being even more mesmeric than card-laying; the eerie atmosphere will not only set the lady's psychological tomtom beating, but it will also make her afraid to go home alone at night. You will now simply call loudly for a small table—if possible select one with one leg a little shorter than the others —then place four or five persons around the table and have everyone spread his hands out flat, thumbs touching each other and little finger tips touching the little fingers of the persons alongside. This is, you explain, to keep the "electrical body-fluid" unbroken and acting upon the table; this very favorable condition will lure sundry loose spirits to try their hands on an evening's terrestrial conversation. All spirits use the same code, a rather imbecile one; A is signaled by one rap, B is signaled by two, C is signaled by three, and so on down to Z (incidentally a rather tiresome letter to telegraph). But in table-tipping everybody has plenty of time, and no one seems to care if our first spirit telegraphs something like this "WXKLHIQUPGYPGYPOHNOOHNO" for you can easily explain this as the work of either a malicious little spirit who always annoys you at first or the signal of an ancient Persian Prince who has never learned English but who has been trying all of these years to "break through" without, however, any apparent success.

All is now ready except for the dimming of the lights and the placing of a scribe with paper and pencil at a far corner of the room. He will take down any possible messages. You are now able to proceed. With your hands upon the small table and after about three minutes of expectant waiting you will now exert a small pressure upon the rickety table causing it to move an inch or two along the floor. You now exclaim,

"There! Didn't you feel something? I felt something!"

The table moves again. You say with suppressed excitement, "The spirit is approaching."

Then the table begins to rap. (You are merely upsetting its small balance as rapidly and surely as a machine gun.) The short leg is jittering in code against the floor. "I-I-I-I-I-I-I." You now pretend to be angry with the spirit. "What do you want?" you whisper hoarsely into the half-darkness.

IAMDEADTRYTOGETMYMESSAGEITISOF
GREATESTIMPORTANCE.

After the scribe has separated this into English, and it has made a certain disturbing impression, the table will move to a new section of the floor, twisting and turning *en route*. You all move your chairs with it and set up a new base of operations. It will now tap:

XYZLMNOPQRSTOOOOOOOOOOOO

Now this you will have none of. You are severe. "Malicious spirit,

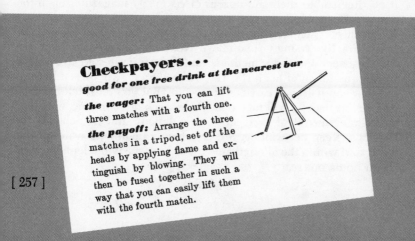

leave us! Let the friendly control break through!" Everybody shivers; the table commences tapping again.

IAMDEADIAMDEADIAMDEADXY
QUTYLXWQZWQXOOOOOOOO!

Again you have to pull the spirit back upon the track, but soon he will really open up and give you all some pretty wonderful advice. If this advice isn't of the kind that will make that lovely blonde on the other side of the table sit up and resolve to make several important changes in her immediate date book, then you should not be head man at a table-tipping party.

NUMEROLOGY

Numerology is another attractive parlor game and it will entice your beautiful victim to sit with you over a page of your penciled numerals for hours upon end. There is nothing to it. All that is necessary is for you to maintain stoutly that you have an older and much more accurate system of Numerology than any Numerology system ever discovered before, yours having come directly from the ancient Chaldeans, whereas all later systems stem from the Phoenicians who had already fairly bungled it, so accounting for the fact that so many people today having their numbers read are deeply dissatisfied with the results thereof. This, you aver, could never happen with your older and more perfect system.

You now write down the letters of her name and quickly, without apparent thought, mark a cipher—any cipher—underneath each letter. It matters not if you should accidentally have the same numeral under B and Q . . . your system is different, remember. You will now do an enormous amount of multiplication, subtraction, and addition, and, if you want, you can throw in a little higher calculus just to impress. At last you are ready to tell her fortune. Make it a good one.

(If you want to throw in a few remarks about her glandular personality at this point you will give her that comfortable feeling that nothing can be concealed from you. She feels as if she were nude before you, incidentally an extremely homelike and relaxing attitude. She will automatically think "Oh what's the use of resisting him, he can see right through me anyway.")

ASTROLOGY

But the really smart fortune teller will soon drop all these infantile pursuits and take up, instead, Astrology. Astrology is really the Big Noise follow-up of after-dinner witchcraft. The method is simplicity itself. Remember there are dozens of Astrology magazines upon the newsstands containing exact information about the stars many years in advance. Therefore should you, at your dinner party, meet the most attractive young girl you have ever seen, be sure to tell her fortune by one of the above methods, and if she is impressed, ask her for the date and hour of her birth. You will make a note of this and assure her that you will now cast her horoscope. But you must tell her that this, unfortunately, will take one whole week of your time, entailing an infinite amount of hard labor, calculations, and tremendous rechecking. Keep her waiting. She will barely be able to wait out the week, and within the allotted amount of time she will telephone you. "Is my horoscope ready?"

It is, you having meanwhile used your typewriter, ten pieces of paper, and a horoscope partially copied from one of the more obscure magazines. That is to say you will not copy it quite exactly but use only the technical positions of the stars and considerable fancy of your own. If you have any trepidations just check one astrology magazine against the other and you will come to note that no one astrologer agrees with the other; therefore, why should you, *another* astrologer, agree with the rest? And upon these ten accompanying sheets you will typewrite just exactly *everything* the stars command her to do day by day for the next three months. We sincerely hope that you will make the stars show the least bit of common ordinary horse sense. After all, she will be following a typewritten list of *your* instructions for three months!

QUIZZES

Many a desperate host has revived a stuffy party by bringing out some clever games and setting his guests against each other in friendly competition. But many another host has driven his guests from his doorstep by the same method. So before you trot out these quizzes, be sure you have the answer to this jack-pot question: will a pencil-and-paper game alienate the relaxed members of the group? will a guessing game show up any embarrassing brain-deficiencies?

If not, why not run these quizzes as spell-downs — choosing up sides and gradually eliminating wrong-guessers until only one contestant remains? Or supply pencils and paper for individual competition, for score. When time and place are right, the games gather momentum so rapidly that you wonder, when you look at your watch, where the evening has gone.

QUIZZES FOR WHIZZES

The classified section of your newspaper was never like this, but let's pretend that for one special edition it consists of the following 50 ads. You will note that each public notice contains an allusion to some literary work; your task is to name that work, whether it be novel, play, short story, opera or poem.

Count two points for each correct answer. Then, as a bonus, award yourself an extra point if you can also name the author or composer.

The total possible score is 150. Don't worry about scoring more than 100. In fact, you're doing very well if you get 92; and anything over 75 is considered good.

ANSWERS ON PAGE 281

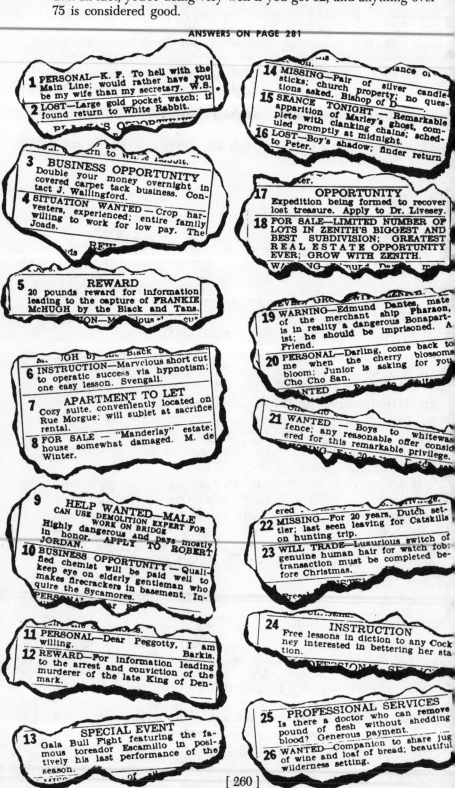

1 PERSONAL—K. F. To hell with the Main Line; would rather have you be my wife than my secretary. W.S.

2 LOST—Large gold pocket watch; if found return to White Rabbit.

3 BUSINESS OPPORTUNITY
Double your money overnight in covered carpet tack business. Contact J. Wallingford.

4 SITUATION WANTED—Crop harvesters, experienced; entire family willing to work for low pay. The Joads.

5 REWARD
20 pounds reward for information leading to the capture of FRANKIE McHUGH by the Black and Tans.

6 INSTRUCTION—Marvelous short cut to operatic success via hypnotism; one easy lesson. Svengali.

7 APARTMENT TO LET
Cozy suite, conveniently located on Rue Morgue; will sublet at sacrifice rental.

8 FOR SALE — "Manderlay" estate; house somewhat damaged. M. de Winter.

9 HELP WANTED—MALE
CAN USE DEMOLITION EXPERT FOR WORK ON BRIDGE
Highly dangerous and pays mostly in honor. APPLY TO ROBERT JORDAN.

10 BUSINESS OPPORTUNITY—Qualified chemist will be paid well to keep eye on elderly gentleman who makes firecrackers in basement. Inquire the Sycamores.

11 PERSONAL—Dear Peggotty, I am willing. Barkis.

12 REWARD—For information leading to the arrest and conviction of the murderer of the late King of Denmark.

13 SPECIAL EVENT
Gala Bull Fight featuring the famous toreador Escamillo in positively his last performance of the season.

14 MISSING—Pair of silver candlesticks; church property; no questions asked. Bishop of D

15 SEANCE TONIGHT — Remarkable apparition of Marley's ghost, complete with clanking chains; scheduled promptly at midnight.

16 LOST—Boy's shadow; finder return to Peter.

17 OPPORTUNITY
Expedition being formed to recover lost treasure. Apply to Dr. Livesey.

18 FOR SALE—LIMITED NUMBER OF LOTS IN ZENITH'S BIGGEST AND BEST SUBDIVISION; GREATEST REAL ESTATE OPPORTUNITY EVER; GROW WITH ZENITH.

19 WARNING—Edmund Dantes, mate of the merchant ship Pharaon, is in reality a dangerous Bonapartist; he should be imprisoned. A Friend.

20 PERSONAL—Darling, come back to me when the cherry blossoms bloom; Junior is asking for you. Cho Cho San.

21 WANTED — Boys to whitewash fence; any reasonable offer considered for this remarkable privilege.

22 MISSING—For 20 years, Dutch settler; last seen leaving for Catskills on hunting trip.

23 WILL TRADE—Luxurious switch of genuine human hair for watch fob; transaction must be completed before Christmas.

24 INSTRUCTION
Free lessons in diction to any Cockney interested in bettering her station.

25 PROFESSIONAL SERVICES
Is there a doctor who can remove pound of flesh without shedding blood? Generous payment.

26 WANTED—Companion to share jug of wine and loaf of bread; beautiful wilderness setting.

7 PERSONAL—REPENT YE SINNERS—save your soul. Apply to the Reverend Davidson of Nebraska.

8 BOATING—Row on beautiful Grass Lake in very boat used by Clyde Griffiths, equipped with new unsinkable device.

29 REWARD—For information leading to identity of my bridegroom, who recently arrived via swanboat.

30 WANTED—Successor to ruler of Tibetan utopia; running water and other ultra modern conveniences.

31 NOTICE—to all sea captains—any ship carrying Philip Nolan is prohibited from permitting him to disembark at any port.

2 INSTRUCTION—Easy and pleasant knitting lessons given in front of La Guillotine. MADAME THERESE DEFARGE.

3 FOUND—Last night upon my doorstep, a baby boy. Reward for information regarding him. Mr. Allworthy.

34 PERSONAL — Gavin, forget your ministerial duties, and meet me in the woods for a gypsy wedding. Babbie.

35 ATTRACTION
CITIZENS OF LILLIPUT, COME ONE, COME ALL, AND SEE THE GIANT WHO HAS BEEN CAST UPON OUR BEACH.

36 WANTED FOR MURDER
Runaway slave by the name of Jim, last seen floating down the Mississippi on a raft.

37 REWARD—For information concerning infant boy named Mowgli, lost in the forest; parents anxious for his safety.

38 ANNOUNCEMENT — Mister Heathcliff is now home from his travels in America and is holding open house at the Grange.

39 OPPORTUNITY
For young men to learn lucrative profession under tutelage of experts; SEE THE ARTFUL DODGER OR FAGIN.

40 GOVERNESS WANTED—To care for ward of Mr. Rochester. Apply at Thornwood.

41 FOR SALE—Pious and faithful slave named Tom. Apply George Shelby of Kentucky.

42 NEEDED—A brave man to impersonate King Rudolph at his coronation tomorrow in Strelsan, thereby foiling his treacherous brother, Duke Michael.

43 AUCTION TODAY
Dorlcote Mill must be sold because of ruin and death of owner; see Tom or Maggie Tulliver for information.

44 PILLORY TODAY—Bostonians can witness the punishment of one Hester Prynne, who with her illegitimate daughter will serve sentence in the public square today.

45 EXPERT TRAINING—For recalcitrant wives, undertaken by Petruchio, who has had great personal success.

46 FENCING LESSONS — Learn the gentlemanly art of self-defense from the best firm in the business. ATHOS, PORTHOS, ARAMIS AND D'ARTAGNAN.

47 DEATH NOTICE—Catherine, beloved wife of Frederic Henry; suddenly. interment in Montreux, Switz.

48 REWARD—For information as to the whereabouts of Fortunato, nobleman and connoisseur of wines, who has disappeared without leaving the slightest trace.

49 WARNING—TRY NOT THE PASS! Dark lowers the tempest overhead. The roaring torrent is deep and wide.

50 FOR RENT
Stately palace in Xanadu, near the river Alph.

HOW ATTRACTIVE ARE YOU TO MEN?

1—Do you bring the names of other men into the conversation to give yourself a sought-after appearance?

Don't. This may give a man a sense of inferiority—he is uncomfortable with you, and soon drifts away to someone else. It may make him wonder how much talking you do about *him*.

2—Do you wear clothes that make you a little more up-to-the-minute than the other women in your set?

Good—provided your taste is reliable and that the clothes suit you. Men may rant about that "crazy hat" but they swell with pride when their lady companions arouse admiring stares.

3—If you are asked to get another girl for a foursome, do you pick one obviously less attractive than you are?

You are unwise to do so. Get the most glamorous girl you know, and both men will be pleased.

4—Do you make a point of building up other women, even those you dislike, in discussing them with a man?

This is sound practice. But don't put it on so thick that it sounds like a line.

5—Do men marvel at your capacity for holding liquor?

A great mistake: it gives you a fast reputation and runs into money —the man's money—besides.

6—How many comfortable chairs are there in your living room?

At least two, I hope. No man can fall in love unless he has a chance to relax and he can't if either of you sits bolt upright.

7—Do you keep men interested by hinting that later—not tonight —you'll be really demonstrative?

This is a low trick and one that a surprising number of men see through at once. If you kiss a man, it should be for your own pleasure and not a reward for him.

8—Do you make things easier for a man by suggesting that he climb into a car first, if he's driving, or by asking him not to stand up when you come into the room?

This is an error—men know that they are supposed to show these signs of consideration to a girl and they respect her more if she takes them as a matter of course.

9—Do you ever embarrass a man by telling him he's good-look-ing or has big muscles or is too, too intelligent?

Try it! Almost any man can stand almost any amount of flattery, however obvious, without embarrassment or suspicion.

10—Do you knit when you are having a cozy, fireside evening with a man?

For some reason, men hate to see a woman doing anything with her hands when talking to her. Undivided attention is best.

11—Do you either play bridge or dance really well?

If not, take steps to correct this at once. You're better off if you do *both* well, but one talent is mandatory.

12—Are you so beautifully groomed that you make the average man feel like a lout when he takes you out?

Fine. Men are extremely critical of any imperfection in a girl's neatness. If he feels like a lout once, the average escort will take pains to be better-dressed himself the next time.

13—Do you, when you have first met a really attractive man, clinch your future acquaintance by some polite variation of "Come up and see me sometime"?

It often helps out on the occasions when the man is too shy to make the first advance himself.

14—Do you keep your friendships warm by chatty calls to your men friends at their offices?

This is fatal.

15—Do you use artificial conversation gambits like "What movie would you choose if you had to see it every week for a year?" to start talk with a shy dinner partner?

A very good plan—someone has to start the conversation and a question like this can keep it rolling for quite awhile.

16—Do you save yourself wear and tear by not troubling to enter-tain men bores?

A grave mistake. Bores have their uses since a clever girl can prac-tice her conversation on them, with nothing much to lose. Besides, they often have attractive friends.

17—Do you suffer from indecision when ordering dinner or drinks in a restaurant with a man?

This maddens them—learn to make up your mind rapidly.

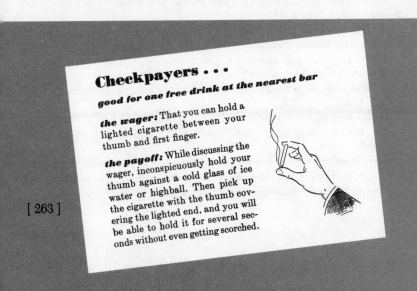

Checkpayers . . .

good for one free drink at the nearest bar

the wager: That you can hold a lighted cigarette between your thumb and first finger.

the payoff: While discussing the wager, inconspicuously hold your thumb against a cold glass of ice water or highball. Then pick up the cigarette with the thumb cov-ering the lighted end, and you will be able to hold it for several sec-onds without even getting scorched.

HOW ATTRACTIVE ARE YOU TO WOMEN?

1—Do you use the continental approach, based on the belief that an immediate pass flatters a woman?

This is the average man's greatest mistake. If a pass, on first acquaintance, doesn't insult a girl it at least bores her.

2—Do you show your real fondness for a girl by telling her about her bad points and advising her how to improve them?

This again is an error. If you must tell her you hate her perfume or how she does her hair, wrap it up in heavy sugar coating.

3—Do you show your devotion to a woman by holding her hand or putting your arm around her when her friends are present?

Please don't. Even a girl who is affectionate in private dislikes public mauling.

4—Can you describe the dress or hat worn by the last two girls you took out?

If not, notice and comment on the next few. Women appreciate having men notice the efforts they make over their appearance.

5—Do you have a double code about drunkenness for men and women when they are together?

If a man has to get drunk, he'll be more attractive if he restricts this behavior to stag company.

6—Do you sometimes take a girl out on parties of four or more, as a change from twosomes?

A good idea. A girl may feel hurt if you never ask her to meet your other friends.

7—Do you make distinctions between the jokes you'd tell a man in the club shower and those you'd tell a girl in a parked automobile?

Almost no women like bathroom jokes or jokes with dirty words.

8—Do you tell a woman she's beautiful, even if she isn't?

This habit hurts nobody and makes a lot of girls happier.

9—Do you ask an attractive girl—who is probably busy most evenings—to call you up sometime when she's free?

Don't do this: you may always ask a popular girl far enough ahead of time to find a free evening.

10—Do you plan your evenings with a woman ahead of time or leave the choice of amusement up to her?

It's much more flattering for a man to announce the evening's program, showing he has given thought to her amusement.

11—Do you believe it necessary in the modern age to push in a girl's chair for her and to light her cigarettes?

These small courtesies mean a lot to a girl.

12—Do you ever tell a girl you love her, under the spell of the moment, when you suspect that you won't tomorrow?

This is a dirty trick and if you do, you ought to be ashamed of yourself. Moreover, the word will soon get around to other women.

13—How many times a week do you shave?

Once a day is minimum, if you care what women think of you.

14—Would you dine a girl expensively and not buy her flowers, or economize on the place and bring her at least a gardenia?

Most women would prefer having flowers and less to eat.

15—If your hostess at a dance is obviously having a whirl, do you consider it necessary to dance with her?

You always should, as a matter of good manners.

16—Do you try to arouse a girl's interest by boasting of your success with other women?

Don't ever do this!

17—Do you consider it a young girl's own business whether she gets tight and is indiscreet when she's out with you?

Keep an inexperienced girl from getting tight, if you have to spank her, and don't let any woman become indiscreet through liquor. Triumphs over drunken women don't help any man.

18—If a girl you're fond of asks you to be nice to her cousin with adenoids and buck teeth do you cut her off your list?

Not pleasant, but if you rally around and give Cousin Belle a whirl, you'll soon be known as the nicest man in town.

19—If you had a quarrel with a girl—in which she is clearly in the wrong—will you wait for her to apologize before calling her up or risk being a door mat and do it first?

Be a door mat—it's easier for you to call a girl than for her to call you.

Checkpayers · · ·
good for one free drink at the nearest bar

the wager: That you can take a drink from an unopened bottle without removing the cork.

the payoff: Select a champagne or vermouth bottle; turn it upside down and pour a shotglassful from another bottle into the indentation at the bottom of the wager bottle. Then take your drink as specified.

365 EXCUSES FOR A PARTY

Here's your new line on parties and why to throw them. There's an excuse for every day of the year, and every one authentic.

January
1—Happy Hangover Day
2—Today the sun reaches its closest point to the earth
3—The Planet Mercury is visible
4—The Anniversary of the OPM working on a rubber rationing program
5—Anniversary of the National Red Cross
6—Swap Day
7—Birthday of Millard Fillmore
8—151st birthday of Lowell Mason
9—On this day in '42 Mickey Rooney applied for a marriage license
10—On this day in '42 Skeezix of the funnies landed a new job
11—Anniversary of the meeting of the Federation of Women's Clubs
12—Anniversary of Saks gigantic sale
13—Buy Defense Stamps Day
14—On this day in '42 the 1 a.m. curfew for bowlers was declared
15—This day in '42 marked the beer shortage in London
16—Anniversary of the 18th Amendment
17—Birthday of Ben Franklin
18—Anniversary of the opening of the Scrap Salvage Office
19—Birthday of Robert E. Lee
20—Inauguration Day
21—On this day in '42 grapes were $6 a pound in London
22—Anniversary of the Hail America Golf Tournament
23—First Anniversary of the U. of Chicago two-year degrees
24—Anniversary of the discovery of gold in California
25—Anniversary of the announcement of the WPB girdle regulations
26—Birthday of Jiffy the Giraffe
27—Anniversary of the tearing down of Honeymoon Bridge at Niagara Falls
28—Annual snowball fight of Rinkeydinks
29—Birthday of William McKinley
30—Birthday of Franklin Roosevelt
31—On this day in '42 Ann Shirley sued for her divorce

February
1—First anniversary of the order prohibiting juke boxes
2—Groundhog Day
3—Birthday of Sidney Lanier
4—Anniversary of the meeting of the American Social Hygiene Association
5—Constitution Day in Mexico
6—Birthday of Babe Ruth
7—Birthday of writer, Charles Dickens
8—Anniversary of the N. Y. Dog Show
9—Feast Day
10—Anniversary of the unification of Upper and Lower Canada
11—Edison Day
12—Lincoln's Birthday
13—Birthday of Grant Wood, painter
14—Valentine's Day
15—Susan B. Anthony Day
16—Mule Day
17—Anniversary of the Parents and Teachers Association
18—Eve of the Marine invasion of Iwo Jima (1945)
19—Anniversary of the International Council for Exceptional Children
20—Birthday of Gloria Vanderbilt Stokowski
21—Anniversary of the dedication of the Washington Monument
22—Washington's birthday
23—Anniversary of the Red Army
24—Independence Day in Cuba
25—Anniversary of the launching of the Kingfish, a submarine
26—Birthday of the writer, Victor Hugo
27—International Day
28—Anniversary of the Chinese Feast of the Lanterns

March
1—State Day in Nebraska
2—Texas Independence Day
3—Anniversary of the Child Labor Law
4—Anniversary of meeting of U. S. Congress
5—Anniversary of the bank holiday
6—Anniversary of the meeting of the American Chemical Society
7—Masaryk Day for Czechoslovakians
8—Farmer's Day
9—Anniversary of the battle between the ships, Monitor and Merrimac
10—Anniversary of establishment of Albany as the capital of New York
11—Anniversary of the Lease-Lend Act
12—Anniversary of the Girl Scouts
13—Anniversary of the discovery of the planet Pluto
14—Birthday of Albert Einstein
15—Anniversary of the abdication of the Czar of Russia
16—Birthday of James Madison
17—St. Patrick's Day
18—Birthday of Grover Cleveland
19—Anniversary of the creation of the National Defense Mediation Board
20—Anniversary of "Uncle Tom's Cabin"
21—Anniversary of the St. Louis Dog Show
22—Emancipation Day in Puerto Rico
23—Birthday of Larry Chittenden
24—Anniversary of Library of Congress
25—Lady Day
26—Anniversary of the Milwaukee Public School Music Festival
27—Anniversary of the Greensboro, N. C. open golf championship
28—Anniversary of the end of the Civil War in Spain
29—Anniversary of Canada's Constitution
30—Seward's Day in Alaska
31—Transfer Day in the Virgin Islands

April
1—Anniversary of the Cherry Blossom Festival in Washington
2—Anniversary of the establishment of U. S. Mint
3—Anniversary of the Pony Express
4—Adoption of Act of Chapultepac, 1945
5—Bette Davis' and Spencer Tracy's birthdays
6—Old Lady Day
7—The birthday of Fala, President Roosevelt's dog
8—Anniversary of Ponce de Leon's Landing in Florida
9—Tommy Manville's birthday
10—Founder's Day in the Salvation Army
11—Anniversary of F. D. R.'s increase of national debt limit
12—Anniversary of the Passage of Halifax Independence Resolution

13—Birthday of Thomas Jefferson
14—Pan American Day
15—Anniversary of American T. & T. stockholders' meeting
16—DeDiego's birthday in Puerto Rico
17—St. Patrick's Day
18—Anniversary of Paul Revere's ride
19—Patriot's Day
20—Hitler's birthday
21—Princess Elizabeth's birthday
22—Arbor Day
23—Birthday of James Buchanan
24—Anniversary of the Drake Relay Races
25—Anniversary of the reunion dinner of the Fossils
26—Wedding Anniversary of King George and Queen Elizabeth
27—Birthday of Ulysses Grant
28—Birthday of James Monroe
29—Birthday of Hirohito
30—Anniversary of the opening of the N. Y. World's Fair

May

1—Labor Day in the Canal Zone
2—Anniversary of the American Booksellers Convention
3—Semi-Pro Baseball Day
4—Rhode Island Independence Day
5—Anniversary of the exile of Napoleon
6—Anniversary of the purchase of Manhattan by Peter Minuit
7—Birthday of Robert Browning
8—Joan of Arc Day
9—Golf Week begins
10—Confederate Memorial Day
11—Birthday of Henry Morgenthau Jr.
12—Birthday of Florence Nightingale
13—Birthday of Joe Louis
14—Ascension Day
15—Anniversary of the Jumping Frog Derby of Calaveras County
16—Raisin Week begins
17—Anniversary of the assembling of the parts of the Statue of Liberty
18—Anniversary of the Norwegian Constitution
19—Spanish Orphan Day
20—Mecklenburg Declaration of Independence Anniversary in North Carolina
21—Birthday of De Soto
22—Maritime Day
23—Anniversary of the opening of the New York Public Library
24—Anniversary of the hanging of Captain Kidd in London
25—Anniversary of the National Spelling Bee
26—Queen Mary's birthday
27—Anniversary of the sinking of the German boat, *Bismarck*
28—Birthday of the Dionne Quintuplets
29—Anniversary of Roanoke College
30—Decoration Day
31—Anniversary of the Johnstown Flood

June

1—Anniversary of the separation of Kentucky from Virginia
2—Anniversary of the stockholders' meeting of the Standard Oil Co.
3—Birthday of Jefferson Davis
4—Feast Day
5—Anniversary of the Ozark "Smile Girl" contest
6—Constitution Day in Denmark
7—Anniversary of Congress' approval of penny postal cards
8—Anniversary of the meeting of the National Confectioners' Association
9—Birthday of Cole Porter
10—Anniversary of the Portland, Ore., Rose Festival
11—Kamehamena Day in Hawaii
12—King George's birthday
13—Anniversary of the landing in France of General Pershing
14—Flag Day
15—Anniversary of Benjamin Franklin's kite experiment
16—Annual convention of the International Brotherhood of Magicians
17—Bunker Hill Day
18—Birthday of James Montgomery Flagg
19—Birthday of Duchess of Windsor
20—West Virginia Day
21—Birthday of artist Rockwell Kent
22—Bolivarian Day
23—Anniversary of the National Baptist Sunday School Congress
24—Midsummer Day
25—Birthday of Jesse Straus, ambassador
26—Anniversary of the American Crow Hunters Association
27—Anniversary of Fair Labor Standards
28—Birthday of Jean Jacques Rousseau
29—Peter and Paul Day
30—Anniversary of the Y.M.C.A.

July

1—Anniversary of President Roosevelt's address to the Democratic Convention
2—Anniversary of the opening of the first elevated railroad in New York City
3—Birthday of Samuel de Champlain
4—Independence Day
5—Anniversary of Optimist International
6—Birthday of John Paul Jones
7—Anniversary of Barnard College opening its first summer session in history
8—Anniversary of Jacob's Pillow Dance
9—Anniversary of the meeting of the Society of American Florists
10—Statehood Day in Wyoming
11—Birthday of John Quincy Adams
12—Birthday of Henry Thoreau
13—Gen. Nathan Bedford Forrest's birthday

14—Bastille Day
15—St. Swithin's Day
16—Birthday of Roald Amundsen
17—Birthday of Manoz Rivera
18—Birthday of Jane Austen
19—Anniversary of the first Woman's Rights Convention
20—Anniversary of the National Shuffleboard Open Championship
21—Anniversary of Belgian Independence
22—Birthday of Mendel
23—Chippewa Day
24—Mormon Pioneer Day
25—Occupation Day in Puerto Rico
26—Birthday of Baron Henry de Rothschild
27—Barbosa's birthday in Puerto Rico
28—Anniversary of the 14th Amendment
29—Mussolini's birthday
30—Dog Day
31—Joseph Lee Day

August

1—Colorado Day
2—John Kieran's birthday
3—New World Anniversary Day
4—Anniversary of the Coast Guard
5—Anniversary of Chautauqua Institution
6—Deadwood Day
7—Anniversary of the founding of the Order of the Purple Heart
8—Anniversary of Daylight Saving time in London
9—Anniversary day of the first locomotive drawn by steam
10—Birthday of Herbert Hoover
11—Anniversary of the crossing of Niagara Falls on a tightrope wire by Blondin
12—Indian Day
13—Occupation Day
14—Assumption Day
15—Napoleon's birthday
16—Battle of Bennington Day
17—Anniversary of Fulton's first steamboat trip
18—Birthday of Virginia Dare, the first white child born in the New World
19—Aviation Day
20—Birthday of Benjamin Harrison
21—Birthday of Princess Margaret Rose
22—Birthday of Claude Debussy
23—Anniversary of the execution of Sacco and Vanzetti
24—Anniversary of Parcel Post
25—Independence Day in Uruguay
26—Anniversary of the 19th Amendment
27—Anniversary of Kellogg Peace Pact
28—Anniversary of the Bureau of Engraving and Printing
29—Birthday of Maurice Maeterlinck
30—Birthday of Huey P. Long

31—Anniversary of the World War II

September

1—Beginning of the oyster season
2—Fiesta of San Esteban
3—Anniversary of the Rooftop Harvest Corn Husking Match
4—Anniversary of the opening of the world's first electric power station
5—Fiesta of Santa Fe
6—Birthday of Lafayette
7—Birthday of J. P. Morgan
8—Magellan arrived from the first trip around the world
9—Admission Day in California
10—Anniversary of the opening of the subway in New York City
11—Manhattan Island was discovered
12—Defender's Day
13—Birthday of Pershing
14—Anniversary of the Gregorian Calendar
15—Birthday of Taft
16—Anniversary of the Cherokee Strip Contest
17—Anniversary of the adoption of the Declaration of Independence
18—Gandhi's birthday
19—San Jose Day in New Mexico
20—Regatta Day
21—Anniversary of the beginning of George Washington Bridge
22—Execution of Nathan Hale
23—Anniversary of the meeting of the Association of Legal Aid
24—Anniversary of the annual horse show in Monterey, California
25—Anniversary of the Assembly of Telephone Pioneers of America
26—Birthday of the King of Denmark
27—Gold Star Mothers' Day
28—Anniversary of the discovery of California
29—Leif Ericsson Day
30—Anniversary of the Munich Pact

October

1—Anniversary of the announcement of Sally Rand's engagement
2—Wedding anniversary of Governor James of Pennsylvania
3—Today the planet Mars is only 38,130,000 miles from the earth
4—Birthday of Rutherford Hayes
5—Birthday of Chester Alan Arthur
6—Missouri Day
7—Anniversary of Northwestern University's Pajama Contest
8—American Tag Day
9—Anniversary of Arkansas' Tribute to a Mule Pageant
10—Anniversary of the opening of the U.S. Naval Academy
11—Anniversary of the first ascension of the Graf Zeppelin
12—Fraternal Day
13—Anniversary of the meeting of the Town and Country Equestrians

14—Anniversary of the Lithuanian Relief Dinner
15—Anniversary of the opening of lecture season of the Women's Athletic Club
16—Mothers' Day at Brookfield Zoo
17—Anniversary of Walgreen's Super-Value Days
18—Alaska Day
19—Anniversary of Medinah Temple Oriental Pageant
20—Anniversary of the Alpha Delta Pi Alumnae Meeting
21—Anniversary of Washington Monument
22—Anniversary of the meeting of the Barbers' Association of America
23—Anniversary of the launching of the submarine *Trigger*
24—Anniversary of Anna Taylor plunging over Niagara Falls in a barrel
25—Anniversary of the opening of George Washington Bridge
26—Anniversary of the Homemakers Conference
27—Anniversary of the New York Subway
28—Anniversary of the unveiling of the Statue of Liberty
29—Anniversary of the Illinois Cornhusking Contest
30—Buy a Doughnut Day
31—Nevada Day

November

1—All Saints' Day
2—Memorial Day in the Canal Zone
3—Secession from Colombia Day in the Canal Zone
4—Anniversary of the National Roller Derby
5—Anniversary of the election of Al Smith as Governor of N. Y.
6—Anniversary of the meeting of the International Kiwanis Club
7—Anniversary of the meeting of the Gold Star Mothers' Club
8—Anniversary of the election of Governor Lehman
9—Mt. Holyoke College Alumni Day
10—Anniversary of the independence from Spain in the Canal Zone
11—Armistice Day
12—Anniversary of the completion of the New York Subway
13—Anniversary of the Smokes for the Yanks Drive
14—Anniversary of the meeting of ASCAP
15—Anniversary of a Notre Dame-Northwestern game
16—Christening Day of King Leopold
17—Anniversary of the English Speaking Union
18—On this day in '40 a box of Churchill's cigars sold for $2,010
19—Discovery Day in Puerto Rico
20—Anniversary of the National Crocheting Contest

21—Anniversary of the Mexican Revolution
22—Birthday of John Nance Garner
23—Repudiation Day in Maryland
24—Birthday of Zachary Taylor
25—Anniversary of the Wheaton Anti-War Rally
26—Anniversary of the meeting of the American Dental Association
27—Anniversary of the meeting of the Snowchasers Club
28—Independence from Spain Day in the Canal Zone
29—On this date Byrd reached the North Pole
30—Bonifacio Day

December

1—Anniversary of the Chicago Stock Show
2—Anniversary of the Monroe Doctrine
3—Birthday of Illinois State
4—Anniversary of the U. of Purdue Queen Contest
5—Birthday of Martin Van Buren
6—Anniversary of the placing of the capstone on the Washington Monument
7—Anniversary of the opening of U. S.-Africa airmail service
8—Anniversary of the American Farm Bureau Federation
9—Birthday of William Henry Harrison
10—Fewer than 14 shopping days until Christmas
11—Anniversary of the Bank Moratorium
12—Anniversary of the American Pioneers Bridge Tourney
13—Anniversary of the Annual Hoosier Dinner
14—Anniversary of the 4H Club meeting
15—Holiday issue of Esquire is on the newsstands
16—Anniversary of the Railway Business Women's Annual Yule Party
17—Anniversary of the first flight of the Wright Brothers
18—Anniversary of the Indiana University Dames Ball
19—Anniversary of the Big Sisters of the Off the Street Club Yule Party
20—Anniversary of Mid-Year Graduation at the U. of Chicago
21—On this day the Pilgrims landed on Plymouth Rock
22—Only 3 shopping days until Christmas
23—Anniversary of W. Wilson Foundation
24—Tom and Jerry Night
25—Merry Christmas
26—Anniversary of the landing of two baby pandas from China
27—Anniversary of the Chicago Bowling Tournament
28—Holy Innocent's Day
29—Birthday of Andrew Johnson
30—Rizal Day
31—Anniversary of the National Football Coaches' Assn. luncheon

ETIQUETTE REFRESHER

Modern etiquette might better be termed "manners," and thus be stripped of its stuffy implications; for it is simply a code of conduct, regularly revised in keeping with the spirit of the times, designed to make social living more pleasant for all concerned. If you are guided by a consideration for others, you need no rule books. There are those, of course, who continue to "go by the book" in all matters of etiquette — even when their friends' tempo of living, their own servant shortages or ordinary good sense should tell them that by following the letter of the etiquette books they are losing the spirit, making life more instead of less complicated. There are also those circles where absence of the most formal (and even the most senseless) of etiquette customs would seem odd. But for the most part the modern male's manners are consistent, have logical reasons for being and are noticeable only in the breech, never in the observance. In short, unless you happen to be a Neanderthal man, all you have to do is be natural.

One of the easiest things to be awkward about is the matter of:

INTRODUCTIONS

It is seldom necessary or even desirable to introduce people casually encountered in public places, and under no circumstances is it advisable if the introduction involves scrambling about and making everyone concerned uncomfortable—as in a restaurant where getting to your feet would involve pushing the table about and stepping into the aisle. It would, it seems to us, be preferable by far to journey through life anonymously.

In most Eastern cities the business of introducing people has been treated with refreshing common sense. Only at house parties, at small dinner parties and similar functions is it considered essential, and then the introduction is made in the simplest possible form. All of the "May I presents" have gone by the board in favor of the more laconic but wholly courteous, "Miss Struthers, Mr. Arbuthnot."

INVITATIONS

The matter of issuing formal invitations is another bugbear. Purveyors of engraving have fostered the idea that we should announce, in courtly language and suitable, hand-cut typography, the most casual of celebrations, the most ordinary of comings or goings. As a matter of fact, the engraved invitation is nothing but a nuisance and may be dispensed with for anything short of weddings, large dances or gargantuan dinner parties. For less formal entertaining, upon the part of a man, the engraved calling card may be used with the nature of the occasion simply written in the corner in longhand.

In this case no reply is indicated. Should there, however, in the case of a small dinner or dance have been an R. S. V. P., the form is equally simple. Just grasp one of your own cards and, writing in the date for which you have been invited, add a phrase like "With pleasure."

And even this effortless method has been largely supplanted—for small and informal entertaining—by the telephone, the telegraph or just plain word of mouth. Let mutual convenience be your guide in issuing invitations; in answering, follow the same form as the invitation itself, be it 3rd person formal engraved or "c'mup and see us."

SHOULD YOU ASK HER IN?

The occasions upon which a man really requires manners, and upon which manners actually evidence themselves, oftentimes have to do with entertaining women who, for one reason or another, are on their own, without immediate background. A well-chaperoned young woman may ask you in for a night cap, whereas a girl living by herself should not be similarly importuned by you. It may all seem very unreasonable but experience will teach you that there's a great deal to be gained in the long run out of walking softly.

After all, in a world where men are popularly supposed to spend their waking hours in devising new methods of making illicit overtures—God knows when they work!—it is a sound idea to employ what manners you can marshal, be your intentions never so overt. If, on the other hand, you are completely innocent of anything beyond a desire to dine in pleasant company, decent manners will save you the trouble of spending valuable time in allaying unfounded suspicion.

Admitting that the gag: "Mother, what is a chaperon?" has a certain humorous validity, it is well known that the species has managed to persist in the face of all opposition. The present-day chaperon remains the staunch prop of outward virtue and the bachelor's bane.

As a bachelor, you will at least occasionally crave feminine companionship and, at least occasionally, you'll have no ulterior motive. Admittedly it is difficult to convince some women of this. That a man carries neither the marriage nor the ultimate seduction of a given female in the back of his mind is quite incomprehensible to them. What, then, can be done?

Our own tendency is toward eclecticism. Rather than to postulate a set of rules of conduct, we incline to judge each case on its, or her, merits. Size up your wench, then go ahead.

Let us first consider that it is your wish to entertain a business woman; perhaps she is a buyer, a customer of yours, possibly she is an advertising copywriter or maybe she is simply somebody's stenographer. In any case she is a female who has had some actual contact with the workaday world and therefore not one to be unduly impressed with your delicate observance of the more threadbare conventions. If your acquaintance with this admirable member of her sex is slight or your entertainment offered for business rather than purely social reasons, there is but one course open to you: take her to a public place, luncheon, dinner or the theatre, escort her home and let it go at that. If, on the other hand, you know the girl well and if, better still, she has been given no reason to believe that you mean to work your wicked will upon her once the opportunity presents itself, there is no reason on earth why you should not ask her to your apartment for a cocktail or a meal or even to look at your etchings, should you chance to have any. All of the delicious shudders and most of the social taboos have been eliminated from the once daring adventure of "visiting a bachelor in his rooms," at least so far as adults are concerned.

It is intended as no reflection upon the business woman that she may be treated somewhat less conventionally than, say, a sub-debutante; rather it is a compliment. No modern woman in her right mind and past the age of consent wishes to preserve the ancient fiction of her fragility in the face of a practical world, and any additional consideration offered the sub-deb is in the nature of a sop to the prejudices of her maternal parent and not as a pretty gesture in the general direction of the girl.

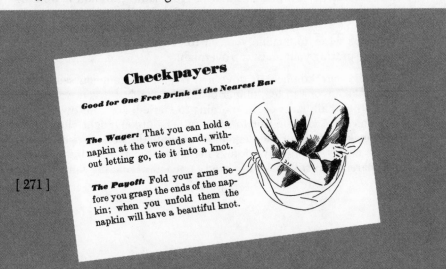

Checkpayers
Good for One Free Drink at the Nearest Bar

The Wager: That you can hold a napkin at the two ends and, without letting go, tie it into a knot.

The Payoff: Fold your arms before you grasp the ends of the napkin; when you unfold them the napkin will have a beautiful knot.

If you wish to entertain so young a girl or one who has received an immoderate amount of sheltering, you may be forced to employ chaperonage of this variety or that. In such a case always bear it in mind that it is the girl and not her mother who is to be made comfortable; a chaperon need not be a dragon and the girl herself will in all probability be the last person in the world to demand such protection. Conventionally, a chaperon should be a married woman, yet it can conceivably be more dangerous for you to harbor a young matron in your rooms (unless you can thoroughly depend upon the understanding of her husband) than to run the risk of starting gossip by having the girl up alone. Perhaps the greatest convenience a bachelor can have is a sister who will permit herself to be pressed into service. For some reason or other no one seems to suspect the man whose sister habitually acts as chaperon-cum-hostess for him; and it is not, you will recall, your own lack of morals but the whisper of the scandalmonger that stimulates you to all this effort in behalf of Mrs. Grundy.

Again, in the case of young girls, it is both sensible and safe to ask them to your apartment in groups of three or more. This practice provides you with a variety of automatic, self-loading chaperon, inexpensive to operate and maintain and involving no additional obligation on your part. Even if your affections happen to be centered upon one of your guests and one alone, you have provided her with more than adequate protection, for unless a girl is of sub-normal intelligence she will never permit her contemporaries to have anything on her; while as to you, your hands, metaphorically, are tied.

If you go in for dinner parties you need not worry overmuch about violating conventions. There is safety in numbers. Nevertheless, and despite all that has been written about the reaction toward social conservation of the rising generation, it is still the part of discretion to keep a weather eye on the drinking and see to it that your younger guests do not imbibe too freely. This is a matter of protection, not parsimony; there is small pleasure to be derived from finding yourself with an eighteen-year-old passout on your hands.

Should you be so fortunate as to have a country place of your own, you may entertain there quite as freely as you might were you married. Of course, if you run to week-end house parties you'll require a married couple to be among those present, but that should work no hardship if you pick them with reasonable care and a working knowledge of their habits. If, on the other hand, your country place consists of a shack in the woods minus adequate bedroom facilities, you'd be wiser to confine yourself to entertainment which does not involve putting your guests up overnight.

Public entertainment is governed largely by common sense. You may take anyone to tea, dinner or the theatre, but if you want to go on in the small hours of the morning to Harlem (or your own town's equivalent of Harlem) or to some rather dubious night club, you'd best make certain of the degree of broadmindedness enjoyed by the lady's family. Shotgun weddings may be out of fashion but a Model "T" parent can still make life pretty uncomfortable for you.

DINING WITHOUT PAIN

Formal dinners, in any save great households, are an anachronism. Very few people, nowadays, are equipped to give them, and if there is any doubt at all in your mind about the ability of your own household to carry off one of these oppressive functions, you may be sure that you'd best not attempt it. In making this decision your position is very like that of the successful young man who thought to spread himself a bit with a yacht and asked an experienced yachtsman what it would cost. "If you have to know how much it costs, you can't afford it," was the reply.

Possibly the most important thing to avoid, in giving a dinner, is the appearance of pretentiousness. Do not attempt, or permit your wife to attempt, anything that is beyond the ordinary limitations of your establishment. If your cook is expected to wait on table, keep the dinner simple. If the handy man doubles in brass as a butler, be certain that he is going to get away with it, and remember it's a hundred to one shot that he won't.

And if, as is more likely, the dinner is completely in your own hands, do your serving from the sideboard or at the table, "family style," or retreat completely to a buffet supper.

You can strain your house to the bursting point and yet bring off a buffet supper successfully. Simply move the dining-room chairs back against the wall, set out several hot dishes and a cold joint or two on the dining-room table and your problem is solved. What carving there is to do is best accomplished beforehand in the kitchen, and the most important task of the waitress if any will be that of removing the empty or partially emptied plates before your guests have a chance either to step on them or sit in them. You won't need to go in heavily for wines. A cocktail may be served beforehand, and a claret cup, set up in a punch bowl on a side table, will do nicely during the meal. Later on, bottles of whisky and brandy, left on another side table with tall glasses and a bowl of cracked ice, will take care of the heartier drinkers.

At a small dinner the problem of whom to invite is a serious one. You do not, in a group of eight, want four noisy people and four quiet ones. A single talker, provided he is not a pedant or a bore or both, should be sufficient. Do not ask all your clever friends to one dinner and the dull ones to another. Nothing annoys a clever man or woman more than a second one; and even the conversationally dull are not complimented at being grouped with their peers. If you are giving a dinner for a business associate of some importance, let him be important. Unless you can provide another guest of real distinction (and a distinction that is either well known or readily recognizable) it is safest to permit your guest of honor to dominate.

After dinner, whatever its service, you can take refuge in bridge, backgammon or games. Of these latter be careful, for many a dinner guest resents being asked to perform feats of memory or erudition on a full stomach. There is always conversation or music upon which to fall back, provided your guests are equipped to perform creditably in either of these arts. The tactful host will be certain of the capacities of his guests or will provide them with more innocent diversion.

BLUEPRINT FOR A COCKTAIL PARTY

The Summonses.—Printed, penned or phoned. (Engraving is impressive but takes weeks.) Can be sizable card or folder, plain or decorated, bearing genial salutations. Or a practical but presentable "informal" (small and folded, titled with your name). States day, time (usually 4-6 or 5-7), and place, with mention of cocktails. And don't forget R.S.V.P. if you care. Invitations should be issued one to two weeks in advance.

Population Estimate.—To be on the safe side, add ten or twenty percent to the number of acceptances. Or, if you're operating without R.S.V.P.'s, count on about 70% of the crowd putting in an appearance. In any case, one sound theory says that the party should either be small enough so everyone can be seated or large enough so that the standees won't prove embarrassing.

Glassware.—You need at least two to a customer of shapes and sizes required by the pouring program: 3 oz. cocktail stemmers (busiest), 10 oz. highball glasses (close competitors), 2 oz. V-glasses for sherry, Old Fashioned glasses (if you're serving that drink), champagne glasses if festivity is ultra.

Beverage Supplies.—Three drinks per person is a fair allowance. You compute the bottles without calculus if you know your clue numbers. Basic 17 is the number of jiggers (1½ oz. each) that a "fifth" bottle (25.6 oz.) will pour. Translated, it means 17 Martinis per bottle of gin, 17 Daiquiris per bottle of rum, 17 Manhattans or Old Fashioneds per bottle of whisky. If brandy or Scotch highballs are of 1-jigger strength, 17 washes up the bottle.

But let's be larger-minded, tripling our jiggers to 51 and throwing away the spare, which would probably be accounted for by spillage anyhow. Now our yardstick is 50 drinks, 3 bottles—offering an easy jump to 200 drinks, 1 case. But the vermouths, dry for the Martinis and sweet for the Manhattans, are still to be reckoned. They operate at half-jigger speed: 34 cocktails (clue 17 doubled) to the "fifth," or 40 to the taller traditional "vermouth bottle" which is 2 oz. short of a quart; 50 cocktails therefore mean 1½ "fifths" of vermouth, or 1¼ traditional size, along with the 3 bottles of liquor; and the case job of 200 would require 6 vermouth "fifths" or 5 traditionals.

Sherry deals are 2 oz., a dozen to the bottle, with a residue of 1.6 oz., which in old Spanish sherries may be dreggy. American sherries run younger and can usually be squeezed to the last drop, providing a starter on the next glass; so count 25 for 2 bottles. Similarly 2 "fifths" of liquor will yield 25 highballs of 2 oz. strength. (More appropriate for a stag affair than a mixed party.) Champagne, straight or cocktailed, is 6-9 to the bottle.

At a big cocktail party, a choice of drinks should be available. It's a safe bet to offer:

1 standard cocktail (Martini, Manhattan or Old Fashioned)
1 other cocktail, either standard or more fanciful
Whiskey and soda, for the long drinkers
An aperitif, for the mild drinkers (sherry or dubonnet)
A non-alcoholic drink for the wagon-riders.

Fruit and Fixings.—Maraschino cherries for Manhattans and Old Fashioneds; pitted olives for Martinis; 1 lime to 2 Daiquiris or 2 Cuba Libres; 2 sizable lemons to 3 Collinses; snips of lemon peel and half-slices of oranges for Old Fashioneds. Large bottle of bitters. Sugar. Bottles of sparkling water, prechilled.

Ice.—More than you could expect of your refrigerator. If you live in a city, phone a cube service; in the country, your ice company will oblige. Shakers and mixing glasses require cracked ice.

Flowers.—By all means, but vased where they won't be knocked over.

Cigarettes.—Invitingly stood up in shot glasses in many strategic spots. Ash trays everywhere. Matches, table lighters.

Canapés.—Single-mouthful propositions, avoiding the necessity of individual plates which men hate to be encumbered with. Platters aren't so huge as to require ten tours of the room to dispose of contents. Late arriving guests draw fresh editions, not sad, soggy remainders.

CONFUSION CONTROL

If you live in an apartment house, you can save yourself a lot of running every time the bell rings, if you leave the front door open. The parking of coats and hats will be simplified if guests, as they enter, can see at a glance where they are to lay their things. Perhaps on tables (or borrowed hat racks) by the door—or placed right out in the hall—if you can trust your neighbors! If coats are to be put in bedrooms, have signs conspicuously displayed bearing arrows, one reading "Boys," the other "Girls." If your party is large and formal, then, of course, you will hire a checker. But if you indulge in such swank, then you're probably going to put yourself in the hands of professionals—caterers, florists and such—and you won't need these helps.

All persons assisting in the operation of this party have definite assignments. Somebody is stationed near the door to greet incomers and start the introductions. Somebody has the job of scouting for empty glasses and whisking them out to the kitchen, where they are promptly washed and put back into service; otherwise the party might get stalled by glass shortage, a calamity exceeded only by that of running out of liquor. Those in charge of pouring have their work simplified for them by fruit juices already squeezed, slices and peels neatly dished, and Martini and Manhattan mixtures prepared in advance or, for convenience, bought bottled. The cracked ice isn't soupy; and cubes aren't left melting in glasses destined for highballs. Shaker productions are presented while still cloudy and foam-edged. To ease congestion at the bar, trays of assorted drinks are passed around. Somebody musical is coaxed to the piano. Songs are joined in. Everybody is of the opinion that it's a swell party. Even its planner contrives to smile through his cares.

Checkpayers . . .
good for one free drink at the nearest bar

the Wager:
A wine glass is resting on two nickels, and a dime is slid between them; you offer to remove the dime without touching the glass or the nickels and without poking in after the coin with any instrument.

the Payoff:
Scratch the tablecloth in the direction of the weave and the dime will magically "walk" out from under.

Granting that you are a bachelor and not a hermit, that you are going to entertain pretty regularly in the apartment and not spend all of your time prowling after a pair of nylon legs, here are a few simple suggestions on what to wear when the friends come around for a few drinks. Wise ones will be as much concerned about their clothes as the amount of vermouth in the Martinis and the composition of the hors d'oeuvres.

Get yourself in the right mood for playing the host by climbing out of your business blues and into the shower. A quick once-over with the razor, a little lotion and you're ready to attack the wardrobe. The pleated chest dress shirt that shows studs and cuff links of black pearl or lapis lazuli is the one you want. With a turned-down collar, wear a butterfly-shaped tie in midnight blue.

Unless you've called in outside assistance, you're going to be doing a few chores, so keep coolness and comfort in mind and wear the lightweight worsted evening trousers of midnight blue with a single braid down each side. The word comfort has real meaning when you're wearing black ribbed nylon socks and patent leather or black suede pumps. The latter, with bright red linings, are gaining favor of late; they won't crack over the instep and they always look well-groomed after a brief brushing.

There is about as much leeway in choice jackets as there is in liquors. Only a few are just right. Tops on the preferred jacket list is the double-chested type of dark maroon velveteen. A modern version of the smoking jacket, it has self-faced broad lapels and four buttons covered with the same fabric as that of the jacket. Some hosts like the same jacket in bright scarlet and others go for blue velvet or velveteen. The main idea is that the host should not only be dressed adequately but should be distinguishable from the rest of the guests who are put at ease by this home-only type of outfit.

If you are one who sticks to the tried and true, your double-chested dinner jacket of the same lightweight midnight blue fabric as the dress trousers is always in good taste. In fact, the lustrous satin facings on the lapels will even give an added formal gleam to your appearance.

A boutonniere is an extra touch of style that doesn't take too much thinking. Wear a white carnation or other flower for the dark red jacket and a red carnation for midnight blues.

Finally, unfold a white linen handkerchief and hold it at the center, allowing the points to hang irregularly. Fold it in half so that the center point falls just below the corner points and tuck it casually into the chest pocket with the center point side toward the body. One corner hanging out like a rabbit's ear or precise arrangement of the points is exactly what you don't want, so keep it casual.

When you don't feel like elbowing your way to a seat in Madison Square Garden, you'll probably have a group of friends over to watch the fights on television. Your clothes problem is simple on a night like this. Replace the suit jacket with a house coat of brocaded silk with satin covered shawl collar. In dark blue or maroon, this coat should be on complementary terms, colorwise, with the trousers and tie. A dark red or blue house coat combines nicely with the trousers of your grey or blue suit. With the dark red or maroon house coat, wear blue, grey or gold neckwear. Dark red, grey and gold ties go well with a blue house coat. If this was the day for the brown suit, brown and green are good coordinating colors.

Recently, hosts also have been wearing the television coat — a loose-fitting, finger-tip length garment with large pockets. It comes in figured foulard or lightweight flannel.

For a cocktail party, prior to a dinner out, a bachelor's business suit, in blue or grey, fills all requirements. Wide-spread collars or tabs on your white shirt dictate the knot of a modestly patterned tie. The former takes a Windsor and the latter is best with a four-in-hand.

It is often a surprise to see just how well the friends look relatively early of a Sunday morning when they come up for brunch. While combining breakfast and lunch, it is also astute to combine the right casual, informal clothes. Assuming that you had enough sleep and have a reasonably clear head, you'll probably select a pair of the old reliable grey flannel slacks and a tweed sports jacket. An Oxford shirt, bow-tie or four-in-hand, and comfortable shoes like loafers or moccasins complete the brunch outfit for Autumn, Winter and Spring.

When the sun begins to spend most of its time on this side of the planet, especially during the very warm summery days, our bachelor friend will replace the light tweed jacket with a linen blazer; the flannel slacks will give way to lighter weight gabardine. Actually, you merely can wear a light sport shirt, a pair of slacks, and moccasins, and still be dressed correctly.

A final word: The objective behind all of this is not to make you into a fashion plate, but rather to give you an opportunity to be a distinctive host with a plate full of canapés in one hand and a fair lass on your arm, with not a single clothes-conscious moment. That's the point, gentlemen: dress your part.

ANSWERS TO BRAIN TEASERS

1. The bookworm consumed only a quarter of an inch. When two volumes are in order from left to right on a bookshelf, the first page of Volume I and the last page of Volume II are separated only by the two covers.

2. Twenty-nine days.

3. Six rungs would still be submerged. The ship with the ladder rises with the tide, of course!

4. The friend that Richard Roe happened to meet was a Wac lieutenant, see?

5. 1, 3, 9, 27 pounds.

6. Smith. The businessman living nearest to the engineer is named Smith, and the engineer's income is exactly a third of his. Therefore, this businessman cannot be the brakeman's namesake as the latter earns $3500 which is not divisible by three. Hence, the brakeman's name is not Smith. Neither is the fireman's name Smith since railway man Smith beats him at billiards and so must be a person with a different name. This leaves the engineer to whom the name Smith may be correctly applied, thus answering the question.

7. If we assume that the third native told the truth about the second, then the second is lying and that makes the first a half-breed. Since two of the natives lied, there are two half-breeds, but it was stated that there was only one half-breed, making our original assumption incorrect. Assuming the other alternative that the third native was lying, the correct conclusion is that the first and second natives are pure-blooded and the third is a half-breed.

8. A's cross was blue. He figured it this way: "If I were white, B would decide he is blue, for otherwise C would see two whites, and would leave the room. Likewise, C would know that he is blue or else B would have gone out. Since both of them stay in the room, I must be blue also."

9. Oh, yes, if you haven't solved the fox, goose, and corn problem, there are two ways of getting them across: He first takes the goose, returns and fetches the fox and takes back the goose. He leaves the goose at the starting point and takes over the corn, and then returns and fetches the goose. Or, for variety, he can take over the goose, return and fetch the corn, at which time he takes back the goose. Then he leaves the goose at the starting point and takes over the fox, after which he returns and fetches the goose.

10. The answer to HOCUS plus POCUS equals PRESTO is 92836 plus 12836 equals 105672.

11. Perhaps the cigarette problem is fair only for cigarette-smokers, but that is a great majority of the literate population these days. The point to it is that the desperate smoker, having made and smoked the six cigarettes he can obviously manufacture out of his collection of butts, will have six butts left from the new cigarettes. Out of those six new butts, he can make and smoke a seventh cigarette. Answer: seven. But don't let any disgruntled victim object that he still has a butt left at that point. The problem clearly states that it takes no less than six to make a smokeable cigarette.

12. As for the man with ten trees and an *idée fixe*, the amateur solver can only juggle and juggle, as if he were playing pigs in clover, until he strikes on the following arrangement:

A five-pointed star with a tree at each angle will do it just as well.

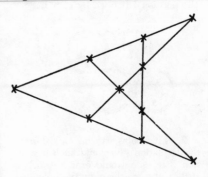

13. It is easy to see that the cyclists rode for exactly one hour. The fly was flying between them at a constant speed of fifteen miles per hour, then, for one hour. Consequently, he flew just 15 miles.

14. How Old Is Ann?—Ann, 16½; Mary 27½.

15. Which plane crashed? — The plane leaving San Francisco would crash. The earth rotates from west to east, and this rotation would add miles to the journey of the eastbound plane, while shortening the westbound plane's trip.

ANSWERS TO KINSHIP PUZZLES

1. The statement that "A man married his widow's sister" is easily explained. A man marries a woman, who dies; he then marries his deceased wife's sister, and himself dies. It is then entirely correct to say "He married his widow's sister," because he did—before he married his widow.

2. The gentleman spoken of by the ladies on the bus was the speaker's uncle.

3. To explain the brother-in-law and father-in-law tangle we had best resort to a family tree. Here it is; let us call the families involved Smith and Jones, just to be original:

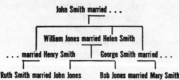

John Smith married . . .

William Jones married Helen Smith

. . . married Henry Smith   George Smith married . . .

Ruth Smith married John Jones   Bob Jones married Mary Smith

4. As for the young man who was Augustus Smith's nephew but not his sister Sophronisba's nephew, well—he was her son.

5. And the family party of seven consisted of two little girls and a boy, their father and mother, and their father's father and mother. This accounts for everybody listed, as you will see if you check on it.

6. The man who was the other man's uncle and nephew at the same time was a son by the following marriage: two men each married the mother of the other, and a son was born to each marriage.

Each of these sons is at the same time the uncle and nephew of the other. I might state that there are other ways of getting the same answer; but this one is the simplest.

SOLUTIONS TO COIN TRICKS

1. It can be done in two moves, as shown below. Move coin 1 around as indicated by the arrow; then carefully slide coin 4 out of its place and up to the position left open by coin 1.

2. Five coins can be moved from the formation given into such a position that each would exactly touch a sixth, if it were there, by the following four moves (See diagram below): Move coin No. 1 to dotted position 1; coin No. 2 to dotted position 2; slide coin No. 4 up to the place originally occupied by coin No. 2; and move coin No. 1 back to its original place.

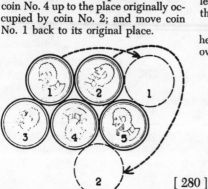

3. In the case of the five nickels and five pennies, to get them together move the following pairs, considering that the two blank spaces are numbered 11 and 12, and that the numbers refer to the spaces and not to the coins. If the directions, for instance, call for No. 2 to be moved, to space No. 6, say, then that coin becomes No. 6. Move 2 and 3, 7 and 8, 4 and 5, 10 and 11, and 1 and 2. As there are always only two blank spaces it need not be specified where these moves are made to.

4. The three-nickels-and-three-pennies puzzle is solved like this: move a nickel, then two pennies, then three nickels, then three pennies, then three nickels, then two pennies, then one nickel. The nice thing is that these moves are so easy to remember: 1, 2, 3, 3, 3, 2, 1, and alternating nickels and pennies. In a very short time you can learn to make the change so quickly that a watcher can't follow your moves.

5. To get the coins alternating heads and tails in three moves, turn over pairs 3-4, 4-5, and 2-3.

[280]

QUIZ ANSWERS

1. *Kitty Foyle* by Christopher Morley;
2. *Alice in Wonderland* by Lewis Carroll; 3. *Get Rich Quick Wallingford* by George R. Chester; 4. *The Grapes of Wrath* by John Steinbeck; 5. *The Informer* (novel by Liam O'Flaherty, movie directed by John Ford); 6. *Trilby* by George du Maurier; 7. *Murders in the Rue Morgue* by Edgar Allan Poe; 8. *Rebecca* by Daphne du Maurier; 9. *For Whom the Bell Tolls* by Ernest Hemingway; 10. *You Can't Take It With You* by Moss Hart and George S. Kaufman.

11. *David Copperfield* by Charles Dickens; 12. *Hamlet* by Shakespeare; 13. *Carmen* by Bizet; 14. *Les Miserables* by Victor Hugo; 15. *A Christmas Carol* by Charles Dickens; 16. *Peter Pan* by James M. Barrie; 17. *Treasure Island* by Robert Louis Stevenson; 18. *Babbitt* by Sinclair Lewis; 19. *The Count of Monte Cristo* by Dumas; 20. *Madame Butterfly* by Puccini.

21. *The Adventures of Tom Sawyer* by Mark Twain; 22. *Rip van Winkle* by Washington Irving; 23. *The Gift of the Magi* by O. Henry; 24. *Pygmalion* by G. B. Shaw; 25. *The Merchant of Venice* by Shakespeare; 26. *The Rubaiyat of Omar Khayyam*, translated by Edward Fitzgerald; 27. *Miss Thompson* (novel by W. Somerset Maugham) or *Rain* (play by John Colton and Clemence Randolph); 28. *An American Tragedy* by Theodore Dreiser; 29. *Lohengrin* by Wagner; 30. *Lost Horizon* by James Hilton.

31. *The Man Without a Country* by Edward Everett Hale; 32. *A Tale of Two Cities* by Charles Dickens; 33. *Tom Jones* by Henry Fielding; 34. *The Little Minister* by James M. Barrie; 35. *Gulliver's Travels* by Jonathan Swift; 36. *The Adventures of Huckleberry Finn* by Mark Twain; 37. *The Jungle Book* by Rudyard Kipling; 38. *Wuthering Heights* by Emily Brontë; 39. *Oliver Twist* by Charles Dickens; 40. *Jane Eyre* by Charlotte Brontë.

41. *Uncle Tom's Cabin* by Harriet Beecher Stowe; 42. *The Prisoner of Zenda* by Anthony Hope; 43. *The Mill on the Floss* by George Eliot; 44. *The Scarlet Letter* by Nathaniel Hawthorne; 45. *The Taming of the Shrew* by Shakespeare; 46. *The Three Musketeers* by Alexandre Dumas; 47. *A Farewell to Arms* by Ernest Hemingway; 48. *The Cask of Amontillado* by Edgar Allan Poe; 49. *Excelsior* by H. W. Longfellow; 50 *Kubla Khan* by Samuel Taylor Coleridge.

DRINK

. . . AND BE MERRY